Henry V and the Earliest English Carols: 1413–1440

As a distinctive and attractive musical repertory, the hundred-odd English carols of the fifteenth century have always had a ready audience. But some of the key viewpoints about them date back to the late 1920s, when Richard L. Greene first defined the poetic form; and little has been published about them since the burst of activity around 1950, when a new manuscript was found and when John Stevens published his still definitive edition of all the music, both giving rise to substantial publications by major scholars in both music and literature. This book offers a new survey of the repertory with a firmer focus on the form and its history. Fresh examination of the manuscripts and of the styles of the music they contain leads to new proposals about their dates, origins and purposes. Placing them in the context of the massive growth of scholarly research on other fifteenth-century music over the past fifty years gives rise to several fresh angles on the music.

David Fallows taught at the University of Manchester for thirty-five years until his retirement in 2011. He is author of *Dufay* (1982), *Josquin* (2009), several critical editions and many articles about the 'long' fifteenth century from Zachara da Teramo to Henry VIII – some of them reissued in two Variorum volumes of his essays published by Ashgate (1996 and 2010).

Henry V and the Earliest English Carols: 1413–1440

David Fallows

LONDON AND NEW YORK

First published 2018
by Routledge
2 Park Square, Milton Park, Abingdon, Oxon OX14 4RN

and by Routledge
711 Third Avenue, New York, NY 10017

Routledge is an imprint of the Taylor & Francis Group, an informa business

© 2018 David Fallows

The right of David Fallows to be identified as author of this work has been asserted by him in accordance with sections 77 and 78 of the Copyright, Designs and Patents Act 1988.

All rights reserved. No part of this book may be reprinted or reproduced or utilised in any form or by any electronic, mechanical, or other means, now known or hereafter invented, including photocopying and recording, or in any information storage or retrieval system, without permission in writing from the publishers.

Trademark notice: Product or corporate names may be trademarks or registered trademarks, and are used only for identification and explanation without intent to infringe.

British Library Cataloguing-in-Publication Data
A catalogue record for this book is available from the British Library

Library of Congress Cataloging-in-Publication Data
Names: Fallows, David, author.
Title: Henry V and the earliest English carols : 1413–1440 / David Fallows.
Description: Abingdon, Oxon ; New York, NY : Routledge, 2018. | Includes bibliographical references and index.
Identifiers: LCCN 2018001650 | ISBN 9781472421920 (hardback) | ISBN 9781315610900 (ebook)
Subjects: LCSH: Carols, English—England—15th century—History and criticism. | Henry V, King of England, 1387–1422—Knowledge—Music.
Classification: LCC ML3652.2 .F35 2018 | DDC 782.280942/0902—dc23
LC record available at https://lccn.loc.gov/2018001650

ISBN: 978-1-4724-2192-0 (hbk)
ISBN: 978-1-315-61090-0 (ebk)

Typeset in Times New Roman
by Apex CoVantage, LLC

 Printed in the United Kingdom by Henry Ling Limited

For Dagmar, who listened, and who helped me to understand Englishness, besides much else

Contents

Acknowledgements ix
Abbreviations x
Notes on musical examples and text citations xii
Musical examples and figures xiii

1 'Straightforward songs' 1

2 The musical repertory 5

3 Definitions and terminology: carol, burden, refrain, chorus, verse 12

4 The musical form and virelai forms in general 19

5 Burdens and double burdens 33

6 Fauxbourdon 43

7 Metre and rhythm 52

8 The main poetry sources 56

9 The earliest English poems in carol form 60

10 Monophony for the carol 68

11 Add. MS 5666 76

12 Awareness of the carol, 1: 1600–1890 80

13 Composers 88

14	Social context, 1: The Royal Court and Political Propaganda	92
15	Social context, 2: Orality and the Polyphonic Carol	104
16	Social context, 3: The Notion of Communal Song	111
17	Awareness of the carol, 2: 1891–1901	114
18	The date and origin of Ritson	120
19	The date and origin of Egerton	134
20	The date and origin of Trinity	149
21	The date and origin of Selden	154
22	Chronology	161
23	The later carols	167
24	Binchois, Dufay and the *contenance angloise*	169
25	Awareness of the carol, 3: 1902–2017	179
26	'Blessid Inglond ful of melody'	183

Bibliography	185
General index	196
Index of carols	201
Index of other songs and poems	204
Index of manuscripts	206

Acknowledgements

For a wide variety of erudition, information, encouragement and scattered advice, I am indebted to Jane Alden, Bruce Barker-Benfield, Nicolas Bell, Margaret Bent, Michael Benskin, Danilo Curti, Helen Deeming, Marco Gozzi, Barbara Haggh-Huglo, John C. Hirsh, LeAnn House, David Howlett, Paul A. Laird, Grantley McDonald, Christopher Mehrens, Stefano Mengozzi, Christopher Page, Joshua Rifkin, Ephraim Segerman, Gareth Stainer, John Stevens (of course), Leah Stuttard, Carol Wakefield, Melanie Wald-Fuhrmann, Andrew Wathey and Peter Wright. It was Laura Macy, then the commissioning editor for Ashgate music books, who first suggested that my original plan for an article (about the date of Ritson) should really be a book. Three dear friends paid me the immense privilege of reading the entire typescript and making suggestions that have greatly improved the book: Margaret Bent, Fabrice Fitch and my wife, Dagmar Hoffmann-Axthelm. But in particular I cannot forget my first attempts to sing quantities of this music with Tony Barnes in 1964: thank you, Tony, for helping to change my life.

Chorlton-cum-Hardy and Basel, 2017

Abbreviations

1 Modern editions

EEC

    The early English carols, ed. Richard Leighton Greene (Oxford: At the Clarendon Press, 1935; revised and expanded edition 1977)

MC

    Mediæval carols, ed. John Stevens = Musica Britannica 4 (London: Stainer and Bell, 1952; revised edition 1958; further revised edition, prepared by David Fallows, 2018)

2 Musical manuscripts

Trinity

    Cambridge, Trinity College, MS O. 3. 58: the Trinity carol roll; music ed. in *MC*, nos. 2–14; all first published in Fuller Maitland [1891]. Online scans at: https://diamm.ac.uk

Selden

    Oxford, Bodleian Library, MS Arch. Selden B. 26, fols. 3–33; carol music ed. in *MC*, nos. 15–42 plus 11^A – 13^A and 15^A, most of the remainder ed. in Hughes 1967; all published in facsimiles and transcribed in Stainer 1901. Online scans at: http://image.ox.ac.uk

Egerton

    London, British Library, Egerton MS 3307; carol music ed. in *MC*, nos. 44–75 and 15^A; remainder ed. in McPeek 1963 and (mostly) in Hughes 1967. Online scans at: https://diamm.ac.uk

Ritson

    Joseph Ritson's manuscript: London, British Library, Add. MS 5665; carol music ed. in *MC*, no. 76–119; remainder ed. in Lane and Sandon 2001. Online scans at: https://diamm.ac.uk

3   Text manuscripts

Audelay

> The poetry collection of the chantry priest John Audelay, *c.* 1426, Oxford, Bodleian Library, MS Douce 302; modern editions in Whiting 1931 and Fein 2009.

Sloane

> London, British Library, Sloane MS 2593; modern editions in Wright 1856 and Palti 2008.

OxEng

> Oxford, Bodleian Library, Eng. poet. e. 1; modern editions in Wright 1847 and Palti 2008.

Hill

> Richard Hill's commonplace book, early sixteenth century: Oxford, Balliol College, MS 354; modern edition in Dyboski 1908. Online scans at: http://image.ox.ac.uk

Ryman

> The poetry collection of the Canterbury friar James Ryman, dated 1492: Cambridge, University Library, MS Ee. 1. 12; modern edition in Zupitza 1892, with commentary in Zupitza 1894–7.

Notes on musical examples and text citations

Note on musical examples

These are in quartered note-values and mostly reduced to a single stave with a view to showing as much music as possible within as little space as possible. As a result, they are in no sense *Urtext*: particularly in the matter of whether accidentals are editorial or present in the manuscripts, the examples are not to be trusted. Similarly, notes, words and text-underlay are adjusted without comment.

Note on text citations

These are in the nearest possible modern English equivalent, generally following the orthography John Stevens used in *MC*. That was not an easy decision: it is absolutely not common practice for Middle English texts (though it is perfectly standard for Shakespeare). But there was no uniformity of English orthography in the fifteenth century, and the particular orthography of any one source (determined less by what the copyists had in front of them than by where they had learned to spell) tells us nothing useful about the pronunciation of the texts. Besides, the original orthography of all carol texts is available in *EEC*. Most important of all, it seems to me that the habit of retaining manuscript orthography has limited modern appreciation of the texts; and, even though my main theme is the music and its underappreciation, another point is that the texts are often superb and underappreciated. I would also draw attention to comments on the carol *Pray for us, thou Prince of Peace* in chapter 15 as an example of how scholars have transcribed the manuscripts with painstaking precision without considering whether they make any sense.

Musical examples and figures

Musical examples

2.1	*Hail, Mary, full of grace*, MC 2. Complete	7
3.1	*Alleluia, Pro virgine Maria*, MC 28. Complete	16
4.1	*Salve festa dies* (chant)	20
4.2	*Douce dame jolie* (Guillaume de Machaut)	23
4.3	*Ecce, quod Natura*, MC 37. Complete	27
4.4	*Ecce, novum gaudium* (Theodoricus Petri)	28
4.5	*As I lay upon a night*, MC 11[A]. Complete	29
4.6	*Verbum caro factum est* (Theodoricus Petri)	30
4.7	*Verbum caro factum est* (Trento 92)	32
5.1	*What tidings bringest thou?*, MC 27. Complete	35
5.2	*Deo gracias, Anglia*, MC 29. Complete	40
6.1	*There is no rose*, MC 14. Complete	44
6.2	*Te eternum Patrem*, from *Te Deum*, MC 95. Burden II only	47
6.3	*Qui condolens in teritu* (Dufay). Opening only, in two versions	48
7.1	*Worship we this holy day*, MC 94. Burden I only	55
10.1	*Parit virgo* (Cambridge 9414)	71
10.2	*Abide, I hope it be the best*, MC 10. Complete	73
11.1	*Now has Mary born a flower* (Add. MS 5666). Complete	77
11.2	*Puer natus in Betlehem* (Add. MS 5666). Complete	78
12.1	*Deo gracias, Anglia* (Pepys arrangement). Complete	85
14.1	*Princeps serenissime*, MC 62. Complete	98
15.1	*Omnes una gaudeamus*, MC 15[A]. Complete	107
15.2	*I pray you all with one thought*, MC 65. Complete	109
18.1	*Pray for us to the Prince of Peace*, MC 106. Burden I alongside Credo	125
18.2	*Pray for us to the Prince of Peace*, MC 106. Verse alongside Credo	126
18.3	*Marvel not, Joseph*, MC 81. Burden II only	129
18.4	*O blessed Lord*, MC 116. Burden II only	130
19.1	*Enforce we us with all our might*, MC 60. Complete	141
20.1	*Nowell sing we both all and some*, MC 7/16	151

xiv *Musical examples and figures*

21.1	2nda pars of *Tota pulchra es* (Plummer)	158
24.1	*Qui nos fecit ex nihilo* (Venice 145)	175
24.2	Section from Dufay's first *Ave regina celorum*	176
24.3	*Triste plaisir* (Binchois). Complete	177

Figures (between pages 91 and 92)

1. British Library, Egerton MS 3307, fol. 49: *Tibi laus* (*MC* 44) with the decorated initial that opens the carol section of the manuscript
2. Cambridge choirbook fragment: University Library, MS Ll. 1. 11, fol. 32, containing *Nowell, nowell: Out of your sleep* (*MC* 14A)
3. Agincourt carol (*MC* 29), from Oxford, Bodleian Library, MS Arch. Selden B. 26, fol. 17v
4. Cambridge fauxbourdon page: University Library, MS Add. 2764 (1)
5. Cambridge, Magdalene College, Pepys fol. 1 (copy of Agincourt carol) 'PL Ballads 1.4'
6. Pepys: arrangement of Agincourt carol (just first page) 'PL Ballads 1.5'
7. Oxford, Bodleian Library, MS Arch. Selden B. 26, fol. 5 with original ruling and quod j.d.
8. Ritson (British Library, Add. MS 5665), fol. 16v, with apparent ascriptions to Smert and Trouluffe

1 'Straightforward songs'

Only after I had known and loved this music for nearly twenty years did I begin to see that its early history had been misunderstood.[1] Another quarter century after that, I saw that its later history had also been misunderstood.[2] And ten years later still – in the course of eventually writing this book – it became clear that the social context of the carols had been misunderstood about as badly as possible.[3] Those matters all have a serious impact on our view of the earliest English carols. But at the same time I also felt sure that scholars had not just underestimated the repertory but, more seriously, quite overlooked its true place in the story of western music. This book tries to put those things right.

But it is also a book about why I love the English carols of the early fifteenth century. They were what first brought me unavoidably to the music of those years. For a young music student filled with excitement for Beethoven and Brahms, then for Schoenberg and Webern, then for Stockhausen and Boulez, there was about these carols a muscular energy coupled with an elusive charm that opened up new worlds. Not just that: there was a freshness of colour and a broader cultural resonance that repeatedly evoked a community. And above all there was the simplicity, the directness of expression, the sheer lack of pretension that made so much of the music instantly attractive. It was not my first encounter with medieval music, but it was the decisive one.

Across more than forty years I have written much about the music of the fifteenth century but almost nothing about the English carol. Nor was I alone. In those years little has been published on the topic – just entries in dictionaries and encyclopedias, otherwise a handful of short articles on newly discovered manuscripts,[4] but not much else.[5]

---

1 As argued particularly in chapter 9.
2 As argued particularly in chapter 18.
3 As argued particularly in chapter 14.
4 Among them Seaman and Rastall 1977, Wilson 1980, Griffiths 1995, Camargo 1998, Edwards and Takamiya 2001 and Faulkes 2005. Interestingly, all of these new discoveries, with the single exception of Edwards and Takamiya 2001, concern poems that appear in the polyphonic repertory of carols, so all are included in my revision of *MC*.
5 Certainly there were doctoral theses, particularly those of Paulette Catherwood 1996, Jonathan King 1996, John Zec 1997, Heather Collier 2000, Beth Ann Zamzow 2000, Adele Smaill 2003,

2 Chapter 1: 'Straightforward songs'

There is a good reason for that: it looked as if two scholars had completely covered the subject. One was John Stevens (1921–2002), who edited all the known music in 1952 as Musica Britannica 4: *Mediæval carols* (henceforth *MC*). The other was Richard Leighton Greene (1904–83), who assembled the poetic repertory in his Princeton dissertation of 1929, published it all with Oxford University Press in 1935 as *The early English carols* (henceforth *EEC*), and presented his final expansion of that book in 1977 after over half a century of intensive research and publication on the topic.[6] With everything neatly edited and beautifully organized, elegantly packaged and almost presented with a rose attached to the knot, there seemed nothing else to say. So, briefly, nobody said anything.

A word could be added on the packaging. The 1977 revision of Richard Greene's book is in the most mandarin Clarendon Press manner, done at a time when they were producing what still seem to me some of their loveliest books. My own original copy is totally battered from constant use over forty years, but I recently bought a second copy in mint condition and was once again amazed at its beauty. John Stevens's edition was just the fourth volume in the series Musica Britannica, launched to coincide with the 1951 Festival of Britain, basically celebrating Britain's recovery from World War II – and running now to over a hundred volumes. Initiated by the scholar and conductor Anthony Lewis (aged 35) with the help of the harpsichordist Thurston Dart (aged 30), Musica Britannica was a response to an initiative proposed by the Royal Musical Association. And those volumes were gorgeous – at least that is the way it seemed to me on my first encounter as a student fifteen years later. They epitomized the way the post-war years rejected the excesses of the previous generation. What I felt about them in relation to the elegant volumes of the Neue Bach-Ausgabe (started 1954) and the Neue Mozart-Ausgabe (started 1955), I no longer know: it could well be that I came across these only later. But Musica Britannica seemed to represent the best of what was British: the elegant but economical design; the scholarly integrity combined with compactness and lack of fuss; the opening up of new worlds in music. I report that as a way of helping to put this whole book into perspective.

But there is another reason for the lack of recent literature on the early English carol. With basically just four musical sources, the style seemed hermetically sealed, an English repertory with no relevance to anything else that was going on in European music. That too, I now wish to show, was quite wrong.[7]

Kathleen Palti 2008 and Louise McInnes 2013, all of which contribute to what I have to say here. But only Palti and McInnes have moved from typescript to formal publication on the carol.

6 To give the details: the 1935 book had over 300 pages of edition, followed by 100 pages of notes and preceded by an introduction that described the repertory in another 130 pages. Greene produced a smaller anthology in 1962, partly to take account of the recently discovered Egerton manuscript of carols, but all the same it had 50 pages of introduction, 100 pages of poems and almost 150 pages of notes. After which, it was perhaps only logical that he returned to his original book and recast it in 1977, bringing it entirely up to date, most particularly to take account of new sources and of John Stevens's work on the music. Now the introduction increased to 160 pages and the explanatory notes to 140 pages.

7 As argued particularly in chapter 6 and chapter 24.

As it happens, much of the main scholarly discussion of the topic was in the years 1945–54. The sudden emergence of the manuscript Egerton 3307 after World War II increased the known musical repertory by one-third and brought a burst of serious writing by major scholars, among them Manfred F. Bukofzer, Richard Leighton Greene, Rossell Hope Robbins and Bertram Schofield. The first 1954 fascicle of the *Journal of the American Musicological Society* devoted more than half of its pages to material on the carol, namely the enormous reviews of *MC* from a musical and a literary viewpoint, respectively by Bukofzer and Greene, together with Greene's extended article on the Egerton manuscript and its origins. Literature since then has added little, often repeating material previously published, though a special mention is necessary for Rossell Hope Robbins, co-author (with Carleton Brown) of the *Index of Middle English verse* (New York: Columbia University Press, 1943),[8] editor of *Secular lyrics of the XIVth and XVth centuries* (Oxford, 1952) and author of the most outspoken qualifications of Greene's work.[9]

But it is worth stressing at this point that the main thinking about the English carol of the fifteenth century goes back to Greene's doctoral thesis of 1929. His publications over the next fifty years are in many ways absolutely magnificent; but in other ways they represent cut-and-paste jobs from his initial statement – a paragraph here to clarify something on which another scholar had expressed disagreement, a few added sentences to take account of subsequent research, large quantities of his own further research on the details and intentions of the texts. This all represents the most astonishing commitment and stamina; but the underlying mindset had changed little. It is time to try thinking afresh.

As concerns the music and its manuscripts, it may be fair to say that the discipline of historical musicology was almost in its infancy when John Stevens published *MC*. Before that date the musicologist was an extremely rare phenomenon, particularly in the English-speaking world: Stevens himself was a lecturer in English at the University of Cambridge. Since then there has been a massive growth in highly professionalized musicology worldwide. On the manuscripts and on other

---

8 He was also co-author (with John L. Cutler) of *Supplement to the index of Middle English verse* (Lexington: University of Kentucky Press, 1965), which again brings extraordinary energy to the topic. Perhaps it should be added that the intended replacement, Julia Boffey and A. S. G. Edwards, *A new index of Middle English verse* (London: The British Library, 2005), is less than helpful for the present purposes, not least because it ignores the Ritson manuscript in the belief that it was copied after 1500 (see chapter 18). Rather more useful, because more fully documented, but ignoring (at the time of writing) most musicology published since 1965, is *The DIMEV: an online, digital edition of the index of Middle English verse*, ed. Linne R. Mooney, *et al*. This last has what seems to me the problem that it gives an entirely new numbering to the repertory.

9 Robbins (b. Wallasey, Merseyside, 1912; d. Saugerties, NY, 1990) had university degrees in English (BA Liverpool, PhD Cambridge, 1937) but had studied piano seriously enough to gain the licenciate of the Guildhall School of Music in 1932. That may not suffice to describe him as a musicologist; but he understood far more about music than most literary historians. After finishing his doctorate ('The Middle English religious lyric') he moved to the United States, teaching at various universities and finishing his career as International Professor of English in the State University of New York at Albany (1969–82).

manuscripts of fifteenth-century music there is now a literature of often daunting detail and refinement. On the musical techniques and the social place of the musician in the various decades of the century there is also a vast literature. It is with absolutely no disrespect for what John Stevens achieved that I now try to situate this music in the light of the research that has happened since his edition. In fact, quite the contrary. The volume has been at my side since I first bought it in 1966 (actually rather longer, since I had been singing and studying the music from library copies already for two years at that point); and John Stevens himself gave me so much help and encouragement over the years that I cannot ever forget or adequately repay my debt to him.

The word 'straightforward' in the chapter title comes from the essay that the young Jack Westrup (1904–1975) wrote for the 1932 revision of the Oxford History of Music. Here the future much decorated Heather Professor of Music at the University of Oxford, later author of distinguished books on Purcell, Liszt and Schubert, produced an astonishingly wide-ranging chapter that covered the songs of all European languages up to about 1600.[10] His remarks are less well known than they merit. Here is what he wrote about the carol:

> 'Straightforward', indeed, is the epithet which might well be applied generally to these songs, and it is this characteristic which we like to regard, rightly or wrongly, as typically English. The vocal display of the Italian, and the inconsequent flippancy of many French chansons are both supposed to be opposed to our national temperament.[11]

While I must obviously detach myself from his remark on French songs (which ones can he have had in mind?), the rest seems to the point. This is music that makes its impact with disarming economy of means. But that issue of straightforwardness has a broader cultural resonance, one that will recur several times in the coming pages.

---

10 Incidentally, this chapter shares very little indeed with Westrup's later chapter 'Medieval song', in *The new Oxford history of music* 2: *Early medieval music up to 1300*, ed. Dom Anselm Hughes (London: Oxford University Press, 1954, revised second impression, 1955): 220–69.
11 Westrup 1932: 256–375 at p. 337.

2 The musical repertory

When John Stevens published the music of the English carols in 1952 he prefaced it with the words: 'The collection was first suggested by a scrutiny, from a musical standpoint, of . . . Greene's . . . *The early English carols* (Oxford, 1935), and it was originally designed as a musical companion to his'. But what is truly surprising is that the resulting group of pieces is so stylistically coherent that additions and subtractions were easy to see. Stevens left out the later carols that appear in the Fayrfax book (British Library, Add. MS 5465, *c.* 1500) as being in an entirely different manner;[1] and he added pieces in the Selden and Egerton manuscripts that happened to have texts purely in Latin but had the same musical form. With this done, he produced a volume of the most astonishing musical consistency.

It is worth just pausing there to reflect on the strangeness of the situation. Greene had defined the carol in terms of its poetic form – 'intended, or at least suitable, for singing, made up of uniform stanzas and provided with a burden which begins the piece and is to be repeated after each stanza'.[2] He thereby published a collection of 474 poems. Assembling the ninety of these that had polyphonic music and adding almost thirty more that had the same poetic form but text only in Latin resulted in a group of pieces that are not only uniform in style but quite different from what is otherwise known of fifteenth-century music, so much so that the style is instantly recognizable in strange contexts. That is to say that when Charles Hamm (1960: 214–15) printed a textless piece among the almost 1,900 works in the Trento codices and claimed it was an English carol, there was really no need for discussion.[3] Some years later I did the same (Fallows 1976–7: 66–7) for a piece in the south German Buxheim keyboard tablature of around 1460, again to meet instant agreement.[4] It is an absolutely distinctive style, quite unlike anything else in England or on the continental mainland in those years.

So the features of the style should be easy to define. A very high proportion of the music is in two voices when the norm of the age was three voices. The

---

1 He later published them in Musica Britannica 36: Stevens 1975; they are briefly discussed in chapter 23.
2 Greene 1935: vii; 1977: xi.
3 Modern edition in Fallows 2014: no. 36, alongside a further piece in the same style in the same manuscript, no. 37.
4 Modern edition in Fallows 2014: no. 38.

declamation is by and large homophonic, which is also rare in those years. There is a dancing manner to the rhythmical and metrical structure.

We can see all this in Example 2.1, *MC* 2.[5] The burden starts the work and is repeated after each verse: in this case it has (roughly) the same metre as the verses, each of which ends with a line that rhymes with the end of the burden. The contrast between the three-voice writing of the burden and the two-voice writing of the verses implies the use of chorus for the burden and soloists for the verse. The music is broadly homophonic, resulting in clear declamation throughout. The text is not exactly narrative but tending in that way. And although the music seems of the gentlest it is in highly regular phrases: that is to say that the verse is entirely in four-bar phrases and the burden has four-bar phrases except for the last phrase, which has five bars (a matter to which we must obviously return).

The last two stanzas, not printed in Example 2.1, draw attention to another dominant feature of the carol, the sense of a community taking part in the song:

5

Muchë joy to us was grant
And in earthë peace y-plant,
When that born was this infant
In the land of Galilee.

6

Mary, grant us the bliss,
There thy Sonnës woning is:　　　　　　*dwelling*
Of that we han done amiss
Pray for us pour charité.

And the two last words remind us that French was in the early fifteenth century an active language in England, as it had been since the Norman conquest nearly four hundred years earlier – though things were to change on that front in the reign of Henry V, as we shall see, since it is important for the history of the carol.

Nowhere else in the vernacular music of the fifteenth century is there the alternation of three-voice and two-voice writing between the sections of a single piece; almost nowhere else is so much homophony between the voices or indeed such functional equality between the voices. And, recalling the points made in chapter 1, there is an astonishing expressivity in this apparently simple music.

In terms of manuscripts with polyphony, the story begins with the carol roll in Trinity College, Cambridge, from perhaps around 1420, which in fact opens with the carol in Example 2.1.[6] This is a scroll created by sewing three pieces of

---

5　Numbers given here are those in John Stevens's edition, *Mediæval carols* = Musica Britannica 4 (1952).
6　The entire manuscript was published for the first time in Fuller Maitland [1891].

Chapter 2: The musical repertory 7

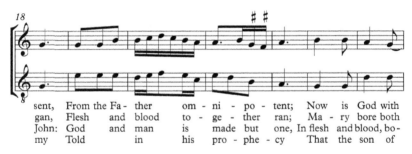

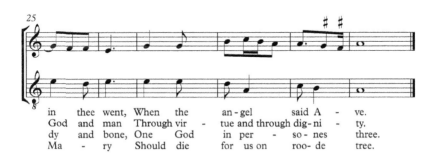

Example 2.1 Hail, Mary, full of grace, MC 2. Complete

parchment together, 2 m long and some 20 cm wide – the format typically used for accounting documents, though quite often portrayed in pictures of angel musicians. On one side there are thirteen carols (*MC* 2–14), all uniformly written in void notation; on the other side there is liturgical material that was added perhaps

8   *Chapter 2: The musical repertory*

twenty or thirty years later[7] – as though the music had ceased to be of much interest although the parchment remained valuable, but suggesting that the carol collection was then in an ecclesiastical institution.

Of those thirteen carols, eleven are identical in their makeup, namely with a burden followed by music for from three to six verses. Of those eleven, all but one are in two voices throughout: just the first has its burden in three voices. Of the other two, the famous Agincourt carol, *Deo gracias, Anglia*, has two burdens, one in two voices, the other in three. The other, *Abide, I hope it be the best*, has two burdens and a slightly different musical style, raising questions that are best left aside for the moment: suffice it to say at this point that the apparent presence of only three verses is contradicted by a later source of the same carol, which has five verses.

The Trinity roll texts are all for Christmas except *MC* 12 (for St Stephen, the day after Christmas), *MC* 8 (the Agincourt carol) and *MC* 10 (*Abide, I hope it be the best*, which has a broadly moralistic text). All, apart from *Abide, I hope*, are in major prolation (that is, 6/8 or 3/8 time in the modern edition).

From there we can move to the Egerton manuscript, a strikingly elegant and uniformly copied book that includes a group of carols beginning at the start of the eighth gathering. The carols proceed from fol. 49 to fol. 72 (*MC* 44–73) with a single interruption, the song *Omnes una gaudeamus* (fol. 68v: *MC* 15[A]), which is in the same musical style but has a different poetic form (also to be discussed later). These pieces are all copied by a single hand, preceded by a single magnificent decorated initial (Figure 1), and all copied with staverulings of eight staves (for four systems of two voices) on the left-hand pages and nine staves (for three systems of the three-voice burden) on the right-hand pages.[8] This copying of thirty-one pieces is plainly a single act. And there are other kinds of consistency here: that the copyist always underlays three stanzas to the music of the verses, moving to the bottom of the page only for any further stanzas.[9]

---

7   Identified by Paulette Catherwood (1996: 57) as the Propers of four masses: *De sancta trinitate, De angelis, Officium Corpus Christi* and *De sancta cruce* (incomplete).
8   On the matter of hands, Greene 1954 and McPeek 1963, as well as the *Census-catalogue* 1979–88, agree that a single musical hand is responsible for everything in Egerton apart from the first piece (fols. 6–7) and the last two (fols. 77v–79: *MC* 74–5). If so, that would mean that the main copying began on the last recto of the first gathering; but in fact Schofield 1946 and King 1996 prefer to think that all the music is by a single hand, and, on balance, I am inclined to agree with them. For text hands, Greene and McPeek (and apparently the *Census-catalogue* 1979–88) agree that hand B did the liturgical section, fols. 8–48v, apart from the two Passions (fols. 15–16v and 20–24v), which they credit to C; and that all the carols and the two closing motets (fols. 49–77) were done by D. Jonathan King (1996: 103) argues for the identity of C and D. The differences are perhaps unimportant in comparison with the main point: that the manuscript is done with astonishing consistency and professionalism throughout.
9   Andrew Wathey (1989: 154; quoted in Catherwood 1996: 125) claimed that this was 'the earliest surviving source [*sc.* of polyphony] ruled as a whole'. I would say that there are enough irregularities in terms of indenting to suggest that the book was not entirely preruled. On the other hand,

Chapter 2: The musical repertory 9

This last brings its own problems, as Jonathan King noted (1996: 107–8). To aid clarity and elegance, the scribe always copied the second line of text in red, using a different quill that was evidently broader and therefore took up more space. There are many examples in John Stevens's edition where attempts to replicate the texting of the manuscript result in second stanzas being implausibly wrong in their underlay.

We must come later to the physical origin of Egerton, because there is an unresolved dispute basically as to whether it was for Meaux Abbey in Yorkshire or for the chapel of St George, Windsor. We can come also to the unrelated question of its date. For the moment it is enough to note that most of these thirty-one pieces are in tempus perfectum (that is, 3/4 time in the modern edition), with ten in major prolation (*MC* 44, 50, 57, 61–3, 65–6, 69, 72), and that all but fourteen (*MC* 44, 47–8, 50, 57–8, 60–63, 65–66, 68–9, 72) have two burdens, one in two voices and the other in three. Both features indicate a date later than the Trinity roll, but – as I shall argue presently – not quite so much later as observers have suggested hitherto. The carols are preceded by a coherent group of liturgical pieces for Holy Week and Easter and followed by an incoherent group of four other pieces, namely two motets and two possible further carols, incompletely copied.

Occupying a place between these two sources, at least in terms of actually mixing the carols in with other material, is the Selden manuscript. This is a much more varied collection of fifty-two pieces: just over half (twenty-eight) are carols but a further six are written in the manner of carols, that is to say in 'pseudo-score', and have the musical style of the carol repertory (*MC* 11[A] – 13[A] and 15[A], plus *Gaude terra tenebrosa*, ed. in Hughes 1967: no. 12, and *Glad and blyth mote ye be*, ed. in Fallows 2014: no. 83).[10] The remaining works are liturgical polyphony, mostly written in choirbook layout, with the three voices distributed across the page. By contrast with the other sources, there seem to be many copyists at work here: no two scholars agree on exactly how many hands are involved, but it cannot be fewer than nine and it is easy to accept E. W. B. Nicholson's view that this was therefore copied at a religious house with a fair number of literate and enthusiastic musicians among its membership.[11] On the other hand, the apparent complete lack of organization rather suggests that its purposes were not official.

Finally, we have the Ritson manuscript, named after the eighteenth-century collector who owned it and then gave it to the British Museum.[12] This is basically different in that it has carol music that is broadly later in style and more discursive.

---

since the ruling is so uniform it may well have been done by the same person who did the music copying. It is ruled in uniform red ink with a single 13 mm rastrum throughout. The nine-stave pages are uniformly 19 cm deep (that is, from the top line of the top stave to the bottom line of the bottom stave) throughout; eight-stave pages are usually about 18 cm deep, but not so uniform. Vertical rules to left and right are in plumb throughout, reaching to top and bottom of page, approximately 14 cm apart. As noted later, Selden seems to have been preruled.

10 The relevance of these two pieces to the discussion was first pointed out by Margaret Bent in Stevens 1967: 286.
11 In Stainer 1901: i.xxi.
12 Joseph Ritson (1752–1803), donated on 7 August 1795, shortly after he had published carols from it in his *Ancient songs* (1790).

Chapter 2: The musical repertory

Plenty of indicators place its copying in the west country, around Exeter Cathedral, and apparently well away from the other three sources. On the other hand, like Trinity and Egerton, it has all its carols together, uniformly copied and uniformly decorated.[13] In the uninterrupted run of forty-four carols here there is not a single piece that does not absolutely conform to Greene's definition of the poetic form. All but two have two burdens, one in two voices and the other in three (apart from one case with the second burden in four voices: *MC* 116). Beyond that, most carols here have an annotation indicating the appropriate feast for its performance, most often 'in die nativitatis' but also 'de sancto Johanne' (the evangelist, celebrated on 27 December: *MC* 77, 106, 115), 'de innocentibus' (28 December: *MC* 78, 93, 94), 'in die circumcisionis' (1 January: *MC* 83), 'de sancta Maria' (*MC* 76, 86), 'sancti Stephani' (26 December: *MC* 92), 'de sancto Thoma' (Becket, 29 December: *MC* 96, 109), 'epiphanie' (6 January: *MC* 108), 'in fine nativitatis' (*MC* 118) and fairly often 'ad placitum' (*MC* 85, 99–100, 104, 110, 112–114, 116–17). Only one lacks any designation, *Salve, sancta parens* (*MC* 84). But, for the rest, it is notable that all the specific indications are for the 'twelve nights' of the Christmas season, from 25 December to 6 January.

While the first three sources share a number of pieces, there is no carol music in Ritson that appears anywhere else (apart from the bizarre case of one carol whose music appears elsewhere with a Credo text and an ascription to Binchois, a matter to be considered in chapter 18). Several of the texts appear with different music in the other sources, but in purely musical terms Ritson is a total outsider. The best of received literature has dated the copying of the Ritson carols *c.* 1470: in chapter 18 I shall argue for a substantially earlier date.

There are so few further sources of early carol polyphony that we can quickly complete the story here. The Oxford fragment MS Ashmole 1393, fol. 69 is a piece of parchment attached to a piece of paper.[14] It contains the carol *Ecce, quod Natura* (*MC* 43) in full-black notation followed by two carol texts (*EEC* 35 and 191). The fragment is hard to date but may be from around 1420.

Also in the Bodleian Library, MS Bodley 88* is a set of twelve parchment strips and fragments formerly used to strengthen the sewing in MS Bodley 88 (a printed book, despite its shelf-mark). When reassembled, they form portions of three leaves containing material of six or seven carols in void notation, including two that also appear in Egerton (*MC* 64 and 67).[15]

In the Cambridge University Library there is a single parchment leaf catalogued as MS Add. 2764 (1). It contains fragments of two carols in full-black notation (*MC* 19[A] and 20[A]; facsimile herewith as Figure 4).

---

13 The carols run from fol. 4v to fol. 53, with two interruptions in plainly later script: fols. 38v–39 and fols. 47v–48.
14 Description and facsimile in Stainer 1901: i.xix and plates 26–8.
15 First described in Greene 1977: 295–6 (though with the erroneous call number Bodley 77). Detailed reconstruction and description with complete facsimile in Fallows 1984, where two of the facsimile pages are printed upside-down: good and correctly aligned scans are now available at https://diamm.ac.uk.

Chapter 2: The musical repertory 11

Finally, in the same library MS Ll. 1. 11, fol. 32 (Figure 2), the first of two parchment flyleaves at the end of a fifteenth-century volume of cases in Law French, contains most of a polyphonic carol not otherwise known (*Nowell, nowell: Out of your sleep, MC* 14[A]), though its burden and first stanza appear with entirely different music in Selden as *MC* 25.

This is the single known case of a carol that is laid out in separate voices rather than in pseudo-score. The leaf, plainly cropped at both top and bottom so originally larger than the rest of the book, contains parts of a carol on the recto and accounts on the verso, both apparently from the middle years of the fifteenth century. The carol page has the discantus at the top, the tenor at the bottom and the text residuum between the two. At least this answers one possible question that arises from the pseudo-score sources, namely whether the discantus should be texted even though it is not underlaid. Here both voices are fully underlaid: this piece is absolutely in the same otherwise unusual style as the other carols and its evidence must surely apply also to the others.

In chapter 23 I shall have a little to say about the later sources, most particularly the glorious music of the Fayrfax book. But those all date from around 1500 or later, and their music has nothing at all in common with the repertory that is the main topic of this book. Also later I shall discuss the few fragments of monophonic music for carol texts. These too have – in my view – nothing at all to do with the material I have just outlined and are best kept apart from the polyphony (though their importance is prime). But otherwise, those eight sources – four of them substantial, the others fragments – provide the music that is my topic.

3 Definitions and terminology: carol, burden, refrain, chorus, verse

Obviously enough, the word 'carol' and its cognates in other languages has had a wide range of meanings across the centuries. In the early middle ages, it often meant 'round dance' and sometimes the associated music;[1] over many centuries it just meant 'a song'; and for the last few centuries in the English-speaking world it has meant seasonal songs, particularly for the Christmas season.

That is why we need to be clear that Richard L. Greene's definition of the word purely in terms of poetic form is closely limited and has a fairly slender documentary basis.[2] Hence also the need to lay out the musical details first of all in chapter 2: the sheer consistency of the poetic form in Ritson and Egerton, as well as in the much smaller Trinity roll, is our evidence that Greene defined a poetic form that existed. And the sheer consistency of the musical style further supports him in trumps. But the case for using the word 'carol' to describe these pieces is weak.

Greene's formal definition is supported nowhere among the musical sources but in just two of the poetic sources: in blind John Audelay's poetry collection dated c. 1426 (Bodleian Library, MS Douce 302) and in Richard Hill's commonplace book from early in the next century (Balliol College, MS 354).[3]

Audelay has a heading in red ink at the beginning of his group of twenty-five poems, all in carol form:

> I pray you, sirs, both more and lass,
> Sing these carols in Christemas.

Only seven of the carols that follow have themes related to the Christmas season, but three of them contain the word 'carol':

> I pray you, sirs, of your gentry,
> Sing this carol reverently

---

1 This is beautifully laid out in Robert Mullally, *The carole: a study of a medieval dance* (2011): 9–31, a description that benefits much from the author's training in medieval philology as well as from the extreme thoroughness of his bibliographical coverage – including, for example, some dozen reviews of Margit Sahlin's erudite but controversial *Étude sur la carole médiévale* (1940).
2 As Greene notes (1935: xxiii–xxiv), the definition seems to have been pioneered – 'has been suggested before, but without emphasis' – by Sir Edmund Chambers (1907: 290–94).
3 The quotations over the next two pages fairly closely match those given by Greene (1935: xx–xxii; 1977: xxx–xxxi); I hope that my different emphasis helps to clarify the situation.

For it is made of King Herry;
Great need for him we have to pray. (*EEC* 428 on Henry VI: stanza 15 of 16)

As I lay sick in my langour,
With sorrow of heart and tear of eye,
This carol I made with great doloure:
Passio Christi conforta me. (*EEC* 369 on the fear of death: stanza 8 of 11)

I pray you, sirs, pour charity,
Redis this carol reverently
For I made it with weeping eye,
Your brother John, the blind Awdley. (*EEC* 310 on St Francis: stanza 13 of 13)

Elsewhere in his manuscript there is just one other poem in carol form, again containing the word (though almost the same as the last stanza of his carol on St Francis):

I pray you all, pour charity
Redis this carol reverently
For I it made with weeping eye;
My name it is the blind Awdlay. (*EEC* 314 on St Winifred: stanza 30 of 30)

Even though the notion of 'singing' is there only in the heading and in the Henry VI carol, several of his other carols appeal to a 'company' or community; moreover, their form is that of the Trinity roll carols, and it would be easy to sing any of Audelay's poems to music from the Trinity roll.[4]

Second, and more convincingly, Richard Hill's commonplace book has three entries in its opening list of contents (p. 7):[5]

Diverys carolles
Item: dyvers good carolles, fol. 203 [= Dyboski, fol. 219; modern pencil p. 459]
Item: dyvers mery carolles, fol. 226 [= Dyboski, fol. 248; modern pencil, p. 503]

Kathleen Palti (2008: 35) adds:

All but five of the manuscript's seventy-eight carols appear in these groups, and within them only four songs are not in carol form.

So in one sense Richard Hill offers the most convincing evidence for calling the form 'carol'. It is only sad that this evidence is from the early sixteenth century and far too late for the music that is the main topic of this book. On the other hand,

---

4 As observed in Copley 1958.
5 These are in Dyboski (1908): no. 120, *a–zz*, on fols. 219v–231, edited as nos. 8–59; no. 73, fols. 177v–178, edited as nos. 2–7 and 87–8, and fols. 248v–249v, edited as nos. 60–62.

the poems in Hill's collection have a wide chronological range, including some of the earliest known carols.[6]

In addition, three printed books of the sixteenth century have the word 'carol' in their title. There are six poems, all devotional, in Richard Kele's *Christmas carolles newely imprynted* of c. 1545,[7] five in carol form though not one of them even mentions Christmas or the Christmas season. The single surviving last page of Wynkyn de Worde's *Christmasse carolles newely enprinted* (1521) has bits of two poems, of which one mentions Christmas and the other is about hunting, though both are in carol form (*EEC* 424B and 132B).[8] The four surviving leaves of *Christmas carolles newely imprinted* contain three Christmas pieces among their five poems, all in carol form.[9] That is obviously not enough material for a judgment, but it looks as though the 'Christmas' toggle had become just the automatic description of pieces in carol form. It may also be that the songs were traditionally sung during the Christmas season, irrespective of whether they had Christmas themes (as remains the case to this day).

But the received story on the carol has been badly deflected by confusion of terminology. In the great statements of the literary scholars Richard L. Greene (1935/1977) and Sir Edmund Chambers (1945) much space is given to round-dances and other early songs called carol or 'carole'. These are very general terms: they may occasionally have concerned a specific dance form (as argued most recently by Robert Mullally), but they have nothing intrinsic to do with the poetic form described (also) by Greene.[10]

Equally, the word 'carol' can mean any song. There are dozens of references, particularly in the fifteenth and sixteenth centuries, to payments for a carol: to associate these with payments for pieces in the form defined by Greene leads to a topsy-turvy view of history.

Similarly, several writers give much space to the Franciscans and most particularly to Richard Ledrede's *Red book of Ossory* from the fourteenth century, where the sacred poems are specified to be sung to the tunes of (lost) secular songs; but this is a tradition that stretches across Europe. It may have its roots in the Franciscans but it has no relationship with the carol as defined by Greene and as endorsed by the style of the surviving English polyphony.

The word 'burden' is even more problematic, historically and philologically speaking; it has been queried many times.[11] Greene used the word for the defining element of the carol, namely the passage that appears at the start and is repeated

---

6 Just one further carol text includes the word 'carol', in a Welsh manuscript from around 1500: *EEC* 10: stanza 3 of 5.
7 San Marino, The Huntington Library, Rare Books 56461; facsimile in Reed 1932: plates 1–16. Updated descriptions are in Greene 1977: 339–41 and Palti 2008: 99–102.
8 Oxford, Bodleian Library, Rawlinson 4° 598 (10); facsimile of the verso only in Reed 1932: plate A.
9 Oxford, Bodleian Library, Douce fragments f. 48; facsimile in Reed 1932: plates G–N.
10 Mullally 2011: 9–31. The case has also been made with some power by Adele Smaill (2003: 1–81). Robbins (1959b: 582) trenchantly called it 'a red herring that blends ill with the smell of incense'. The problem continues in more recent literature, as for example Chaganti 2008.
11 Perhaps first in Jacquot 1953: 100. Also in Wulstan, *An anthology of carols* (1968), 'Preface'; then in Wulstan, *Tudor music* (1985): 58.

after each stanza.[12] But its earliest use in a sense that could be related to that of the carol is in the late sixteenth century.[13] So to all intents and purposes it is an invention of Greene. But it is useful – more useful, for example, than the word 'refrain'. That is because many carols have both a burden and a refrain at the end of the individual stanzas or even within them, as in *MC* 28:

B

| Alleluia, | Alleluia, |
| Pro virgine Maria. | for the virgin Mary. |

1

Diva natalicia	The divine birth
Nostra purgat vicia,	cleanses our faults,
Alleluia,	
Ne demur ad supplicia:	lest we be given over to punishment.
Alleluia.	

2

Nato sacrificia	To the new-born
Reges dant triplicia,	the kings give triple offerings
Alleluia,	
Herodis post convicia:	after the reproaches of Herod.
Alleluia.	

3

Mortis vincla trucia	The fierce chains of death
Solvit die tercia,	he loosed on the third day
Alleluia,	
Resurgentis potencia:	by the power of one rising again.
Alleluia.	

(Incidentally, it is again worth noting the regularity of the phrases here: the burden has two four-bar phrases plus a two-bar intermission before the last phrase, which could be read – or at least heard – as a four-bar phrase; the verse opens with

---

12 The terms 'bourdon', 'faburden' and 'fauxbourdon' generated an enormous literature, particularly in the years between 1936 and 1955. This is an entirely different matter, covered briefly in chapter 6.
13 Chambers (1945: 86) states that the earliest usage in this sense is from 1589. That may in fact be a misprint, as the *Oxford English dictionary* gives as its earliest citation Francis Bacon's *Religious meditations* (London: Humfray Hooper, 1598): x.123: 'Lucrecius the epicure, who makes of his invectives against religion as it were a burthen or verse of returne to all his other discourses'.

16 Chapter 3: Definitions and terminology

Example 3.1 *Alleluia, Pro virgine Maria*, MC 28. Complete

two four-bar phrases and a two-bar 'Alleluia' with a more irregular concluding phrase, which can be read as an eight-bar phrase. On the other hand, by contrast with *Hail, Mary*, Example 2.1, the music and the text imply a positive dancing atmosphere. It may not be regular enough for actual dancing;, but the spirit is undeniably there.)

Plainly we need to have one word for the defining element, the burden that precedes and follows each stanza, and another word for the repeated material that can appear in or at the end of each stanza but not in any sense defining the carol: this latter we shall call 'refrain'.

In Richard Hill's manuscript we find a word for what we now call the burden: the word 'fote' appears alongside the burden for seventeen carols.[14] Since there

---

14 Hill: pp. 473–80 and 507; ed. Dyboski (1908): nos. 34–5, 37–49, and 95–6.

is apparently only one (even later) use of the word in this context, Hill must be considered with caution.[15] On the other hand, even bearing in mind that Greene's terminology, and his distinction between the two, are essentially his own, we shall continue to use the words 'burden' and 'refrain' as he defined them.

Finally, we must consider the word 'chorus', which appears several times in the surviving musical sources of the carol:[16]

Selden

Ah, man, assay (*MC* 17) for the full ('refrain') section at the end of the verse
Goday, my lord (*MC* 18) for the full ('refrain') section at the end of the verse
Alleluia: Now well may we mirthës make (MC 20) for burden II
What tidings bringest thou? (*MC* 27) for the full ('refrain') section within the verse (see Example 5.1)
Deo gracias, Anglia (MC 29) for burden II
Alleluia: A newë work (*MC* 30) for burden II and three refrains
Ave Maria: Hail, blessëd flower (MC 36) for burden II

Egerton

Qui natus est de virgine (MC 51) for burden II

Bodley 88*

That holy [Martyr Steven] (reconstructed fol. II = MC 22^A) for burden II
Verbum Patris hodie (reconstructed fol. III = MC 67) for burden II
Verbum Patris hodie (reconstructed fol. IIIv = MC 67) for the full ('refrain') section within the verse

Cambridge Add. 2764(1)

Farewell lo (*MC* 20^A), for burden II

Ritson

Johannes assecretis (MC 77*)* for burden II
Sonet laus (*MC* 78) for burden II

---

15 Greene (1935: cxxxiii; 1977: clx) cites [Richard] *Huloet's Dictionarie, newelye corrected, amended, set in order and enlarged . . . by John Higgins* (London: In aedibus I. Marshii, 1572), s.v. 'Foote of a dittie, or verse, which is often repeated. Versus intercalaris. *Refrainctes de balades*'. In fact, it is already present in the first edition, *Abcedarium anglicolatinum, pro tyrunculis Richardo Huloeto exscriptore* (London: William Riddel, 1552), s.v. 'Fote, or repete of a dittye, or verse, whiche is often repeated, *versus intercalaris*'. But that hardly counts as authority for using the word 'foot' in preference to 'burden' for this particular phenomenon.
16 Bowers, 'To chorus from quartet' (1995): 19.

Nowell, nowell: The boarës head (MC 79) for burden II
O clavis David (MC 91) for burden II
For all Christen soulës (*MC* 118) for the full ('refrain') section within the verse

Most of these are for the second burden, the one in three voices; and that must be why Bukofzer (1950: 153–9) used the word 'chorus' for what Greene called the three-voice burden. Since four of these are for 'refrain' sections within the verses, it is obviously dangerous to use it for the carol burdens. In a single carol text copied into a book owned by Professor Toshi Takamiya in Tokyo, certainly dating from after 1489, the word 'chorus' precedes the burden and appears after the end of four of the seven stanzas: plainly for that late copyist 'chorus' meant 'burden'.[17]

On the other hand, those uses of the word 'chorus' are part of the uniqueness of the carol repertory. If we for the moment accept that the music of both Selden and Egerton is from before 1430 (though the arguments will follow only later), then the appearance of the word is far earlier than in any other polyphonic music. Of course, the concept existed far earlier: the entire church chant repertory is based on the juxtaposition of soloist and the full *schola*; and the earliest history of polyphony is almost entirely for solo voices juxtaposed with a *schola* for chant sections. Current opinion is that most polyphony in the early fifteenth century was still for solo voices. And it should perhaps be no surprise that the earliest surviving polyphony with clear indications of a chorus should be in the simpler style represented by the carol.

One final note on terminology must concern 'verse' and 'stanza'. In what follows, the word 'verse' is never used in the sense of a single line. In general, the words 'verse' and 'stanza' mean the same thing in this book: I use the word 'verse' where it is used by Stevens and Greene, though I prefer the word 'stanza', which I tend to use in all other circumstances. (Perhaps 'strophe' would be the better word, but it does not appear in the carol literature; and this book aims to build on the available literature, despite its questioning so many of the basic tenets proposed in that literature.)

---

17 As noted in Edwards 2001, with the surprising view that this is the earliest use of the word in that sense and the even more surprising information that the *Middle English dictionary* glosses 'chorus' only in the sense of 'the northwest wind' – though without noting that the Latin word has an enormously longer history, even in England.

4 The musical form and virelai forms in general

Among the loveliest poems of late antiquity, perhaps from the fourth century, is the spring-song *Pervigilium veneris*. It has ninety-three lines but opens with a refrain that recurs eleven further times in the course of the poem, albeit at irregular intervals:[1]

> Cras amet qui nunquam amavit,   Let him love tomorrow who has
>   never loved,
> quique amavit cras amet.   and let him who has loved love
>   tomorrow.

The poem is far longer than any of our carols with polyphony, but the essence of the form is plainly there: a broadly general refrain precedes and follows a series of stanzas that fill the picture with more detail.

By and large, the early English carol has a burden of one or two lines;[2] and the stanzas most often have four lines, three rhyming with one another and the last rhyming with the second line of the burden – or occasionally identical with the second line of the burden. Sometimes the stanzas have only two lines, sometimes five, but only rarely anything else.[3]

The design is there in the earliest layers of the Gregorian chant repertory, particularly in the Introit, with its alternation of antiphon and psalm verses. But it is also present in several processional hymns. The Easter processional hymn *Salve, festa dies*, credited to Venantius Fortunatus, c. 600, is entirely written in elegiac couplets, but the available chants have different music for the

---

1 The edition by J. W. Mackail for the Loeb Classical Library (first edition 1912) plausibly cuts the poem into four-couplet stanzas, each followed by the refrain; the editor also remarks (p. 343) that 'It is the earliest known poem belonging in spirit to the Middle Ages'.
2 As Robbins observed (1942), the frequent appearance of four-line burdens in *EEC* is largely because Greene has written down the text of both burden I and burden II; only a single burden is essential to the poetic form.
3 Greene (1935: xl and 1977: lv) states that only twenty-two of his carols have stanzas of more than seven lines.

20 *Chapter 4: The musical form*

verses than for the opening couplet, which repeats after each following pair of couplets.

> Salve, festa dies, toto venerabilis aevo,
>   Qua deus infernum vicit et astra tenet.
>
> Ecce, renascentis testatur gratia mundi
>   Omnia cum domino dona redisse suo.
>
> Qui crucifixus erat Deus ecce per omnia regnat,
>   Dantque creatori cuncta creata precem.

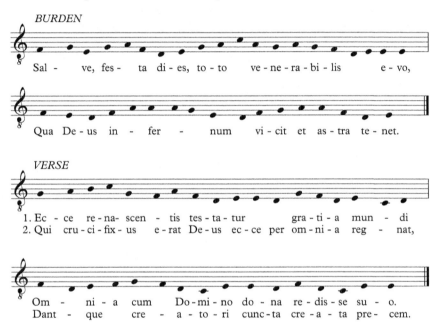

Example 4.1[4] *Salve festa dies* (chant)

The same is the case with the Palm Sunday processional hymn *Gloria, laus et honor*, credited to Theodulph of Orleans, *c.* 810, and famously appearing in the liturgical portion of Egerton.[5]

> Gloria, laus et honor tibi sit, rex Christe, redemptor,
>   Cui puerile decus promptsit hosanna pium.

---

4 The music here is from *Graduale sarisburiense*, ed. W.H. Frere (London: Bernard Quaritch, 1894): plate 116. Another version appears in *Hymnen (I): Die mittelalterlichen Hymnenmelodien des Abendlandes*, ed. Bruno Stäblein = Monumenta monodica medii aevi 1 (Kassel and Basel: Bärenreiter-Verlag, 1956): no. 1008. If I understand correctly, there is no source earlier than the fourteenth century for the full melody as printed here.

5 The text here is from *Hymnen (I)*, just cited: no. 1011 (and appears in a slightly different version in *Liber usualis*: 588–9). Once again, though, Stäblein mentions no source earlier than the fourteenth

Israel es tu rex, Davidis et inclita proles,
   Nomine qui in domini, rex benedicte, venis.

Coetus in excelsis te laudat caelicus omnis,
   Et mortalis homo, et cuncta creata simul.

Thus in both cases the music treated as a burden has precisely the same poetic form as the music treated as verses. In fact, it is hard to find the 'burden plus verses' form in sources much before 1300, but that phenomenon is definitely to be found in the *Cantigas de Santa Maria* credited to King Alfonso the Wise of Castile (1221–84) as well as in the Italian *laude spirituali* of around the same time.

But it is worth outlining a few details of the early history of the three *formes fixes* that dominated French song in the fourteenth and fifteenth centuries – the rondeau, the ballade and the virelai. All made their first appearances in the years around 1300.[6] The rondeau, the most compact and circumscribed of the three, accounts for perhaps a quarter of French polyphonic song in the fourteenth century and well over half in the fifteenth century; it continued to be favoured by poets well into the second half of the sixteenth century.[7] The ballade, with roots going back to the Pindaric odes and the *grande chanson courtoise* of the troubadours and trouvères, was perhaps the most universal form, with its broad AAB stanza-structure; by the fourteenth century it was traditionally in three stanzas, all ending with a refrain-line.[8] But the most interesting form, in some ways, is the one we call virelai.[9] It was also the loosest in design, turning up in many varied forms and in particular turning up in Iberian poetry with the names '*cantiga*' and '*villancico*' as well as in Italian poetry with the name '*ballata*';

---

century with different music for the first couplet and the remaining couplets, though he does note an eleventh-century Beneventan source with the same music for all couplets including the first. A further case is the Maundy Thursday processional hymn *O Redemptor, sume carmen*, ed. in *Hymnen (I)*: no. 1025, for which he finds two sources from around 1200 with different music for the first couplet.

6 As argued for the first time in Willi Apel, 'Rondeaux, virelais, and ballades in French 13th-century song', *Journal of the American Musicological Society* 7 (1954): 121–30. Obviously there are earlier vestiges of these forms, which was part of Apel's point – with particular reference to Friedrich Gennrich's *Grundriss einer Formenlehre des mittelalterlichen Liedes* (Halle: Niemeyer, 1932).

7 I outlined a history of this in the article 'Das mehrstimmige Rondeau des Mittelalters', in *Die Musik in Geschichte und Gegenwart . . . zweite neubearbeitete Ausgabe*, ed. Ludwig Finscher, *Sachteil* 8 (Kassel, etc.: Bärenreiter and Stuttgart, etc.: J. B. Metzler, 1998): cols. 541–9.

8 I outlined a history of this in the article 'Mehrstimmige Ballade des Mittelalters', in *Die Musik in Geschichte und Gegenwart . . . zweite neubearbeitete Ausgabe*, ed. Ludwig Finscher, *Sachteil* 1 (Kassel, etc.: Bärenreiter and Stuttgart, etc.: J. B. Metzler, 1994): cols. 1129–34.

9 Sadly, my planned trio of articles on the *formes fixes* for the revised *Die Musik in Geschichte und Gegenwart* was aborted when the article 'Virelai' was commissioned elsewhere and adopted a viewpoint quite different from my own. But some hint of my plans can be seen in the much briefer article 'Bergerette', in *op. cit.*: cols. 1411–13.

loosest of all its manifestations is the one Richard L. Greene called the English 'carol'.

The virelai often had two stanzas in the fourteenth century.[10] Example 4.2 (a monophonic virelai chosen primarily because the complete music takes up less space but also because it is one of Machaut's most unforgettable melodies) shows the most characteristic details. Like the carol, it opens with the burden (called *refrain* in French literary theory of the time), which is repeated after each stanza. But the remaining details are never found in the carol repertory: that the music of the *refrain* is repeated after the *couplet* with new text, the *tierce*, that matches the rhymes of the *refrain*; that the *couplet* proper has music that is always repeated with new words; that the entire poem in this case is in the voice of a single singer who is wooing a single woman, whereas the carols give plenty of evidence that the burden was for a chorus while the verses are for soloists and of the entire performance witnessing the presence of a community. Only in the *Cantigas de Santa Maria* do we find the contrast implied in the carols: here normally the text of the refrain is a general moralistic statement, whereas the stanzas typically tell the story. But the carol stanzas almost never tell a story: like the majority of lyric poetry, they are static.

Within that framework, the major difference in the Portuguese-Galician *cantigas* of the thirteenth century and the Italian *ballate* of the fourteenth century is that these had a more sophisticated rhyme scheme for their equivalent of the French *tierce*, called *vuelta* in Spanish and *volta* in Italian: here, the rhymes begin with those of the *couplet* (*mudanzas*; *piedi*) and 'turn' towards the rhyme scheme of the refrain. This never seems to happen in the French virelai repertory, where the *tierce* always has the same rhymes as the *refrain*. And it absolutely never happens in the English carol.

---

10 Most modern studies state that the virelai has three stanzas, as in this example by Machaut, and that there is also a single-stanza form called the bergerette which replaced it in the fifteenth century. But the musical record contradicts this. From the beginning of the fourteenth century through to about 1480 there are a little over two hundred surviving songs in this form apart from the works of Machaut; and they divide more or less equally before and after about 1420. Only three of those before 1420 have the full three stanzas. One seems to me very much in the style of Machaut and could well be his; the others are by Solage from the late fourteenth century and by Matteo da Perugia early in the fifteenth century. Eight have two stanzas, and the rest have only one. Of course, musical sources cannot always be relied on to transmit the complete poem, but the overwhelming weight of the evidence is that the three-stanza form in music of the fourteenth century is more or less confined to Machaut (who in any case called his virelais 'chansons baladees'). The literary record in fact favours the two-stanza form in the years around 1400. On the basis of autograph or near-autograph sources, Christine de Pizan always has two stanzas, as does Charles d'Orléans in his four early virelais (though he actually called them *caroles*); Froissart normally has two. The only named poet apart from Machaut to exploit the three-stanza variety is Eustache Deschamps, who described himself as Machaut's pupil: he has seventeen with three stanzas, but eighty-four with two stanzas and eighteen with one stanza. By contrast, most carols have four or more stanzas.

Chapter 4: The musical form 23

Example 4.2[11] *Douce dame jolie* (Guillaume de Machaut)

The upshot of this is that it makes sense to view the English carols as within the broad formal genre we call 'virelai/*ballata*/*cantiga*' but as being essentially different in several important respects: in having a looser form, most particularly avoiding musical repeats within the stanza, in having no repeat of the refrain with different words.[12]

Among distinctive details of the English carol as it appears in the literary sources are the layout of the poem on the written page, with the burden often appearing to the right of the main texts, as though to define its recurrence. The point here is that the layout makes it clear when the burden is repeated; and from the surviving music we know that the music for the verses contains no repeat before the next statement of the burden.

---

11 Taken, with two tiny adjustments, from *The works of Guillaume de Machaut: second part*, ed. Leo Schrade = Polyphonic music of the fourteenth century 3 (Monaco: Éditions de l'Oiseau-lyre, 1956): 168. The second and third stanzas of text are omitted here.
12 In this context, the pieces considered in Frank Ll. Harrison, 'Benedicamus, conductus, carol' (1965), seem to be irrelevant. The manuscript Aosta, Seminario Maggiore, cod. 11 (*olim* 9-E-19, later C3 and apparently also D16), originating in Aosta during the fourteenth century, includes four pieces that Harrison gives the heading 'Carol' (nos. 18–21 in his list, transcribed on pp. 47–8 from fols. 83–85v). Nos. 18–20 do indeed look like monophonic carols, but all three have repeated music at the opening of the verse and two of them have a *tierce*. They are certainly within the virelai genre, but they are not carols as defined by Greene and accepted here, although all four pieces have Christmas texts.

That, in short, is the key difference between the carols and the surviving repertories of French virelais, Iberian *cantigas* and Italian *ballate*. All those other forms have a verse that includes a musical repeat.[13] Interestingly enough, the form that comes closest to that of the carol is the Andalusian *zajal* and *muwashshah*, dating back to at least the twelfth century: all the music is lost, so we cannot be sure what was repeated, but the verse forms very often follow the *AB cccb* design that accounts for a great majority of the English carols.[14]

As a matter of fact there is an Irish poem, perhaps of the ninth century and perhaps earlier, that beautifully matches the form of the carol and even has the characteristic that there can hardly have been a musical repeat in the verse:[15]

| Cluchi cách, gaine cách | Game was all and sport was all |
| co roich Fer Diad issin n-áth. | until my meeting with Fer Diad at the ford. |

1

Inund foglaim frith dúinn,	The same instruction we had,
innund rograim ráth,	the same power of guarantee,
innund mummi máeth	the same tender foster-mother we had
ras slainni sech cách.	whose name is beyond all others.

| Cluchi cách, gaine cách | Game was all and sport was all |
| co roich Fer Diad issin n-áth. | until my meeting with Fer Diad at the ford. |

2

| Inund aisti arúath dúinn, | The same nature we had, |
| inund gasced gnáth. | the same fearsomeness and weapons. |

---

13 Often that repeat includes cadences on different pitches (what the French called *ouvert* and *clos*), but the principle remains the same.

14 The classic discussion of the Andalusian influence on Spanish and French poetry remains Pierre Le Gentil, *Le virelai et le villancico: le problème des origines arabes* (Paris: Société d'éditions 'Les belles lettres', 1954). More recent summaries are in David Wulstan, 'The muwashshah and zagal revisited', *Journal of the American Oriental Society* 102 (1982): 247–64, and Manuel Pedro Ferreira, 'Rondeau and virelai: the music of Andalus and the *Cantigas de Santa Maria*', *Plainsong and medieval music* 13 (2004): 127–40.

15 This comes from the prose epic *Táin Bó Cúalnge*, ed. George Sigerson, *Bards of the Gael and Gall* (3rd edition, Dublin: Talbot Press, 1925): 119–20, with translation from Cecile O'Rahilly, *Táin Bó Cúalnge from the book of Leinster* = Irish Texts Society 49 (Dublin: Dublin Institute for Advanced Studies, 1967): 234. The three known manuscripts are from the eleventh or twelfth centuries, but the epic is believed to have been written in the eighth century. My knowledge of the text comes from James T. Munro, 'Andalusi-Arabic strophic poetry as an example of literary hybridization', in *Medieval oral literature*, ed. Karl Reichl (Berlin and Boston: Walter de Gruyter, 2012): 601–28, at pp. 623–5.

Scáthach tuc dá sciath	Scáthach gave two shields
dam-sa is Fer Diad tráth.	to me and to Fer Diad.
Cluchi cách, gaine cách	Game was all and sport was all
co roich Fer Diad issin n-áth.	until my meeting with Fer Diad at the ford.

3

Inmain úatni óir	Beloved was he, the golden pillar,
ra furmius ar áth.	whom I laid low at the ford.
A tarbga na túath	O strong one of the tribes,
ba calma ná cách.	you were more valiant than all others.
Cluchi cách, gaine cách	Game was all and sport was all
co roich Fer Diad issin n-áth.	until my meeting with Fer Diad at the ford.

The poem continues for five more stanzas, though the transmission becomes increasingly difficult. I add these first three stanzas not just as a curiosity but as a hint that this formal feature may have a far wider history, particularly in the unwritten traditions. Obviously the story of the king's son Fer Diad and how he died at the ford has nothing in common with any carol, or any *zajal* or even any *cantiga*, at least in rhetorical terms. But formally this is closer to the carol than anything in the virelai, *ballata* or *cantiga* repertory.

Perhaps the closest repertory is the Italian *lauda spirituale*, as represented in two musical manuscripts, both confined to monophony: the forty-six *laude* in the late thirteenth-century manuscript, Cortona, Biblioteca Comunale, MS 91; and the eighty-nine generally more florid melodies in the somewhat later manuscript, Florence, Biblioteca Nazionale Centrale, Banco Rari 18.[16] While forms vary, the most often encountered form here is with a two-line refrain and a four-line stanza rhyming *aaaB*, that is, each stanza having its own rhyme but ending with a rhyme that matches the refrain, which is to say that they have precisely the form that appears in the majority of English carols.[17] Occasionally the stanzas include a musical repeat, but generally they do not.[18] On the other hand, the *laude* differ from the polyphonic carols in having a far wider range of topics, in particular saints from all times of the

---

16 The fundamental treatment of the topic is in the luxurious edition by Fernando Liuzzi, *La lauda e i primordi della melodia italiana* (Rome: La Libreria dello Stato, [1935]). More recent editions are *Il laudario di Cortona*, ed. Luigi Lucchi (Vicenza: Libreria Internazionale Edizioni Francescane, 1987) and *The Florence laudario: an edition of Florence, Biblioteca Nazionale Centrale, Banco Rari 18*, ed. Blake Wilson and Nello Barbieri = Recent researches in the music of the middle ages and renaissance 29 (Madison: A-R Editions, 1995). I have not yet seen *Il laudario di Cortona*, ed. Marco Gozzi and Francesco Zimei, 2 vols. (Lucca: LIM, 2015).

17 The matter is well explored by John Zec (1997: 82–90). He, however, finds the closest analogy between carol and *lauda* in the monophonic carol *Nowell: Tidings true* (*MC* 4^).

18 For this enquiry, the most convenient edition of the music is in Martin Dürrer, *Altitalienische Laudenmelodien: das einstimmige Repertoire der Handschriften Cortona und Florenz*, 2 vols. (Kassel, etc: Bärenreiter, 1996), which has the massive advantage of resisting any theory about the

church year; their texts, as the word '*lauda*' implies, are largely taken up with varieties of praise, with virtually no narrative; and their music is monophonic.

To see any direct line from the Andalusian forms or from the thirteenth-century *cantigas* to the carol would be to throw common sense out of the window. The French virelai and the Italian *ballata* were certainly known in the England of the early fifteenth century; and the rational view would be to see the English carols as distantly and vaguely influenced by them but at the same time thoroughly distinctive and in a form not found outside England. There may be a direct link in the *laude*, however, since there was a substantial Franciscan presence in fourteenth-century England, though Robbins has noted (1940: 237–8) that the Franciscans had very much ceased to be a driving force in England at the time of the polyphonic carols that are our concern here.[19]

Even so, there are a few slightly odd forms within the musical repertory of the English carol, and it is worth glancing at them to help clarify the situation.

Ecce, quod Natura

This is the only carol to appear in three musical sources. It is the closest we come to a pure virelai in the carol repertory, though with Latin text. Its three sources cope with the form differently: the Selden MS is the only one to lay it out more or less as continental sources lay out their virelais, though the details of its notation are horrible; both Ashmole 1393 and the Egerton MS try makeshift arrangements to fit the music and the poetry together, as though quite unaware of any continental virelai tradition.

But although Bukofzer (1950: 152) and Stevens (*MC*: 119) both describe this as a continental virelai, it is importantly different from almost all known virelais in that the two couplets that open the verse do not carry the same music: here there are four phrases of music for the first four lines of the verse, whereas all French virelais and Italian *ballate* have just two lines of music for two lines of text, repeating the music for the next two. On the other hand, it does follow the pattern of the Spanish *cantigas* and the Italian *ballate* in having a *vuelta* or *volta*, a turning portion, where the text moves from the rhyme of the couplets to the rhyme of the refrain (burden). It also resembles the virelai, as cultivated by Machaut and Deschamps, in having three stanzas. Example 4.3, accordingly, lays out the music rather differently from the other carols presented in this book. Essentially, sections, 1, 4, 7 and 10 are the burden and the three verses are sections 2 and 3, 5 and 6, and 8 and 9.

---

rhythms of the music and simply aligning the musical phrases against a numbered grill according to the structure of the poetry.

19 The standard statement on this topic is David L. Jeffrey, *The early English lyric and Franciscan spirituality* (1975), praised by Greene (1977: cl) as 'indispensable for any further study of the subject'. Jeffrey agrees with Robbins that the Franciscan influence in England was much reduced after the Black Death (see Jeffrey 1975: 273–5), some time before the evolution of the carols I am discussing here.

Chapter 4: The musical form   27

Example 4.3[20] *Ecce, quod Natura*, MC 37. Complete

But perhaps the most important feature of *Ecce, quod Natura* is that an older poem has been adjusted to create a carol. In each stanza, the last line of the *piedi* is repeated to become the first line of the *volta*. As it happens, we have a continental source for the poem, Theodoricus Petri's *Piæ cantiones*, first printed at Greifswald in 1582 (fol. B8r–v), though the poem must be far older. Petri's version puts the opening burden to the end of each stanza, which must surely be its original form. On the other hand, he also has the repeat of line 4, as in the English carol. Example 4.4 omits the second and third stanzas, which closely correspond to those in the English carol sources. The music, unsurprisingly, is quite unrelated to the English version; it hardly looks as though it could be earlier than the sixteenth century.

20 This follows the Selden version, *MC* 37; the variants in the two other sources make for fascinating comparison, not offered here but offered later through other carols in chapter 15.

28 *Chapter 4: The musical form*

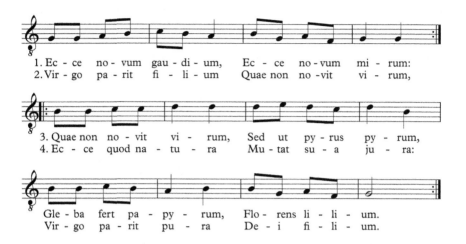

Example 4.4 Ecce, novum gaudium (Theodoricus Petri)

As I lay upon a night

There is just one pure musical virelai in the carol repertory, *As I lay upon a night*, in the Selden manuscript, rejected by John Stevens from his main repertory but printed as *MC* 11[A]. Here the music of the verse is indeed repeated to new words and followed by a repeat of the burden music, also with new words. (Example 4.5 omits verses 2–5.)

But even though the music is in the form of a virelai the text is nothing of the kind. As is clear from an earlier purely poetic source (the fourteenth-century preaching-book of John of Grimestone), it is a succession of sixteen quatrains, rhyming *abab/cdcd* and so forth.[21] They comprise a perfectly standard dream narrative, in which the poet sees the Holy Family and Joseph describes what has happened. But the text used for *MC* 11[A] cuts off after quatrain eleven, just before Joseph explains that the child is from God; that is to say that the Selden version with polyphonic music never actually gets to the point of the story. It is a plain example of adapting an existing poem for new musical purposes.

Whether John Stevens was right to relegate this marvellous piece to his appendix is another question entirely. In style, and in manuscript context, it is beyond question a carol; in musical form it is a virelai; in poetic form it is a narrative in quatrains. Putting it into the appendix draws attention to some of its anomalies.

---

21 It is printed in Brown 1924: no. 58.

Chapter 4: The musical form 29

Example 4.5 As I lay upon a night, MC 11[A]. Complete

Verbum caro factum est

Slightly different is the case of *Verbum caro factum est*, a poem that goes back at least to the twelfth century, though in a large number of slightly (and often substantially) differing forms.[22] For our purposes, perhaps the best version of the poem to take is again that printed in Theodoricus Petri's *Piæ cantiones* (1582): fols. A8v–B1.

That the last two lines of the verse repeat exactly the music of the burden and end with the same words as the burden puts this poem far more exactly into the category of virelai; but the lack of a musical repeat within the first half of the verse

---

22 An exceptionally good and erudite summary is offered in John Julian, *A dictionary of hymnology* (London: John Murray, 1892, second expanded edition, 1907): 1216, signed by James Mearns (1855–1922), the assistant editor of the dictionary. A more recent article, tracing the liturgical origins of the refrain, is Dom Anselm Hughes, 'In hoc anni circulo', *Music and letters* 60 (1974): 37–45, published in the year of his death at the age of eighty-five and perhaps his last article. In fact, to judge from the article on him in *The new Grove dictionary* (2001), this appears to be the first article he published in a musicological journal, though this accreditation as one of the major musicologists of the twentieth century is incontestable.

30   *Chapter 4: The musical form*

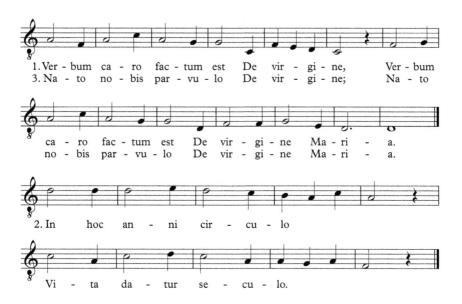

Example 4.6 Verbum caro factum est (Theodoricus Petri)

aligns it more with the carol repertory. So does the poem,[23] in which each stanza consists of four lines, the first three rhyming with one another (but not with those of any other stanza) but the last matching the second line of the burden.

B

Verbum caro factum est
De virgine Maria.

1

In hoc anni circulo
Vita datur seculo,
Nato nobis parvulo
De virgine Maria.

2

O beata femina,
Cuius ventris Gloria

---

23 Taken here from *Piæ cantiones*.

Mundi lavat crimina
De virgine Maria.

3

Stella solem protulit,
Sol salutem contulit,
Carnem veram abstulit
De virgine Maria.

4

Fons de suo rivulo
Nascitur de populo,
Quem tulit de vinculo
De virgine Maria.

5

Laus, honor, virtus, Domino,
Deo Patri et Filio,
Sancto simul paracleto,
De virgine Maria.

The earliest known version of this poem was copied around the year 1100 in the St-Martial manuscript Paris, Bibliothèque nationale de France, f. lat. 1139, fol. 48, with a parallel text in Provençal (thereby making it a key document in the early history of troubadour song). From the diastematic neumes one can read a melody that is not exactly identical with that in *Piæ cantiones* but close enough to be recognizably the same. What is different in this St-Martial manuscript, however, is that the 'Verbum caro' burden is not present. The burden seems to make its appearance for the first time in another BNF manuscript, f. lat. 1343, fol. 40 – copied perhaps for the Sicilian royal court in the late thirteenth century.[24] Beyond that, no fewer than eleven Italian polyphonic settings from the fifteenth century and the sixteenth are printed in Francesco Luisi, *Laudario giustinianeo* (Venice: Fondazione Levi, 1983): ii.194–206.

Intriguingly, the one setting that Luisi did not print is the version in the manuscript Trento 92, specifically with fauxbourdon and offering plenty of clues that this could in fact be English, albeit perhaps a little later than the carols we otherwise know. Once again, one could observe the regularity of the phrases: burden of

---

24 Printed in *Cantus fractus italiano: un' antologia*, ed. Marco Gozzi = Musica mensurabilis 4 (Hildesheim, etc: Georg Olms Verlag, 2012): ex. 11. The same volume contains three more musically related settings (ex. 20, ex. 62 and ex. 63).

32 Chapter 4: The musical form

Example 4.7 Verbum caro factum est (Trento 92)

4+4 bars, verse of 4+5+4+4 bars. It is also worth noting, though we shall return to the point in more detail, that the middle voice is easily reconstructed, though not by the normal (received) rules of fauxbourdon: for bars 6 and 7, as well as bar 21, the middle voice cannot be a 4th below the discantus; it must be calculated from the tenor (where the indication stands), being a 3rd higher but a 5th higher at cadences – as to be discussed further in chapter 6.

The aim of this chapter was to show that the English carol belongs broadly within the category known elsewhere in Europe as the virelai/*ballata*/*cantiga* but is at the same time fundamentally different from any – absolutely any – of the others. That is not by any means to claim that the poets and composers of the English carols were stunningly brilliant originators; but it is to say that what they produced is entirely different from what their contemporaries elsewhere produced; and it is also to say that the musical individuality of the carol style in music happens to correspond to an individuality in poetic form.

5 Burdens and double burdens

Here we must raise two questions that concern only the musical form and cannot be answered from the poetry sources. They are also questions that address another way in which the carol is unlike any other known musical form from the middle ages, anywhere in Europe.

A majority of the surviving carols have two burdens, usually the first in two voices and the second in three. In all cases but two, the two burdens have the same text;[1] in a few cases the music of the two burdens is identical, though in most cases they are musically related.

John Stevens (1952 etc.) referred to them as 'burden' and 'burden II', which can occasionally be confusing; but it would be more confusing to invent a new terminology, so I retain them in what follows (shortened as B and BII), just occasionally using the term burden I to clarify. I remark only in passing that Bukofzer (1950: 153–9) refers to BII as 'chorus', which is doubly confusing in terms of the available terminology in the sources, as explained earlier (pp. 18) but underlines that his view of the relationship between the two burdens coincides with mine, namely that B is basically for soloists, as happens in so much chant, whereas BII is for more singers. What is not entirely clear, and therefore merits a brief discussion, is how often both burdens were sung. But first we must briefly consider the history of the double burden.

Among the thirteen carols in Trinity, only two have a double burden, namely the Agincourt carol (*MC* 8) and the strange moral carol *Abide, I hope* (*MC* 10); the rest, all associated with the Christmas season, have but a single burden. All the Trinity carols are in major prolation, apart from *Abide, I hope*. The significance of this is that in general major prolation (3/8 or 6/8) gave way to perfect time somewhere in the second or third decades of the fifteenth century.

---

1 One exception is the carol *Te Deum* in Ritson (*MC* 95), where the two-voice burden has the text 'Te Deum laudamus in te confitemur' and the three-voice burden (with identical music albeit expanded to three voices by faburdon) has the continuation of that text 'Te eternum Patrem omnis terra veneratur' – to be discussed later as Example 6.2. The other is the puzzling *O clavis David* (*MC* 91), in which the three-voice burden seems to add another couplet to the text of the two-voice burden.

Chapter 5: Burdens and double burdens

Among the twenty-eight carols in Selden, there are eleven with double burdens; only three of these are in major prolation, namely *Alleluia: Now well may we mirthës make* (*MC* 20), *Nowell, nowell: In Bethlem* (*MC* 38) and *Nowell, nowell: Out of your sleep* (*MC* 25). *MC* 25 is a special case in that it is in major prolation with perfect time (9/8 in modern transcription); and *MC* 38 is a special case in that the music appears already in Trinity without the three-voice burden.

Among the thirty carols in Egerton, there are fifteen with double burdens, none of them in major prolation. That further supports the tentative view that single-burden carols are among the earliest layer of the surviving polyphonic carols.

Among the forty-four carols in Ritson, all have a double burden apart from *Proface, welcome* (*MC* 107), *For all Christen soulës* (*MC* 118) and the complicated case of *O clavis David* (*MC* 91). That implies that by this point a double burden was de rigueur for carol settings (at least for the copyist of Ritson) and once again emphasizes the point that this kind of double treatment is not found anywhere else in European polyphony of the fifteenth century (or indeed the fourteenth). And the rest of the pattern seems to imply that the use of a double burden took off only slowly. By and large, musical style appears to confirm the view that the carols with only a single burden are among the earliest to survive.

What does appear to be the case – here and in continental pieces of related nature, particularly the Portuguese-Galician *Cantigas de Santa Maria* – is that the refrain generally implies choral singing whereas the verses are for soloists. That is clarified in certain carols, for example in *What tidings bringest thou?* (*MC* 27: Example 5.1), where the chorus section within the verse repeats material from the burden and actually has the heading 'chorus'.[2] Besides, the dramatic power of this is palpable: the people ask the messenger for news, which the messenger brings, and they ask for more news, which he again gives. Perhaps it was originally part of a theatrical performance: the same could be suggested for several other carols, among them the Ritson carols *Nowell, nowell: who is there* (*MC* 80), *Marvel not, Joseph* (*MC* 81) and *Proface, welcome* (*MC* 107). That the music for the messenger is in two voices and therefore (presumably) performed by two singers, does nothing to dilute its dramatic impact – though that is, for me, among the details that make the English carol special among the vernacular (and indeed Latin) polyphonic repertories of the fifteenth century.

Two more stanzas follow, in which the messenger reports Mary's greeting to the new-born child and the wonder that the Lord should now have done this thing for mankind.

As concerns how often the burdens were sung, John Stevens, in the revised version of *MC* (1958), was absolutely clear and consistent: that the two-voice

---

2 Bukofzer (1954: 64) stated that this carol 'displays what may be called an extended virelai form', arguing that the *tierce* begins with the words 'Such wonder tidings ye mow hear', but that it is interrupted by the chorus insertion and another line. Given the lack of any musical repeat within the *couplet*, it seems to me that, as in so many other cases, the virelai pattern rather hovers distantly in the background here.

Example 5.1 *What tidings bringest thou?*, MC 27. Complete

36 Chapter 5: Burdens and double burdens

burden should be followed by the three-voice burden before every stanza and again at the end of the song.[3] This results in a performing sequence: B BII V$_1$ B BII V$_2$ B BII V$_3$ B II. I wish to suggest otherwise, namely that in general the two-voice burden was sung only at the outset of the carol, thereafter replaced by the three-voice burden, BII, with the resulting sequence: B BII V$_1$ BII V$_2$ BII V$_3$ BII.[4]

But his entire thinking about double burdens was changed by Bukofzer's review (1954) of the first edition; and there are plenty of signs that Stevens was rather too easily persuaded by Bukofzer – who still stands as probably the sharpest mind in modern times to have tackled the music of the fifteenth century.

In the first edition of *MC* (1952), John Stevens had included a table in the 'key' to his Analytical Index (1952: 138), which listed five different singing orders for the carols; and in the body of the Analytical Index (1952: 126–37) there was a column into which he entered the number of the singing order he deemed appropriate for each song. For the 1958 revision he eliminated this column entirely, reducing the number of columns in the Analytical Index from thirteen to twelve, with the explanation (1958: xii) that 'Bukofzer's arguments convinced me that I had been greatly over-elaborate in my suggestions about the performing order of the carols and that I had failed to grasp one of the basic principles involved'. As a result, he offered basically only two performing orders for the carols, always presented (as also in the 1952 edition) on the page with the music.[5]

Bukofzer's review (1954: 76–7) began with the assertion that three of Stevens's five categories 'are needlessly confusing and take away musical variety'. He never explained why. He then asserted that 'extensive repeats are characteristic of all the fixed forms; those of the carol are indeed mild in comparison with the rondeau in which the first section is heard six times before one is through with the first verse'.[6] This, I suggest, is a thoroughly misleading remark: the multi-verse rondeaux to which he is referring are the monophonic rondeaux found, for example,

---

3 There is a useful discussion in McInnes 2013: 24–35.
4 Robbins, 'The burden in carols' (1942: 18), proposed that the two burdens may be alternatives, 'that is, one or the other to be sung, according to the occasion or the ability of the performers, but never to be sung concurrently': he offered no support for that counterintuitive opinion. Twenty years later (Robbins 1961: 8), he took a more lenient view, allowing 'considerable latitude' but insisting: 'provided that the alternation of stanzas (by the soloists) with burdens (by the chorus) is always maintained'. Most other commentators have supported the flexible view, but I insist that the appearance of double burdens is not otherwise attested in European polyphony of the fourteenth or fifteenth centuries and that it therefore merits more intensive investigation.
5 Partly because I so often disagree with the performing orders proposed by John Stevens, for my 2018 revision I have relegated this information to the commentary.
6 Earlier, Bukofzer (1950: 154) had asserted that 'The great, if not excessive, amount of repetition resulting from this practice would be quite in keeping with the style of the popular refrain forms such as the *lauda* and the *frottola*'. A reflection of those remarks appears in John Stevens's *New Grove* article (1980: 167): 'What now appears an excessive amount of repetition is characteristic of the medieval *formes fixes* and may have seemed both normal and necessary in the 15th century'. I beg to differ.

in the twelfth fascicle of the Notre-Dame manuscript 'F',[7] where the stanzas are extremely short. But his main argument seems to be:

> The chorus section [by which he means BII], no matter whether it comprises the whole or only a part of the burden, is a varied answer and not a self-sufficient section like the burden. It cannot therefore replace the burden.

It is hard to see what he was saying here. There is no case where burden II is less complete than burden I. Perhaps he was referring to the brief choral interjections, like the one just seen in Example 5.1; but if so his comments are plainly irrelevant to the question on hand.

In his famous essay on 'The beginnings of choral polyphony', Bukofzer (1950: 176–89, at p. 187) quoted the two burdens of *Qui natus est de virgine* (*MC* 51) to show that the two-voice burden was rather more florid than the three-voice burden; and he concluded that the former was composed for soloists whereas the latter was for a chorus. There are few other examples that could have made the point so well, but his discussion failed to note one other extremely important feature of *Qui natus est*: the verse ends with a precise repeat of the last five bars of B, namely the bars that are most florid in relation to BII. That again seems a case where the music is calculated on the basis of B being sung just once, by solo voices, with the best bits of its music repeated at the end of each verse. This in fact happens quite often among the carols that have two burdens:

Selden

Ave Maria: Hail, blessëd flower (*MC* 36): almost the entire B appears at the end of the verse, with same text.

Egerton

David ex progenie (*MC* 46): the last 6 bars of B (total 11 bars) repeated at end of verse, with new text.
Sol occasum nesciens (*MC* 49): the entire B written out at end of verse, with same text.[8]
Qui natus est de virgine (*MC* 51): last 5 bars of B (total 13 bars) repeated at end of verse, with same text.
Ivy is good (*MC* 55): last 8 bars of B (total 19 bars) repeated at end of verse, with new text.

---

7 These are now all published in *Notre-Dame and related conductus: opera omnia: 1pt conductus: the Latin rondeau repertoire*, ed. Gordon A. Anderson = Gesamtausgaben X/8 (Henryville, Ottawa and Binningen: Institute of Medieval Music, [1978]).
8 I take this to be an exceptional case, directing that the two-voice burden be sung in its entirety after each verse.

Anglia, tibi turbidas (*MC* 56): last 6 bars of B repeated at end of verse, with same text.
Saint Thomas honour we (*MC* 59): last 4 bars of B (total 13 bars) repeated at end of verse, with new text.
Omnis caterva fidelium (*MC* 70): the last 4 bars of B repeated at end of verse, with new text.
Parit virgo filium (*MC* 73): the last 10 bars of B (total 14 bars) repeated at end of verse, with same text.

Ritson

In every state, in every degree (*MC* 85): the last 9 bars of B (total 14 bars) repeated at end of verse, with same text.
Have mercy of me (*MC* 88): the last 6 bars of B (total 12 bars) repeated at end of verse, with new text.
Regi canamus glorie (*MC* 89): the last 5 bars of B (total 11 bars) repeated at end of verse, with new text.
O clavis David (*MC* 91): last 5 bars of B repeated at end of verse, with new text.
Psallite gaudentes (*MC* 93): last 7 bars of B (total 12 bars) repeated at end of verse, with new text.
Letare, Cantuaria (*MC* 96): last 6 bars of B (total 23 bars) repeated at end of verse, with new text.
Spes mea in Deo est (*MC* 99): all but first bar of B repeated at end of verse, with same text.
I pray you all (*MC* 100): last 9 bars of B (total 15 bars) repeated at end of verse, with same text.
Tidings true (*MC* 102): last 7 bars of B (total 15 bars) repeated at end of verse, with same text.
Do well and dread no man (*MC* 104): last 6 bars of B (total 13 bars) repeated at end of verse, both as a melisma.
Alleluia: Now may we mirthës make (*MC* 105): entire B (total 7 bars) repeated at end of verse, with new text.
Jesus autem hodie (*MC* 108): last 5 bars of B (total 14 bars) repeated at end of verse, with new text.
Jesu, fili virginis (*MC* 111): last 8 bars of B (total 13 bars) repeated at end of verse, with same text.
Jesu, for thy mercy (*MC* 112): entire B (total 12 bars) repeated at end of verse, with same text.[9]
To many a well (*MC* 114): last 4 bars of B (total 14 bars) repeated at end of verse, both as a melisma.
Pray for us, thou Prince of Peace (*MC* 115): last 7 bars of B (total 10 bars) repeated at end of verse, with same text.

---

9 I take this, too, to be an exceptional case, just like that of *MC* 49.

O blessed Lord (*MC* 116): last 8 bars of B (total 13 bars) repeated at end of verse, with same text.
The best rede (*MC* 117): last 9 bars of B (total 13 bars) repeated at end of verse, with same text.

My conclusions, reached fairly slowly, are: (a) that we must obviously resist the temptation to see all carols as identical, despite the much shorter time frame that I shall be proposing for composition of most of the Trinity-Selden-Egerton carols; and (b) that it seems natural to understand these carols and their double burdens alongside liturgical music and the role of the intoner. Much chant begins with a few notes for a soloist (whether a priest or a leading singer), basically to establish the pitch for the rest of the *schola*. In that context, it is perhaps logical to see the two-voice burdens as establishing the pitch-level and introducing the carol. Once the choral three-voice burden is established, that remains the burden. I begin to think that one burden is enough between the stanzas and the form can actually gain power if the two-voice burden is heard only once, as an introduction to the new carol, particularly when so much of the two-voice burden is precisely repeated in so many of the surviving carol verses. Others apparently feel likewise: among the available recordings of the carol repertory there are very few that follow the directions given by John Stevens in the second (1958) edition of his collection.

The remaining question is whether burden II should be sung between the burden and the first verse. Here the Selden manuscript may offer an answer. In Egerton and Ritson there is a special page layout, with the two-voice music on the left-hand page and the three-voice music – whether a three-voice burden or three-voice 'chorus' passages inserted within the verse – all put together on the right-hand page. From these there is no clear information about the singing order. But the far less carefully copied Selden manuscript has burden II immediately after burden I in *Alleluia: A newë work* (*MC* 30: fols. 21v–22); *David ex progenie* (*MC* 34: fols. 24v–25); *Nowell, nowell to us is born* (*MC* 38: fol. 27v); *Laus honor virtus gloria* (*MC* 39: fol. 28); *Veni, Redemptor gencium* (*MC* 41: fol. 29); and *Abide, I hope* (*MC* 42: fol. 29v). The same happens in the Bodley 88* fragments of *Verbum Patris hodie* (*MC* 67). I take that as evidence that the normal opening gambit was to perform burden I with soloists, then burden II with chorus, after which the carol alternates verses and burden II.

On the other hand – and endorsing the view that a certain flexibility is in order – there is an interesting solution in the famous Agincourt carol, where burden I opens as unison, moving into two voices and burden II then expands a little on that entirely in three voices. Example 5.2 takes the version in Selden rather than that in Trinity printed in *MC*. Those familiar with the Trinity version will note an important variant at the start of burden II: whereas Trinity begins with the two lower voices on d and a, Selden begins with them both on g, a note that fits far better as a continuation from the end of the verse. One further detail of Selden is that the last words of the verse, 'Deo gracias', are written in red ink, as is the entire text of burden II and the word 'chorus' alongside burden II. I take this to mean that those last two words of the verse are to be sung also by the chorus, who move easily into three voices for burden II. It is an important and perhaps

40 *Chapter 5: Burdens and double burdens*

unanswerable question how far the presumably later copy in Selden, with its doubled note-values, is a rewriting or a reconsideration of the earlier version. I would simply point out that the Trinity copy also lacks stanza 3, which seems important for the continuity of the story. On the other hand, there are several details of the Trinity text that seem far better (particularly in terms of metre), and I have incorporated them into Example 5.2.

Example 5.2 *Deo gracias, Anglia, MC* 29. Complete

Chapter 5: Burdens and double burdens 41

Example 5.2[10] (Continued)

Two more verses follow:[11]

5

There lordës, earlës and baron
Were take and slain and that well soon,
And some were led into London
With joy and mirth and great renown:
Deo gracias.

6

Now gracious God, he save our king,
His people and all his well-willing;
Give him good life and good ending,
That we with mirth may safely sing:
Deo gracias.

10 Text variants: 2/1 forsooth **Trinity**] the sooth for **Selden**; stanza 3 entirely omitted **Trinity**; 4/1 went him forth our king **Trinity**] forsooth, that knight **Selden**; 4/3 marvellously **Trinity**] mighty **Selden**; 4/4 both field and victory **Trinity**] both the field and the victory **Selden**.
11 Text variants: 5/1 lordës, earlës and baron **Trinity**] dukes and earls, lord and baron **Selden**; 5/2 take and slain] slain and taken **Trinity**; 5/2 well] full **Trinity**; 5/3 led] brought **Trinity**; 5/4 mirth] bliss **Trinity**; 6/1 Now gracious] Almighty **Trinity**; 6/1 save] keep **Trinity**; 6/3 And give him grace withouten ending **Trinity**; 6/4 Then may we call and **Trinity**.

All the same, the other pieces in Selden and the one in Bodley *88 do seem to suggest that it was normal for burden II to receive its first statement after burden I. The tiny detail of a g-chord in the Selden version of the Agincourt carol against the d-chord in Trinity is hardly enough to contradict the source evidence, though it may just suggest that the Agincourt carol was one of the earliest with a double burden. And perhaps the difference is not of enormous importance. People will perform the music as they see fit. But I insist that performing both burdens after each verse is both counterintuitive and musically superfluous.

6 Fauxbourdon

Famously (or, in the view of some commentators, infamously), John Stevens added fauxbourdon middle voices to the burdens of several carols in *MC*. There was no indication to specify this, but he justified it by saying (p. xvi): 'An additional part for "fa-burdening", printed small, is occasionally supplied in accordance with the improvisatory practice of the period'.

Stevens did not say so, but there seem to be four details that support his procedure. The first is that one of the carols actually has a written-out middle voice in fauxbourdon style, *Hail, Mary, full of grace* in both Trinity and Selden (*MC* 2 and 31: Example 2.1), and I shall suggest why in a moment. The second is the Ritson carol *Te Deum* (*MC* 95), in which the second burden has the annotation 'Ffaburdon Te eternum' (Example 6.2). The third, not previously noted, is the fragmentary carol in Cambridge, University Library, MS Add. 2764 (1), where the bottom of the page ends with what is plainly the middle voice of a three-voice burden (Figure 4). Since that middle voice is texted, there can be nothing lost from the bottom of the page. The lowest voice – the 'fa-burden', to use the terminology of the time – was an unwritten voice to be derived by singing a 3rd below the written voice or a 5th at cadences:[1] no other surviving example of fauxbourdon is written that way though the technique is unavoidable.

But the fourth detail is to me the most convincing, namely that there are so many carols for which fauxbourdon fits beautifully to the burden but far less well to the verse: that is to say that the burdens are carefully composed with intervals of an 8ve, a 6th or a 5th between the two written voices, whereas the verse sections include 3rds and unisons, leaving no room for a voice between them. This is true of no fewer than six of the thirteen carols in the Trinity roll (*MC* 3, 5, 6, 7, 11, 14).

This really cannot be a coincidence, and it seems to be as close as we can get to evidence that John Stevens was right to add those extra voices. Two more such

---

[1] The only fifteenth-century English description of fauxbourdon (or 'faburden') is in the manuscript copied by John Wylde for the Abbey of Waltham Holy Cross: British Library, Lansdowne MS 763, fol. 116–116v, most recently transcribed and elucidated in Trowell 1959: 47–52. This treatise describes everything in terms of unwritten voices above and below a borrowed chant. As it happens, there is in fact no surviving piece that matches the practices described in that early source; but this piece – though not based on chant – comes closer than anything otherwise known.

Example 6.1 *There is no rose*, MC 14. Complete

Chapter 6: Fauxbourdon 45

examples appear in the Selden manuscript (*MC* 21, 22, in addition to Selden copies of *MC* 7 and 11); and there is one in both Selden and Egerton (*MC* 28/69: Example 3.1), for which John Stevens did not add a fauxbourdon voice. All these pieces are in major prolation, thus probably in the earliest layer of the carol repertory.

In the case of *Hail, Mary, full of grace* (*MC* 2; Example 2.1), the middle voice needed to be written because there is a moment in the burden where tenor and discantus meet on a unison: that is to say that the filling in of the middle voice was not automatic, as it was in the other cases. But the agreement of its two manuscripts in having the burden in three voices and the verse in two tends to support Stevens's approach in the other cases.

There is just one carol in which both the burden and the verse take fauxbourdon equally well. This is *Ecce, quod Natura* (Example 4.4), the only carol to survive in three sources: *MC* 37 needs emendation if the fauxbourdon is going to work (not made by Stevens, but there in Example 4.4); and there are a couple of troublesome spots in *MC* 43. (But given that this is to some extent an oral repertory, as attested by the variants between musical sources and as discussed further in chapter 15, that should be no surprise.)

For the rest, the contrast between the burdens that invite expansion by fauxbourdon and the verses that do not seems once again to indicate the presence of a fuller group of performers for the burdens than for the verses.

Most readers will know that there is an enormous literature on fauxbourdon, starting with the doctoral dissertations of Manfred Bukofzer (1936) and Thrasybulos Georgiades (1937), hitting its peak in the years after World War II with articles around Heinrich Besseler's magisterial *Bourdon und Fauxbourdon* (1950) and receiving a new burst of energy in the late 1950s with the contributions of the next generation, notably Brian Trowell and Ernest Trumble.[2]

The earliest carols are scarcely mentioned in this literature, partly because the word 'fauxbourdon' does not appear in the sources.[3] At one point Ernest Trumble argued – sensibly enough in the circumstances – that the entire discussion had been confused by including pieces that did not carry the word 'fauxbourdon'. He thus began a projected three-volume study (of which only the first was ever published) with a list of 175 pieces that actually include the word.[4] In response to

---

2 Usefully summarized in Hoffmann-Axthelm 1972. I should add that the standard 'received story' on fauxbourdon goes back to Hugo Riemann, *Geschichte der Musiktheorie im IX.–XIX. Jahrhundert* (Leipzig: Max Hesse, 1898): 141–54, 'Gymel und Fauxbourdon'. Riemann drew heavily on the statement in the second volume of Sir John Hawkins's *General history of music* (London: T. Payne, 1776).

3 The honourable exception is Hugo Riemann, *Handbuch der Musikgeschichte: Zweiter Band: Erster Teil: Das Zeitalter der Renaissance bis 1600* (Leipzig: Breitkopf & Härtel, 1907): 198, citing the carols in Selden and adding: 'In sehr vielen Fällen aber wenigstens für längere Strecken ist die Einführung einer Fauxbourdon-Mittelstimme ohne jeden Zwang möglich'. Why nobody seems to have picked up on that comment (except for possibly John Stevens) is a major mystery. A passing comment by Wooldridge (1905), cited in chapter 25, may also be relevant.

4 Trumble, *Fauxbourdon, an historical survey* (1959). See also Trumble, 'Authentic and spurious fauxbourdon' (1960).

this, Brian Trowell later pointed out that there 'are 37 cases where a composition inscribed "faux bourdon" in one source lacks the designation in another'.[5] That actually accounts for almost all the fauxbourdon-titled pieces that appear in more than one source (which, according to Trumble's list, amount to forty). There are therefore risks involved in Trumble's policy of excluding from consideration all pieces that lack the inscription. A far safer criterion would be to choose pieces in two voices that are consistently separated by an 8ve, a 6th or a 5th (this last interval to be discussed in a moment).

In all these cases John Stevens added the middle voice by running it a 3rd higher than the tenor, or a 5th higher at the beginnings and ends of phrases. This is in sharp contrast to scholarly views of the earliest fauxbourdon pieces on the continent, where the unwritten voice is a 4th below the discantus – as a result of which the two written voices cannot be a 5th apart, only a 6th or an 8ve. And the Ritson carol that actually includes the word 'faburden', *Te Deum laudamus*, also works in the 'English' way, with the unwritten voice being taken from the bottom voice, not from the top voice. That is worth mentioning because the distinction is another point that seems not to be mentioned anywhere in the enormous literature on fauxbourdon;[6] also because Bukofzer in his last article on the topic claimed that this passage could not possibly work in fauxbourdon because adding the middle voice created far too many impossible dissonances, and that was because he had tried to derive his unwritten voice from the top voice, taking it consistently down a 4th:[7] in my revision of John Stevens's edition, I have adjusted his reconstruction of the unwritten voice to make it more precisely match the details of the bottom voice, which works perfectly, as in Example 6.2. And once again it is the flawlessness that convinces me that this is the only correct solution.

Since Besseler, historians appear to have agreed that the earliest piece in that style is the postcommunion of Dufay's Mass *Sancti Jacopi*, in Bologna Q15, and perhaps composed in 1427.[8] The main thrust of Besseler's argument was that Dufay was carefully avoiding strings of 6/3 triads – as though he knew of the technique but did not yet want to stoop so low. But there are other pieces that stand a good chance of being earlier, among them a Kyrie by Grossin (who is documented at Paris in 1418 and 1421) and a Magnificat *primi toni* by Radomski. There are also two movements (Sanctus and Agnus) in this style in the plenary mass credited to 'Reginaldus Libert' in Trento 92, the composer widely identified with the Reginaldus Liebert who was master of the choristers at Cambrai Cathedral in 1424; and nobody would be surprised to learn that the cycle dated from the years around 1420 – though the general simplicity of the style in this mass makes dating estimates particularly hard.

---

5 Brian Trowell, 'Fauxbourdon' (1980a: 434).
6 I detect a hint of recognition of the difference and its importance in Trowell 1959: 63n54.
7 Bukofzer, 'Fauxbourdon revisited' (1952: 32–3).
8 Besseler, 'Der Ursprung des Fauxbourdons' (1948); Besseler, 'Dufay Schöpfer des Fauxbourdons' (1948a: 30–1); Besseler, *Bourdon und Fauxbourdon* (1950: 13–15).

Example 6.2 Te eternum Patrem, from *Te Deum*, MC 95. Burden II only

What is true is that none of the earliest continental fauxbourdon pieces is in major prolation, which is the case with all the early carol examples.[9] What is also

---

9 To clarify: this is by no means to say that successions of 6/3 triads are not found earlier than the carols. There are plenty of examples among the homophonic works of the Old Hall manuscript (see Bukofzer 1950: 47–8); and these could well be written-out versions of pieces that were only marginally too complex to have been sung without notation. Suzanne Clercx, 'Aux origines du faux-bourdon', *Revue de musicologie* 40 (1957): 151–65 at pp. 163–5, presents two brief passages of 6/3 triads from the work of Ciconia (d. 1412), reaching the conclusion that 'le fauxbourdon est né en italie': again, these are fully written out, and there are plenty of other examples in the music

true is that in the carol examples the middle voice must be derived from the tenor, mainly up a 3rd but up a 5th at cadences, whereas the available modern editions of the earliest continental examples almost all derive the middle voice from the discantus, rigorously put down a 4th.

On the other hand, once one has recognized that the English carols appear to derive their middle voice from the tenor, rather than the discantus, it becomes relatively easy to see that the earliest continental fauxbourdon pieces do the same. It is clear initially from the hymn cycle of Dufay as it stands in the Bologna manuscript Q15. Regularly, the cadential formulae include the 6th degree of the scale, thereby forcing a middle voice fourth lower to have the 3rd degree against the 2nd degree in the tenor, as in bar 4 of Example 6.3a.

These dissonances can perhaps be discounted as a characteristic feature of Dufay's hymns, though they are fairly rare elsewhere in his work. But there are also cases that are harder to ignore. Fairly often the tenor rises from the 6th below the discantus to the 5th, as in bar 2 of Example 6.3: if the middle voice remains a 4th below the discantus, there is obviously a clash, and – far more

Example 6.3a Opening of Dufay's *Conditor alme siderum* (CMM 1: v.11), ed. Besseler, with fauxbourdon derived from the discantus

Example 6.3b Same, adjusted, with fauxbourdon derived from the tenor

---

of the Italian Trecento. Hugo Riemann had made a similar point about Landini's *Per la mi è dolce piaga* (he could have used several other Landini pieces) in *Handbuch der Musikgeschichte: Erster Band: Zweiter Teil: Die Musik des Mittelalters (bis 1450)* (Leipzig: Breitkopf & Härtel, 1905): 330–3, with a musical example that gives the contrapuntal basis in fauxbourdon triads alongside the music. Most of the individual features of the polyphonic carols can be found in earlier music: what is interesting in the present context is their combination in the carol.

Chapter 6: Fauxbourdon   49

seriously – the resulting dissonance in the tenor is what any counterpoint teacher would view as the worst possible part-writing ('footling', my own first counterpoint teacher called it); but if the middle voice is a 3rd above the tenor, it creates a perfectly normal triad and perfect counterpoint. Among the eight fauxbourdon hymn settings of Dufay, six contain precisely comparable cases.[10] It should be no surprise that the fauxbourdon indications in the manuscripts are regularly attached to the tenor, not the discantus. It may seem too glib to remark that the modern editions of Dufay, Grossin,[11] Radomski,[12] Reginaldus Libert[13] and Feragut[14] all have their fauxbourdon movements wrongly resolved, but the reader need only scan these volumes to confirm the correctness of that view. In all cases,

---

10 Trumble, 'Dissonance treatment in early fauxbourdon' (1990: 245–7), seems to recognize the problem, even quoting the doctoral dissertation of Masakata Kanazawa (Harvard, 1966) with its finding (i.48) that out of 536 intervals in Dufay's fauxbourdon hymns 104 produced dissonances and (i.56) 'on the other hand, that the non-fauxbourdon hymns [of Dufay] are only infrequently dissonant'. Trumble even notes (1990: 247) that the problem lies with editors taking their instructions from the much later treatise of Guilelmus Monachus. But somehow he never draws what I would consider the only possible conclusion. Margaret Bent reminds me that most intelligent singers could probably fix these problems after one rehearsal; but I think that the sheer quantity of such cases is the main argument that it is wrong to take the resolution of these pieces from such late theorists.

11 His Kyrie appears in *Early fifteenth-century music*, ed. Gilbert Reaney = Corpus mensurabilis musicae 11 (American Institute of Musicology, 1955–83): iii.42–3, as from Aosta, fols. 54v–55, with 'Tenor faulx bourdon'; the piece also appears in Krasinski (now Warsaw, Biblioteka Naradowa, MS III.8054), fol. 181v, a 3rd lower, and with the discantus annotated 'a discantu', facs. and modern edition in Antiquitates Musicae in Polonia 13–14 (1973–6): no. 12. Impossible dissonances appear in these editions at bars 8–9 (= 22–23); resolving the fauxbourdon voice with intervals a 3rd and a 5th above the tenor turns them all into perfectly normal counterpoint.

12 His *Magnificat primi toni*, in Krasinski, fols. 182–183v, for the verses 'Et exultavit', 'Fecit potentiam' and 'Sicut locutus est', all with the annotation 'Per bardunum' and with the additional annotations 'Hic recipe in quinta et fiet Contratenor', 'Hic recipe in tercia' (!) and 'Hic incipe in quinta contratenorem', ed. in Antiquitates Musicae in Polonia 13–14 (1973–6): no. 13. It is also printed in *Les oeuvres complètes de Nicolas de Radom (fl. 1420–1430)*, ed. Adam Sutkowski (Brooklyn: The Institute of Mediæval Music, 1969): 49–59. Sutkowski resolves the fauxbourdon less rigorously, often moving to the 5ths and 3rd that I propose: the bars where this seems the only possible solution include 18, 21, 23, 103, 107, 192.

13 Fauxbourdon is used for the Sanctus and Agnus of his plenary mass cycle in Trento 92, fols. 62v–63v, with an additional contratenor marked 'sine faulxbourdon' for the Sanctus; the movements also appear, without the extra contratenor and without any indication of fauxbourdon, in the St Emmeram codex, Munich, Bayerische Staatsbibliothek, clm 14274, ff. 71v–72. They are published in *Early fifteenth-century music*, ed. Gilbert Reaney = Corpus mensurabilis musicae 11 (American Institute of Musicology, 1955–83): iii.88–93. Impossible dissonances appear in this edition at bars 16–17, 49–50, 62, 73, 83 and 95 in Sanctus and bars 15 and 41 in Agnus; details that seem puzzling by any criteria include bar 25, 53, 110 in Sanctus. The earlier edition in *Sechs trienter Codices . . . Vierte Auswahl*, ed. Rudolf Ficker and Alfred Orel = Denkmäler der Tonkunst in Österreich 53 (Vienna: Universal-Edition, 1920): 16–18, is far less methodical in its resolution of the fauxbourdon sections.

14 Both pieces in Bologna Q15. They are published in *Early fifteenth-century music*, ed. Gilbert Reaney = Corpus mensurabilis musicae 11 (American Institute of Musicology, 1955–83): vii.100–5. Impossible dissonances appear in the hymn *Lucis creator optime* at bars 6, 14 (where the

the editors have followed the much later instructions of Tinctoris, Guilelmus Monachus, Adam von Fulda and Gafori, rigorously having the middle voice a 4th below the discantus; in all cases uncharacteristic dissonances occur and the musical results are massively improved if the middle voice is a 3rd above the tenor with a 5th at cadences.[15] (It should be added, though, that Rudolf Gerber's 1937 edition of Dufay's hymns in the series *Das Chorwerk* resolves the fauxbourdon voices pragmatically, more or less retaining the 3rds and 5ths above the tenor but certainly never creating musical nonsense, which, I submit, is what we find in Besseler's resolutions.)[16]

One key finding in the discussions on fauxbourdon was the assertion of the philologist Hermann Flasdieck that the English word 'faburden' could not possibly have evolved from the French 'fauxbourdon'.[17] In any case, the word 'faburden' is documented already in the fourteenth century, long before any trace of the word 'fauxbourdon'. Moreover, Trowell added the point that the equivalent words in German, Spanish and Italian all derive from the English, not the French word. We must return to the matter of chronology. But for the moment it looks as though the

---

discantus rhythms must be corrected to crotchet, dotted-crotchet, quaver) and in the Magnificat at bars 2, 4, 23–4, 29, 30, 40, 43, 45 and 50; there is no obvious resolution to bar 51.

15 The fauxbourdon pieces by Binchois seem not to yield uncharacteristic dissonances if resolved by taking the middle voice a 4th below the discantus. There is one exception, the curious case of the *Ut queant laxis* setting, printed in Kaye's edition as no. 49: Venice, Marciana IX.145, presents just the tenor and the contratenor with the annotation 'Tenor faulx bordon'; Munich, Bayerische Staatsbibliothek, clm 14274, presents the discantus and tenor with no annotation. The contratenor in Venice is regularly a 4th below the discantus in Munich, but the counterpoint works far better if, once again, but against the apparent evidence of the manuscripts, the middle voice is a 3rd above the tenor and a 5th higher at cadences.

16 It may be worth adding a word about the postcommunion to Dufay's mass *Sancti Jacopi*, considered by Besseler to be the first surviving fauxbourdon piece. Although – just this once among the earlier generation of fauxbourdon – the instructions are quite unambiguous in saying that the unwritten voice should be a 4th below the discantus it actually works far better if you run it in 3rds and 5ths above the tenor, most particularly in those sections where the tenor stands alone and the discantus rests. Whether that means that the copyist of Q15 had a poor exemplar, or misunderstood what he had before him, or that I am applying totally inappropriate criteria is a question for readers to answer for themselves. It may be of interest to note that the two documentably later Dufay pieces with passages in fauxbourdon – the motet *Supremum est mortalibus bonum* (1433) and the pseudo-legal disputation *Juvenis qui puellam* – work perfectly if the unwritten voice is a 4th below the discantus, as do the sequence settings *Lauda Sion salvatorem* and *Isti sunt duae olivae* as well as the *Magnificat* (8. toni). The same is the case with all the fauxbourdon pieces by Johannes Brassart.

17 Hermann M. Flasdieck, 'Franz. *faux-bourdon* und frühneuengl. *faburden*: ein sprachwissenschaftlicher Beitrag zur europäischen Musikgeschichte', *Acta musicologica* 25 (1953): 111–27; Hermann M. Flasdieck, 'Elisab. *faburden* "fauxbourdon" und NE. *burden* "Refrain"', *Anglia* 74 (1956): 188–238 – itself in part a response to the differing views of many language scholars reported in Gustav Kirchner, 'Französisch "faux-bourdon" und frühneu-englisch "faburden" (H. M. Flasdieck): eine Erwidering', *Acta musicologica* 26 (1954): 85–7. Flasdieck's conclusions are pithily summarized in Trowell, 'Faburden and fauxbourdon' (1959): 45.

examples of apparent fauxbourdon in the earliest layer of English carols are likely to be earlier than the earliest continental examples. Moreover, it seems entirely clear that the earliest continental fauxbourdons follow the pattern of the English carols in making sense only if the unwritten voice is calculated above the tenor, not below the discantus.

7 Metre and rhythm

Central to the enquiry here is the metrical style of the earliest carols. Most of them have a strikingly periodic design. *Ecce, quod Natura* (Example 4.3) is rigorously structured in four-beat phrases throughout, as is *As I lay upon a night* (Example 4.5). But more common is the design that is mainly of four-beat phrases but includes irregularities. *There is no rose of such virtue* (Example 6.1) has extra rests between the two phrases of the burden; and its verse begins with a five-beat phrase. *Hail, Mary, full of grace* (Example 2.1) is in regular four-bar phrases except at the end of the burden. And *Alleluia, Pro virgine Maria* (Example 3.1) has rather more irregularities, even though the structure and style encourage listening that expects four-beat phrases, regularly frustrated. There are many similar cases: *Nowell, nowell: In Bethlem* (MC 3) has its burden entirely in three-beat phrases, followed by a verse that begins with two three-beat phrases and then continues in four-beat phrases; *Now may we singen* (MC 5) has a burden made up of two five-beat phrases and a verse that is entirely in four-beat phrases; *Eya, martyr Stephane* (MC 12) and *Nowell sing we both all and some* (MC 16) are both entirely in four-beat phrases apart from the second line of the verse, which has five beats; the Agincourt carol, *Deo gracias, Anglia* (Example 5.2) runs entirely in four-beat phrases except for the first phrase of burden II, which has five beats. In all these cases, the ear becomes accustomed to the four-beat phrases and is lightly tickled by the insertion of the occasional surprise.

While this may all be fairly natural for the music of the seventeenth and eighteenth centuries, it needs to be clear that it is most unusual in the known music of the fourteenth and fifteenth centuries. Broadly speaking, phrases here seem carefully to have avoided regular design or any hint of a dance background. From the fourteenth century, the few exceptions all seem to have made it into the list of modern performers' and listeners' favourites: Machaut's *Douce dame jolie* (Example 4.2) is entirely in four-beat phrases and utterly exceptional; Landini's *Ecco la primavera* is in three-beat phrases apart from one two-beat phrase in the *ripresa* and a four-beat phrase at the start of the *piedi*; the anonymous English *Beata viscera* (Polyphonic music of the fourteenth century 14: no. 43) is in four-beat phrases throughout, as are a handful of English motets based on four-beat tenors (Polyphonic music of the fourteenth century 14: nos. 45, 59, 60 and 61). These are very much exceptions.

In all these cases, it is reasonable to infer a dance background, though almost none is regular enough to involve actual dancing. What must be assumed is that the unwritten dance music of the middle ages was in regular phrases and that these few written examples are either conscious parodies of that dance music or composed on the borderline between the written and unwritten traditions: each of the pieces just cited perhaps occupies its own position on that spectrum. Part of the fascination of the early carol repertory is that it seems to anticipate the dance basis of so much music of the seventeenth and eighteenth centuries, a phenomenon that does not reappear in the surviving written repertories until the years around 1500, with the Spanish *villancico* and the Italian *frottola*.

But there is more to it than that. Among the three earliest carol sources, nearly all the major prolation pieces have that underlying structure, but it appears in almost none of the perfect time pieces. One exception is the Agincourt carol, which appears in Selden with doubled note-values in perfect time. But otherwise the phrases are so irregular that it is something of a surprise to encounter a carol like *Ivy is good* (*MC* 55), with its burdens mainly in five-beat phrases – some of which are easily construed as four-beat phrases with a one-beat insertion – and the verse mainly in four-beat phrases.

Another detail that should be noted about the major-prolation carols is that most of them have infractions of the notational rule that '*similis ante similem perfecta est*': that is to say that, in major prolation, the first of any pair of *semibreves* should be perfect, worth three *minime*. In effect, that means that the common metrical pattern (in 3/8 time in modern transcription with quartered note-values) quaver-crotchet-crotchet should be written *minima-minima-semibrevis*; but often it is not written in that way, but simply written as *minima-semibrevis-semibrevis*. This occurs mainly in major-prolation carols: *MC* 7, 8, 11, 12, 14, 16, 32, 37, 38, 12[A] and 15[A]; it also occurs, far less often, in perfect-time carols, with *semibreves* and *breves*: *MC* 29, 41 and 42.[1] By and large this is not a problem, because the music is perfectly predictable; and presumably it is written in this lax manner precisely for that reason.[2] But in two cases it makes the confident readings of the music's rhythms impossible: *Alma Redemptoris mater* (*MC* 4) and *Ave domina* (*MC* 24).

A final point about these regular phrases is important, namely that some are far more 'dance-like' than others. I already noted that *Hail, Mary, full of grace*

---

1 It also occurs in quite a few secular songs copied in England, see Fallows 2014: nos. 3–4, 10–13, 15–17, 20–21, 29, 42, 74, 81 and 83, where I have (I believe for the first time) noted all such discrepancies and used the abbreviation 'ss' to denote infractions of the *similis ante similem* rule.

2 Which is why the matter seems hardly to be discussed in the available literature. Margaret Bent's article 'Chirbury' in *The new Grove dictionary of music and musicians*, ed. Stanley Sadie (1980) and in *The new Grove dictionary of music and musicians: revised edition*, ed. Stanley Sadie and John Tyrrell (London: Macmillan, 2001) draws attention to it in Chirbury's compositions; and more recently Peter Wright has noted it in the copying activity of Wolfgang Chranekker; see his 'The contribution and identity of Scribe D of the "St Emmeram Codex"' in *Musik des Mittelalters und der Renaissance: Festschrift Klaus-Jürgen Sachs zum 80. Geburtstag*, ed. Rainer Kleinertz, et al. (Hildesheim: Georg Olms, 2010): 283–316, at pp. 288–93.

(Example 2.1) seems to imply the gentlest of motion; the same could be said of *There is no rose* (Example 6.1). And I drew attention to the contrast in the eager exchanges between chorus and soloists in *What tidings bringest thou* (Example 5.1). These carols have an outgoing sense of community and of communication that is relatively rare among the other surviving polyphony of the fifteenth century. Perhaps it is worth adding that Machaut's *Douce dame jolie* (Example 4.2) is far too often performed as though it were a rowdy dance piece, whereas its text clearly states that it is a song of the gentlest possible seduction.

But in this context it is worth noting another metrical feature of the later carols, particularly the more florid pieces in Ritson. A good example is *Worship we this holy day* (MC 94). The two-voice burden begins harmlessly enough with a single five-bar phrase, which is the structure found throughout the verse; but then it moves into a long rambling melisma, which John Stevens transcribes in 7/8 time. It is hard to think of a more sensible way of transcribing this passage;[3] and similar passages appear elsewhere in the Ritson carols (though this is an extreme case).

It is entirely in line with what we have proposed about the relationship between two-voice and three-voice burdens that the three-voice burden II here should be far more regular: unsullied 3/4 throughout, a four-bar phrase for the first line and an eight-bar phrase for the second. And it is in line with the practice of the time that the verses, again presumably for solo voices, are in regular five-bar phrases, evidently planned as such, with the declamation at the start of each line leading the ear to expect a four-bar phrase.

One reviewer of *MC* did not actually believe these irrational rhythms. He wrote (Gombosi 1953: 32):

> Of course such irregular measures – genuine ones – are of extreme rarity ... I am sorry to say that the vast majority is the result of obvious scribal errors ... Mr. Stevens neglected the rather elementary task of establishing a proper text by eliminating ... such errors.

But the kind of metrical irregularity represented by Example 7.1 is fairly common in English music from the fifteenth century. Moreover, these irregularities have been rather hidden in modern editions by editors understandably aiming to reduce confusion. But they are easy to see in Harrison's edition of the Eton Choirbook, since he was unrepentant in inserting totally irrational time signatures for penultimate bars in quartered note-values.[4] For that reason they merit special study far beyond the few words offered here.

---

[3] In the 1952 edition John Stevens had presented this passage in 3/4 time apart from a 5/8 bar before the last note. The 1958 revision here plainly results from the rethinking caused by Bukofzer's review (1954), though Bukofzer does not in fact mention this piece.

[4] *The Eton choirbook*, ed. Frank Ll. Harrison = Musica Britannica 10, 11 and 12 (1956, 1958 and 1961): vol. 10, pp. 111, 113, 114 (all Davy), 123 (Cornysh), 124, 127 and 129 (all Browne); vol. 11, pp. 21, 23 (twice, all Huchyn), 27, 29 (both Wilkinson), 35 (Fayrfax), 67, 68, 70, 74, 85, 98, 99, 101, 116 (all Davy) and 147 (Cornysh); vol. 12, pp. 31 (Browne), 60 (Cornysh), 64 (twice),

Chapter 7: Metre and rhythm 55

Example 7.1 Worship we this holy day, MC 94. Burden I only

This is extremely rare in the music of the continental mainland. There are pieces with unusual metres (five-beat units, 3/4–6/8 alternations), but always rational in their structure. There are pieces that evaporate to an almost imperceptible end, but always with a clearly identifiable main concluding chord at a logical place. And, most important, there is a musical style that sounds as though it is in triple units but is fundamentally on a two-beat framework, though these pieces can usually be understood in terms of a gracious juxtaposition of phrases, often setting up a light metrical expectation that is then frustrated. But there is almost nothing in this music or in the works of Josquin, Obrecht or Isaac to match the sheer unpredictability of the English pieces. Even the two reigning mavericks of continental music, Johannes Ockeghem and Johannes Regis, have no trace of this fundamental irrationality of metre.

Why such irregularities were favoured in England, why they arose, and why there is so little trace of such rhythmic irregularity in continental music of the time are all difficult questions, indeed questions that scarcely seem to have been addressed. And I cannot see an easy way of addressing them here, so I leave them for some later commentator.

---

68 (all Nesbett), 75, 76 (both Horwood), 90, 92, 95 (all Lambe), 98 (Fayrfax), 104, 105, 106, 108 (twice), 110, 111 (all Stratford), 148 (Fayrfax), 153 (Wilkinson), 159, 160 (both Holyngborne), 176 (Huchyn), 181 and 182 (both Wilkinson).

8　The main poetry sources

As concerns the texts, these were the years of England's most verbose poets: John Gower and John Lydgate are proverbially long-winded; and it is all the more remarkable that the pithy manner of the carol texts came from the same years, perhaps as a reaction against the 'aureate' style that continued in favour for much of the century. However that may be, this condensed clarity in the texts contributes greatly to the fresh and bracing nature of the music.

But now is the moment to explore the poetical sources. The main point of this chapter and the next is to state that many of the hundred-odd sources used and carefully described in Richard Leighton Greene's fundamental *The early English carols* (1977) are only marginally relevant to the topic, because they contain material that concords with the repertory but does not present it in carol form or because they contain only a single carol.[1] Carol texts were often adapted from previously existing poems – hence the need for this book to focus on the musical repertory, which is all absolutely original.

There are surprisingly few poetry sources that contain more than a handful of carols. The core of the poetic repertory is in three anonymous manuscripts and three 'personal' manuscripts. The three anonymous manuscripts have recently been re-edited and reconsidered as a group by Kathleen Palti (2008), who judges all three to have been from Norfolk. They have also been studied as a group by Daniel Wakelin (2006). In earlier literature they were often dubbed 'minstrel' manuscripts, partly because they are all so tiny, though Robbins far more accurately termed them 'portable' manuscripts, for they are all small and fit easily into a decent-sized pocket.[2]

Sloane MS 2593 in the British Library seems to be from the first half of the fifteenth century, the pocket book of Johannes Bardel (fol. 36v), conceivably the monk 'Johannes Bardwell' at Bury St Edmunds (Greene 1962: 172–4, and 1977:

1　Bukofzer (1950: 148) wrote, 'The small number of musical manuscripts (sc. for carols) stands in striking contrast to the large number of literary sources'. I wish to suggest that he was quite wrong and that the number of literary sources that are strictly relevant to the history of the carol is also small.

2　As outlined by Andrew Taylor (1991).

306–7).³ Palti (2008: 73) says the *Linguistic atlas* locates it further north on the basis of its dialect, near Thetford.⁴ Its pages are 15 × 11 cm. An early (but by no means original) foliation suggests that forty-eight leaves are missing at the front. It contains seventy-four song texts, all copied by a single hand: three are in Latin (nos. 36, 65 and 66); fifty-three are in carol form. Only two appear in the musical collections, nos. 50 (*MC* 21) and 64 (*MC* 4 = 23); and we shall see later that many of the others have a tone that entirely separates them from the polyphonic carols. I see nothing to put it any later than 1420; but that is perhaps a matter for literary historians to consider after they have seen my evidence for dating the musical sources earlier than hitherto.

MS Eng. poet. e. 1 in the Bodleian Library (OxEng) must be later.⁵ It contains seventy-seven song texts, among them sixty-three carols written by two copyists. Its pages are 15 × 13 cm. Greene proposed that it was from Beverley Minster (1962: 179; 1977: 318); more recent research prefers Norfolk. Rather more of the poems here appear in the musical collections:⁶ E14 (*MC* 2^A), E24 (*MC* 15 = 65, 100), E31 (*MC* 5^A), E44 (*MC* 26, 97), E49 (*MC* 7, 16), E54 (*MC* 13, 106, 115). It also contains three songs with monophonic notation (two printed as *MC* 4^A and 10^A; the other reproduced in Stainer 1901: i.99, with edition ii.182) as well as 'two for which tunes are indicated' (Palti 2008: 84).

MS S. 54 (259) in St John's College, Cambridge, contains only seventeen full texts plus a fragment: fifteen are in carol form. There are two copyists and the pages are 15 × 10 cm. Only no. 8 appears in a musical collection and that with monophonic music (*MC* 1^A).⁷

The three 'personal' collections have the advantage that they are easier to date and to locate. One of the earliest informative sources is Oxford, Douce 302, the parchment collection of over fifty poems apparently dictated in the late 1420s by the blind chantry-priest John Audelay at the Augustinian house of Haughmond Abbey, the ruins of which lie three miles north-east of Shrewsbury.⁸ Of its twenty-

---

3 The earliest complete edition, still very useful, is in Wright 1855. It is also edited complete in Fehr 1902 and in Miller 1975. More recent discussions are summarized by Palti (2008: 26), to which it is worth adding the description in Karin Boklund-Lagopoulou, *'I have a yong suster': popular song and the Middle English lyric* (Dublin: Four Courts Press, 2002): 63–86. But the earliest publication of pieces from this manuscript are by Ritson (1790), who tentatively assigned it to the reign of Henry V, a view endorsed in the partial edition by Thomas Wright (1836).

4 Angus McIntosh, M.L. Samuels and Michael Benskin, *A linguistic atlas of late mediaeval English*, 4 vols. (Aberdeen: Aberdeen University Press, 1986) – now supplemented by the website *eLALME* (2013).

5 Greene (1977: 317) dated it to the second half of the fifteenth century; but Wakelin (2006: 28) proposed that it may be from the early sixteenth century. Complete edition in Wright 1847 (at which point the manuscript was still his own property) as well as Palti 2008.

6 The numbers with 'E' are those used in Palti 2008.

7 Modern edition in James and Macaulay 1915 as well as in Palti 2008.

8 Audelay's MS was first discussed in Halliwell, *The poems of John Audelay* (1844) and in Wülfing, 'Der Dichter John Audelay und sein Werk' (1896); Wülfing apparently prepared an edition for the Early English Text Society (as noted in Chambers and Sidgwick 1910–11: 478), though the Early

58   Chapter 8: The main poetry sources

six carols (twenty-five of them in a discrete section) only one is known from musical sources, *MC* 11/27.[9] It is from Audelay that we have our main definition of the carol, which is why this manuscript was discussed earlier. The date '*c*. 1426' arises from the inscription two-thirds of the way through the book:[10]

> Finito libro . . . Iste liber fuit compositus per Johannem Awdelay capellanum qui fuit secus et surdus in sua visitacione . . . Anno domini millesimo cccc visecimo vj.

As bad luck would have it, the carols are all in the last third of the book, therefore after it was 'finished' in 1426, but it looks very much as though it was copied in a relatively short space of time; so '*c*. 1426' must stand.

The second is the collection of the Canterbury friar James Ryman, dated 1492: Cambridge, University Library, MS Ee. 1. 12. It is on parchment, which is rare in 1492, particularly for a private manuscript. With over 100 carols, it provides almost a quarter of the carols in *EEC*. That is to say that the sheer quantity of Ryman's output results in a slightly skewed view of the genre as a whole, if seen through Greene's edition: commentators have tended to describe him as one of the dullest poets of the fifteenth century (which is a strong claim, considering the competition), though there are signs that critics have been more sympathetic in recent years.[11] But the Ryman carols are all from a date long after the available music had been composed and copied: its only concordance with the musical sources is the text for *MC* 7, which appears here with monophonic music (*MC* 7[A]), as does *MC* 8[A].

The third is the commonplace book of the London merchant Richard Hill, now Balliol College, MS 354, with dates that give the impression that he assembled it between about 1508 and 1536.[12] This is an amazing ragbag of bits and pieces, all apparently entered as and when they seemed interesting. (It is also hard to use, with various different foliations and numberings: in my experience, only the

---

English Text Society edition appeared rather later as Whiting 1931; a far fuller and more copiously annotated edition is *John the blind Audelay: poems and carols*, ed. Susanna Fein (2009).

9   Greene (1977: 372) doubted Audelay's authorship, suggesting that 'The spirited rhythm is so much superior to Audelay's usual metres that his original authorship must be regarded as doubtful'. Contrary views are offered in Stanley (1997) and Smaill (2003: 517).

10   Whiting 1931: 149.

11   Greene (1935: cxxv–cxxvii; 1977: cliv–clv) and Chambers (1945: 97) were unkind about Ryman's gifts. For more recent positive evaluations, see in particular Reichl (2003) and Hirsh (2012). But the greatest supporter of Ryman was surely Julius Zupitza, who not only provided a complete edition (1892) but followed it with an enormous commentary (1894–97), running to 265 pages – an achievement of mindboggling detail that makes Ryman himself seem comparatively witty and compact.

12   The earliest proper description is in Flügel 1903: 94–285. The standard edition is Dyboski 1908, which however resequences the material. See also Collier 1997 and Collier 2000 as well as Karin Boklund-Lagopoulou, '*I have a yong suster*': *popular song and the Middle English lyric* (Dublin: Four Courts Press, 2002): 202–33.

modern pencil pagination is helpful.) Essentially there are three groups of carols here, on pp. 374–80 (Dyboski, no. 73), pp. 459–84 (Dyboski, no. 120), and pp. 503–510 (Dyboski, nos. 130–145). Particularly the largest collection is laid out very formally: when there is space at the bottom of the page, other material has been added, usually in a different hand; but the rest of the material is all in carol form. In several ways, this main collection is the most formal statement of the coherence of the form apart from the musical sources Egerton and Ritson; several writers have suggested that they were copied from a single earlier exemplar. Certainly a large portion of its contents was over a century old when the manuscript was copied.

9 The earliest English poems in carol form

The aim of this chapter is to explore what seem to be the earliest examples of carol poetry, particularly those in the six fourteenth-century manuscripts listed by Greene.[1]

As concerns what is probably the earliest poem that Greene printed, *Blow northern wind* (*EEC* 440), in the 'Harley lyrics' from fairly early in the fourteenth century, G.L. Brook noted that its burden 'with its simplicity and repetition, is probably popular in origin, and is quite different in style from the rest of the lyric'.[2] Expanding that, one might add that the body of the poem is of praise for a lady, whereas the burden looks like the words of a woman:

B

Blow northern wind,
Send thou me my sweeting.
Blow northern wind.
Blow, blow, blow.

10

For her love I cark and care;	*grieve*
For her love I droupne and dare;	*languish and lie awake*
For her love my bliss is bare,	
And all I wax won;	*grow pale*
For her love in sleep I slake;	*become weak*
For her love all night I wake;	
For her love mourning I make	
More than any man.	

---

1 Enumerated in Catherwood 1996: 325.
2 G.L. Brook, *The Harley lyrics: the Middle English lyrics of MS. Harley 2253* (Manchester: Manchester University Press, 1948, 4th edition, 1968): 6.

One could also add that the indication of the return of the burden appears only after the first two stanzas, out of ten. But how the burden and the stanzas became joined must remain a mystery: they can have nothing to do with one another.

The next poem that has been taken as evidence of the early history of the carol is in the Bodleian Library, MS Bodley 26 (with its last stanza also in the London University Library, MS 657, also of the fourteenth century). This is the unforgettable piece that opens:

> Hand by hand we shall us take,
> And joy and blissë shall we make,
> For the devil of hell man hath forsake,
> And Godës son is maked our make.

Each of the three stanzas is followed by an indication to repeat the lines opening 'Hand by hand'. The problem here is that the first stanza has the same monorhyme pattern as the burden, already a suspicious feature:

> A child is born amongës man,
> And in that child was no wam;　　　　　　*stain*
> That child ys God, that child is man,
> And in that child our life began.

Stanzas 2 and 3, on the other hand, are not only entirely different in form, with six lines rhyming *aabaab*, but plainly written as a pair, and moving from the first person of the previous stanzas to a hortatory second person:

> Sinful man, be blithe and glad:
> For your marriage thy peace is grad　　　　　*proclaimed*
> When Christ was born;
> Come to Christ; thy peace is grad;
> For thee was his blood y-shed
> That were forlorn.

> Sinful man, be blithe and bold,
> For even is both bought and sold
> Evereche foot.　　　　　　　　　　　　　　*every*
> Come to Christ; thy peace,
> For thee he gave a hundredfold
> His life to bote.　　　　　　　　　　　　　　*as remedy*

Greene had two suggestions about this (1935: 355; 1977: 345–6): that the poem may be viewed as having been 'made up of two originally different sets of verses', which I would very much endorse, since the two four-line stanzas are specifically about Christmas day and the two six-line stanzas merely invite 'sinful man' to follow Christ; and his second suggestion was 'that the short third and sixth lines were omitted in error from stanza 1, perhaps through confusion with the four-line form of the burden', which seems to me a touch unrealistic, particularly bearing in mind that stanzas 2 and 3 contain between them many repetitions and parallelisms that are entirely absent in stanza 1. Irrespective of whether one believes either of Greene's explanations, this is a very confused poem from which no clear conclusion can be drawn concerning the early history of the carol – though nobody can regret the opportunity to print and read it again.[3]

Elsewhere, Greene (1935: cxli) wrote of the burden: 'These pious lines are plainly an imitation of the burden of some song for a round dance'. That may be true of this particular quatrain, but is rarely true of anything in the main carol repertory.[4] This is a clear example of the danger that can arise from confusing the carol, as defined by Greene himself, with earlier dance-forms.

Another poem copied early is *Of one that is so fair and bright* (*EEC* 191). This appears in two manuscripts of the thirteenth century: British Library, Egerton MS 613, and Cambridge, Trinity College, MS B. 14. 39. But those two copies lack any indication of a burden. The burden appears in a manuscript of perhaps around 1420, Bodleian Library, MS Ashmole 1393 (the same isolated leaf that contains the words and music of *Ecce, quod Natura*, *MC* 43). Here the eight-line stanzas in the two earlier manuscripts are each reduced to their first four lines, to which are added two further stanzas and the burden *Enixa est puerpera*. Evidently the earlier poem has been adapted to become a carol only in the fifteenth century.

Turning to *Now springs the spray* (*EEC* 450), surviving in the fourteenth-century manuscript at Lincoln's Inn, MS Hale 135, this is a *ballata* in the purest continental style.[5] It has a three-line refrain (rhyming *aba*), two-line verses (rhyming *cd*) and a three-line *volta* (rhyming *dda*) that is obviously followed by a statement of the refrain. That the poem has three stanzas further endorses its status as a *ballata*. It is irrelevant for any study of the carol repertory.

With those early apparent carols eliminated we come to Greene's main witness, the commonplace-book of John of Grimestone (Edinburgh, National Library of Scotland, MS Advocates 18.7.21), copied apparently in Norfolk and dated 1372.[6]

---

3 It could be added that this poem is a key document in the literature on the importance of sermons for the history of the carol, as particularly explained by Siegfried Wenzel (1986). Louise McInnes (2013: 243–50) mentions the view expressed in a private communication from the literary historian Alan Fletcher: 'I can't readily see how it [*sc.* the sermon alongside which the poem is copied] fits with the carol at all, and I begin to suspect that the carol was simply copied into a spare space on the verso of the folio'.

4 Robbins (1959b: 576) prefers Margit Sahlin's interpretation of these lines (1940: 58) as depicting 'a church lullaby sung around the crib'.

5 As first noted by Manfred Schöpf (1969: 396). In addition he points out that *EEC* 180 (in OxEng and Sloane) is a rondeau and that *This enders night* (*EEC* 150) is a pure virelai. I would add that *Man of might, that all had i-dight* (*EEC* 424.1) is a *ballata*, complete with *volta*.

6 The entire manuscript includes 246 lyrics, enumerated by Edward Wilson (1973). Further on Grimestone and his collection, see the chapter 'The oeuvre of friar John of Grimestone' in Siegfried Wenzel, *Preachers, poets, and the early English lyric* (1986): 101–34.

Chapter 9: English poems in carol form

Greene lists four carols as appearing here. *EEC* 157D, is a poem in eighteen rhyming couplets, to which three different burdens were added in two manuscripts from the fifteenth century and in one print of *c*. 1550. That is understandable, for it is a striking poem that puts words into the mouths of John, Mary and finally Christ on the cross, opening:

> Mary, mother, come and see:
> Thy child is nailed to a tree,
> Hand and foot; he may not go;
> His body is wounden all in woe.

That writers in the fifteenth century chose this poem (written entirely in rhyming couplets) and adapted it to become a carol should surprise nobody; but in the fourteenth-century manuscript it is absolutely not a carol.

Three other poems in Grimestone's book look like genuine carols. *EEC* 271 is found only here; but it has a quatrain as the burden (which more or less never happens in the polyphonic carol repertory), and has four six-line stanzas, each followed by the word 'Lovely' to denote the return of the burden. With striking originality, it addresses a tear in Christ's eye.[7]

> Lovely tear of lovely eye,
> Why dost thou me so woe?
> Sorful tear of sorful eye,
> Thou breakst mine heart a-two.

The theme and tone of this intimate poem share nothing with any of the known carols with polyphony. But the form is plainly there.

EEC 155 is in pure carol style, with a two-line burden followed by seven stanzas of four lines, the last of which rhymes with the burden. It is entirely in the mouth of the Virgin Mary, who in the course of the poem takes responsibility for taking the forbidden apple and in the burden soothes her Son:

> Lullay, lullay, little child,
> Why weepest thou so sore?

Indications for a repeat of the burden appear after only stanza 2 and stanza 5, but plainly the repeat was intended after all stanzas.

EEC 149 is more complicated. The body of the poem is in thirty-seven quatrains, rhyming *abab*. It opens with the narrator:

> As I lay upon a night
> Alone in my longing,

---

[7] Wenzel (1986: 135–7) explores this poem, which in his view 'surely represents one of the peaks of achievement in the Middle English religious lyric'.

> Me thought I saw a wonder sight,
> A maiden child rocking.

Then Jesus asks who he is and what his future holds. From stanza 6 Mary answers that she knows nothing except what the angel Gabriel has told her and what happened after his birth; then the baby Jesus continues the story through to his crucifixion and his joining the Father in heaven. It is a marvellous poem, and no wonder that it was recopied, albeit in shortened versions: in the St John's College manuscript it has nine stanzas; in Harley 2330 it has only five; and in Cambridge, University Library, MS Add. 5943 it has only a single stanza, but here it does have monophonic music (*MC* 1^A). All four manuscripts open with the burden:

> Lullay, lullay, la lullay,
> My dear mother, lullay.

The manuscript with the music actually lacks the second line of the burden, but there is plenty of music to carry that line. Moreover, even though the Grimestone manuscript indicates the repetition of the burden only after stanza 37, the other three manuscripts have that indication for the first stanza (all three), the second and third (St John's and Harley), and the fourth and fifth (Harley).

It might be mentioned that one further poem in Grimestone appears with music in carol style in Selden: *As I lay upon a night: Her looking was so lovely* (*MC* 11^A: Example 4.5), with a poem of sixteen quatrains all rhyming *abab* and the Selden music in the form of a virelai. Since neither the original poem nor the Selden music is in carol form, this is irrelevant here, but a splendid example of how a fifteenth-century composer took a fourteenth-century poem and adapted it to create a new piece of music.

Two more poems in carol form have been proposed by Robbins (1957) and others,[8] although they do not appear in Greene's collection, and indeed he firmly rejected them. They are among the translations from Latin assembled by Friar William Herebert, copied in about 1318.[9]

In addition, there is one more apparent carol text from the fourteenth century not reported in the literature on carols. It is in the British Library, Royal MS 12 E 1, fol. 194v.[10] The burden reads:

> Think, man, of mine harde stundes;
> Think of mine harde woundes.

---

8 Including Palti (2008: 50–2).
9 British Library, Add. MS 46919, fols. 205–211v, ed. in Stephen R. Reimer, *The works of William Herebert, OFM* (Toronto: Pontifical Institute of Medieval Studies, 1987): 113–16. The case for their being carols was first put in Robbins, 'Friar Herebert and the carol' (1957); Greene (1977: cliii) explained his reasons for not including them. The poems concerned are 'Wel, herying and worship be to Christ' and 'My folk what have I do thee', printed in Brown 1924: nos. 14–15. The first is a straight translation of the Latin hymn *Gloria laus et honor*, already discussed; the second has very irregular stanza lengths.
10 Printed in Brown 1924: no. 3.

And the first stanza reads:

> Man, thou have thine thought on me,
> Think how dear I bought thee;
> I let me nailen to the tree:
> Harder death ne may non be.
> Think, man, all it was for thee.

Two further stanzas follow, both with five lines but with different rhyme-schemes.

One further carol seems, from its content, to refer to events in Norfolk in the 1360s. This is the carol with the burden 'Man, be wise, and arise,/ And think on life that lasteth ay' (*EEC* 357, in Sloane). It has eight four-line stanzas, the last line of each rhyming with the burden. In stanza 3 it evidently refers to the two plagues of 1348–9 and 1361–2; stanza 5 refers to a 'windës blast/ that made many a man aghast' and blew away several steeples; and stanza 7 refers to 'Lightning at Lynn did great harm/ of tollbooth and of friary Cam' (namely the Carmelite friary). By good luck, a fragmentary chronicle of King's Lynn survives from the years 1340–77 and refers to both the events in stanza 5 and in stanza 7, the former being exceptional winds in 1361 and the latter a major lightning strike in 1363 – described in the chronicle as 'combussit ecclesiam et chorum Carmelitarum Lenn et tolbothe in eadem villa eodem tempore'.[11] It is tempting to think that the writer of the chronicle also wrote the carol, with the specific mention of the tollbooth; but it is a reasonable assumption that the poem was written shortly after 1363.

Moving into the early fifteenth century, there is the carol on the death of Archbishop Richard Scrope, in 1405. Its burden reads (*EEC* 425):

> Hay, hay, hay, hay,
> Think on Whitsun Monday.

With the first of its four stanzas reading:

> The bishop Scrope that was so wise,
> Now is he dead, and low he lies;
> To heaven's bliss yet may he rise,
> Through help of Marie, that mildë may.   *maid*

Here the nature of the burden is of a line to be sung, with its first word repeated after each stanza; and the stanza is in absolutely standard carol form, with monorhymes and a last line rhyming with the burden. It may have been written soon after his execution for treason, though it must be said that his fame increased

---

11 British Library, Add. MS 47214, fols. 18v–20, with the relevant details on fol. 19v, transcribed in Antonia Gransden, 'A fourteenth-century chronicle from the Grey Friars at Lynn', *The English historical review* 72 (1957): 270–8; the association of those last two details with the carol is made in Wakelin, 'Lightning at Lynn' (2001).

massively over the years after his death, not just through the openhandedness of Henry V but particularly through the return of York to power under Edward IV.[12] All we can say for certain about this poem is that it was written after his execution on 8 June 1405 and that the sole copy is from the second half of the fifteenth century (Greene 1977: 328).

Finally, we should note the case of an apparent carol in Anglo-Saxon Canterbury discussed by Christopher Page (2010). As described by the biographer of St Dunstan, a writer who calls himself only 'B' but was evidently writing in the tenth century, Dunstan had a vision of heavenly virgins dancing and singing a hymn but repeating the opening couplet after each other couplet 'in the manner of human virgins' (*more humanarum virginum*). The hymn they are singing is *Cantemus socie Domino* by Sedulius, a poem with a most unusual form: it is entirely in elegiac couplets, fifty-five of them; but all except the first couplet are epanaleptic, namely with the last half of every pentameter precisely replicating the first half of the preceding hexameter.[13] As Page argues, it is most remarkable that we have here an apparent reference to the way 'human virgins' sing and dance, that they do so to a hymn in which the first stanza is different from all that follow and that they apparently keep repeating that first stanza. But the hymn *Cantemus socie Domino* dates from the fifth century. It really cannot be relevant to the history of the English carol.

For the rest, we have seen that most of the pre-1400 carols printed by Greene fall at the first hurdle: in *Blow northern wind* (*EEC* 440) the burden seems entirely unrelated to the verses; in *Hand by hand* (*EEC* 12) the first stanzas has the same metre as the burden whereas the second and third stanzas have a different form; in *Enixa est puerpera* (*EEC* 191) the burden is absent from both pre-1400 manuscripts; *Now springs the spray* (*EEC* 450) is in the purest *ballata* form; *Mary, mother, come and see* (*EEC* 157) has three different burdens in its three post-1400 sources but none in the pre-1400 source. *Hay, hay, hay, hay* (*EEC* 425) laments the execution of Archbishop Scope in 1405, but may in fact have been written rather later when he became more of a popular idol.

We are then left with five poems: *Think, man, of mine harde stundes*, with a two-line burden and five-line stanzas, but no indication for a repeat of the burden and no rhymes shared between the burden and the stanzas; *Man, be wise, and arise* (*EEC* 357) seems indeed to describe events at Kings Lynn in 1361 and 1363 and is in classic carol form but again has no indication for a repeat of the burden though the last line of each quatrain rhymes with the second line of the burden; *Lovely tear of lovely eye* (*EEC* 271), in Grimestone's book of 1372, looks indeed like a carol, thought it is a highly original poem sharing nothing in its mood with

---

12 See in particular J. W. McKenna, 'Popular canonization as political propaganda: the cult of Archbishop Scrope', *Speculum* 45 (1970): 608–23.
13 F. J. E. Raby, *A history of Christian-Latin poetry from the beginnings to the close of the middle ages* (Oxford: At the Clarendon Press, 1927): 109, unforgettably remarked that 'It is unnecessary to comment on this exercise of perverse ingenuity'.

the main carol repertory. *Lullay, lullay, little child* (*EEC* 155), also in Grimestone, looks even more like a carol, also does *Lullay, lullay, la lullay* (*EEC* 149), though the stanzas rhyme *aaab* and do not rhyme with the burden.

These five earlier pieces apparently in carol form share one detail, namely that they all hark back to the forms discussed in chapter 4, the broader style represented by processional hymns and *cantigas*. When put alongside the twenty-five all in carol form presented by John Audelay in *c.* 1426 and the thirteen in the Trinity carol roll, they amount to very little, and little enough that they could be mere accidents. With Trinity and Audelay, however, the genre existed.

That, I should add, is the truth that dawned on me only after loving this music for twenty years. Of the hundred or so manuscripts that Greene describes, very few are from before 1420, and astonishingly few of the poems there are in anything remotely resembling carol form. Then quite suddenly, with the Trinity roll and with John Audelay's manuscript, we have a genre that plainly exists and plainly has a distinct identity.

10 Monophony for the carol

Given that so many carol texts address the assembled company and invite them to take part in the singing, it is a touch surprising that almost everything that we have of carol music is polyphony – not stunningly sophisticated polyphony in some cases, but all hard enough that it is clearly not intended for untrained or unrehearsed singers. That makes the scrutiny of the few tiny monophonic remnants all the more urgent.[1]

But before we come to those, it may be as well to note the poems in Sloane, with no music but probably the second earliest text manuscript containing a substantial number of poems in carol form. First of all, there are many burdens here that are plainly designed for singing. (The same is the case in the other two collective fifteenth-century text sources containing carols, OxEng and St John's.) None of these lines could possibly have been written that way if it were not intended for singing, possibly even for singing to a well known tune. (The numbers with 'S' are those used in Palti 2008.)

S7   Gay gay gay gay: Think on dreadful doomesday.
S9   Jesu, Jesu, Jesu, Jesu: Save us all through thy virtue,
S10 Now go guile, guile, guile, Now go guile, guile, now go guile go.
S14 Man, beware, beware, beware, And keep thee that thou have none care.
S17 Gay, gay, to be gay, I hold it but a vanity.
S19 A, a, a, a: Nu[n]c gaudet Maria
S23 Alleluia alleluia alleluia alleluia alleluia alleluia Deo patri sit gloria.
S24 Nowel el el el el el el el el el el: Mary was gret with Gabriel.
S45 Nowel el el el el el el el el el el el el el
S46 A, a, a, a: Nunc gaudet ecclesia
S57 Nowel, el, el, el, Now is well that ever was woe.
S60 Nowel el el el el el el el el el el el el el
S63 Keep thy tongue, thy tongue, thy tongue. Thy wicked tongue worked me woe.

1 They are also treated in McInnes 2015.

No group of burdens can more eloquently endorse the statement of Frederick Raby, quoted by Greene (1977: cxvii):[2]

> It is important to remember one obvious thing. The peoples of Europe did not live without song, and for thousands of years they had had their songs of love and of death, their drinking-catches and their ballades. It is the continued flow of this stream of popular poetry, which has now perished as though it had not been, that must be taken into account in any attempt to obtain a reasonable view of the Latin lyric. The vernacular song was always there, whatever might happen to its learned counterpart.

But the second point to make about those Sloane burdens is that there is nothing like this anywhere in the known polyphonic carols. Certainly, there are a few that repeat the word 'Nowell' once or twice (*MC* 3/18, 25, 79, 80), but nothing remotely like what we have here. Interestingly, though, there is one other related text, with the burden:

Man assay, assay, assay, And ask mercy while thou may.

Aside from the two polyphonic settings (*MC* 17, 110), this does survive also with a monophonic melody (*MC* 17[A]), and one could also argue that one of the polyphonic settings (*MC* 17) comes close to the monophonic style in its basic simplicity. But even those few cases do not come close to the repetitiveness of the burdens just quoted from Sloane.

It is also true that the Sloane carols tend to have more stanzas than the surviving polyphonic carols. Only three polyphonic carols have more than six stanzas, whereas there are eighteen of these in Sloane. That is to say that, by and large, the polyphonic carol repertory is rather separate from the little we can discern of the main monophonic carol.

And the most particular kind of text that absolutely never appears in the polyphonic repertory is those that are humorous or that concern women and marriage – for the most part misogynistic. Similarly, the polyphonic carols include nothing that could be described as a drinking-song.

John Stevens printed nine monophonic settings of carols in *MC*. It is perhaps easiest to start with James Ryman's collection, Cambridge, University Library, Ee. 1. 12, because it is dated (1492), and its problems are uniform.

Sing we now (*MC* 7[A]: fol. 1) and *Of thy mercy* (*MC* 8[A]: fol. 46v) are the same melody except that 7[A] ends on the pitch G and 8[A] ends on F. They both give music for the burden alone, unrhythmized and not particularly attractive, with no hint about how the verses may have been sung. They are both syllabic apart from a

---

2 F. J. E. Raby, *A history of secular Latin poetry in the middle ages* (Oxford: At the Clarendon Press, 1934, 2nd edition, 1957): 326–7.

70 *Chapter 10: Monophony for the carol*

single syllable in each (one two notes, the other three notes). The two melodies are compared and discussed by Karl Reichl (2003: 214–5, with facsimiles of the pages on pp. 225 and 227). There is also a melody on fol. 1v for the non-carol song *I heard a maiden wepe for herë sonnÿs passion* (ed. in Reichl 2003: 217, with facsimile on p. 226): this is a similar unrhythmized melody, but at least it has four lines, to fit the four lines of each of the song's fourteen quatrains. It is hard to see anything in either of those melodies to set the company alight. For what it is worth, the manuscript also has three textless duos in stroke notation on fol. 8,[3] on six four-line staves described by Brian Trowell as follows:[4] (a) *Salvator mundi Domine*, faburden with chant;[5] (b) *Miserere mihi Domine*, faburden with chant;[6] and (c) unidentified piece.[7] Why they should be there is anybody's guess, but they hardly seem relevant to the matter of carols. Moreover, the Ryman manuscript, dating from the 1490s, is unlikely to be any help in the search for monophonic roots of the carol genre.

Similarly monophonic and unrhythmized are two further melodies: *MC* 9[A] is for the love-song *Though I sing and mirthës make* in Gonville and Caius College, Cambridge, MS 383/603 (*EEC* 441), apparently from the late 1480s, with a heading 'le bon l. don', which could hint at a French origin for the melody;[8] *Of all the enemies* (*MC* 10[A]) is in the famous text manuscript in the Bodleian Library, OxEng, for a poem of moral counsel (a facsimile is in *MC*: xix). Both of these, like the ones in Ryman, have music for the burden only.

Moving on to melodies that can be used, two appear in the MS Hunter 83 in the University of Glasgow, hard to date because so mixed, but probably from the end of the fifteenth century.[9] It contains only two carols, written in two different hands, both with music. Here at last are pieces that can be performed. I have never heard *Salve sancta parens* (*MC* 6[A]): the burden is in unrhythmized pitches, though the verse has metrical rhythm and a tune of sorts – perhaps a voice-part for polyphony, though the metre is C (imperfect time, minor prolation), otherwise unknown in the polyphonic carol repertory. *MC* 5[A] is the evergreen favourite *Nova nova: Ave fit ex Eva*.

MC 4[A] is also in the Bodleian Library manuscript OxEng, with a catchy melody for *Nowell, nowell: this is the salutation of th' angel Gabriel* (fol. 41v), preceded by the non-carol melody *Psallimus cantantes* (fol. 40v): facsimiles of both appear in Stainer (1901: i, plates 99–100).

It needs to be clear that all the melodies described so far are from sources well into the second half of the fifteenth century and therefore substantially later than

---

3 Online scan (of this page only) at https://diamm.ac.uk.
4 Trowell 1980: 76 and nos. 77, 136 and 155 in his list of faburdens.
5 Curtis and Wathey 1994: O 450.
6 Curtis and Wathey 1994: O 344.
7 Curtis and Wathey 1994: X 8.
8 This is the multi-language commonplace book of Wymondus London, apparently the man who was a student at Magdalen College, Oxford, in 1484–5, as explained in Greene 1977: 324–5.
9 First described in Robbins 1943; they are also discussed in McInnes 2015.

Example 10.1 Parit virgo (Cambridge 9414)

the dates that I shall propose for the polyphonic sources. There are just two that may be earlier.

Probably a lot earlier, in fact perhaps from around 1400, are the three melodies that John Stevens printed as *Lullay, lullay: As I lay* (*MC* 1[A]), *Lullay, my child* (*MC* 2[A]) and *I have loved* (*MC* 3[A]). The latter two are from that astonishing tiny book in the British Library, Add. MS 5666, all of whose contents appear to be somehow related to Christmas, and which receives a brief description in the next chapter; but 3[A] looks more like the start of a *chanson d'aventure* (hence Greene putting it in his appendix as App. viii); and 2[A], like 1[A], is really a lullaby.

MC 1[A] is at least singable, with three stanzas. But of the material explored so far the only ones that look plausible as the music for monophonic community singing are *Nowell, nowell: this is the salutation* (*MC* 4[A]) and *Nova nova: ave fit ex Eva* (*MC* 5[A]).

Three further carol melodies have come to light more recently. *Man assay* (*MC* 17[A]) is in Oxford, Lincoln College, MS Lat. 89, where the music is among a group of polyphonic Kyrie fragments.[10] This is in fact the most plausible of all the melodies, though the manuscript is likely again to date from the later fifteenth century. The second is a palimpsest, *Think we on our ending* (*MC* 18[A]) visible only under ultraviolet light written twice, above and below the text of the carol.[11] The third came to light to late to be printed in the revised *MC*, so it is presented here.[12] It is a setting of *Parit virgo filium*, a Latin text known from several continental sources as well as from the polyphonic setting as *MC* 63. Also copied twice, at the bottom

---

10 Described in Seaman and Rastall 1977. But the text is independently reported and transcribed in Greene 1977: 215.
11 Cambridge, Trinity College, MS R. 14. 26; discussed in McInnes 2013: 241–2.
12 Cambridge, University Library, MS Add. 9414, on fol. 1v and fol. 7v. I am grateful to Andrew Wathey for bringing this to my attention and sharing his transcription.

72 Chapter 10: Monophony for the carol

of two different pages in a chant book, the melody is too fragmentary for confident analysis.

In addition to these, there are four cases among the polyphonic carols in Selden where much of the music is in unison, though written out twice, once for each voice – a phenomenon I have not noticed elsewhere in fifteenth-century music. In all four, the two-voice polyphony is composed in a third-based style with the two voices intertwining, slightly like *Lullay, lullow* (*MC* 1), though that is in major prolation whereas these are all in perfect time. And in all four there is a three-voice burden II, much more in the traditional style of the time. In *Alma Redemptoris mater* (*MC* 23) the first half of burden I is in unison, as are all three lines of the verse, prior to the refrain with the words *Redemptoris mater*. In *Alleluia: A newë work* (*MC* 30) burden I is mostly in parallel thirds with overlapping voices, whereas burden II adds a third voice above them, and the verse material is almost entirely unison, though all written out in two voices, with occasional interruptions by a three-voice 'chorus' (so marked), which is mostly in pure fauxbourdon style. In *Veni, Redemptor gencium* (*MC* 41), the main body of the verse is in unison, moving into two voices only for the refrain line at the end. The first burden has the two voices overlapping; again, it is only in burden II that the three-voice texture follows normal principles.

Ave Maria: Hail, blessëd flower (*MC* 36), has part of the first burden and part of the verse in monophony, with most of the rest of the first burden and verse in close two-voice writing. This carol stands out from the group in that no music is written twice. But in all other respects these four carols form a stylistically distinct group that seems to hint at an earlier stage in the evolution of the carol. That all of them are in perfect time, whereas most of the other earliest carols are in major prolation, does not necessarily mean that they are later: after all, there are many perfect time pieces in the first layer of the Old Hall manuscript. But we must return to these pieces in chapter 21.

There are two further pieces with monophonic elements, both of them in Trinity as well as in Selden. The most famous is the Agincourt carol (Example 5.2): here the first half of burden I is in unison before moving into polyphony – again written out in full in both voices (see Figure 3 for Selden).

But it is worth stopping for a moment on *Abide, I hope it be the best* (*MC* 10 and *MC* 42). Only burden I is monophonic, but it seems to be written a 4th too low in both manuscripts (Trinity and Selden): in Example 10.2 it is restored to what I believe must be its correct pitch. Beyond that, it looks as though in Selden burden II is also written a 4th too low: at least, it is in a lower range than the other three-voice music and at the Trinity pitch we thereby have all four sections ending with a cadence on F: Example 10.1 uses the Trinity pitch for burden II. But we have another transmission problem here, namely that the music of the burden appears not to match the text: in an effort to rectify the situation, I have added repeats of the second half of the burden text.

But the most puzzling feature of *Abide, I hope it be the best* is that there seem to be two separate sets of music for the verse – one in two voices and one in three. This is a unique case and seems to me to suggest that the form was at that point still

Example 10.2 Abide, I hope it be the best, MC 10. Complete

74 Chapter 10: Monophony for the carol

Example 10.2 (Continued)

in development, that a composer was trying out various patterns, all of them without parallel in the other known polyphony of the fourteenth or fifteenth centuries.

On the other hand, with the work laid out as in Example 10.2, the familiar phrase structures of the earliest carols are again clear to see and hear. The two burdens are each of eight beats; the first verse is of twelve; and the second verse opens with a five-beat phrase before concluding with two four-beat phrases. That is to say that the single piece in Trinity that is written in perfect time is in all other respects similar to the remainder. Its traces of monophonic structure similarly suggest that this may well be among the earliest pieces in Trinity.

Further support for that view may be in the circumstance that the burden text is identical to the first line of the verse – once again as though an existing poem had been adapted to create a new form, namely that of the carol. Perhaps there is added evidence of this in the survival of two further stanzas in the Selden copy:

    Under the bush ye shal tempest
    Abide, till it be over-go.

    For a long time your heart shall brast;   *burst*
    Abide, I counsel you do so.

The very inconsequence of those two stanzas draws attention to the main structure of the entire poem: it is a series of unrelated maxims counselling patience, each cast with the same metre and rhyme scheme. None has any connection with Christmas or indeed Christianity.

But the main thrust of this chapter has been to assert that there was plainly a tradition of unwritten monophonic carols, a tradition that is almost beyond recovery. Among the remnants that we have, there is no stylistic pattern. On the other hand, if we look at the four Selden carols that are partly monophonic we do indeed see considerable stylistic consistency. That may indeed contain clues to the earliest layer of the polyphonic carol repertory.

11 Add. MS 5666

While on the topic of the predecessors of the polyphonic carol and the traces of vernacular monophony, it is as well to add a statement about the extremely odd and tiny manuscript in the British Library, Add. MS 5666. Its main interest for us is that it contains *MC* 1, *Lullay, lullow: I saw*, the single piece in John Stevens's volume that stands out as being entirely different from the rest in musical style. Its gentle ambulating 9/8 metre is shared only with the Selden carol *Nowell, nowell: Out of your sleep* (*MC* 25); its progression mostly in thirds between the two voices, and its two voices in the same range are shared only with the duet sections of the four partly monophonic Selden carols discussed in the preceding chapter. But the familiar detail here is the phrase-structure: the burden comprises four four-bar phrases; and the verse is of three four-bar phrases.

In terms of script and external details, the manuscript looks as though it is from the first decade of the century, so ten or fifteen years older than the others. *MC* 1 could be a precious hint of the fourteenth-century roots of the polyphonic repertory; or it could be something else entirely. Since it has only two verses, there may be some doubt as to whether it is really a carol, particularly in view of the rhyming cadences between burden and verse, as interpreted by John Stevens in *MC* 1: that does occasionally happen elsewhere in the carol repertory, but in this case it could well be a hint that the work is (or was originally) a virelai.[1]

In addition, there are two apparent monophonic carols that John Stevens printed as *MC* 2[A] and 3[A], both of them very much in the musical style of the piece printed as Example 11.1.

Since there seems to be no recent published exploration of the manuscript, it is worth spending a few pages describing it.[2] Add. MS 5666 is a tiny book of twenty-

---

[1] Among the English vernacular song repertory there is a large number of pieces that are, in my view, virelais with no *tierce*. See the editions in Fallows 2014: nos. 1–3, 7, 9, 13, 15–17, 22, 26 and their commentaries.

[2] The first description appears in Ritson 1792: xxxvii–xl (done while it was still his own property); other descriptions include Greene 1935: 331–2 (reprinted unchanged in Greene 1977: 308); *Census-catalogue* 1979–88: ii.44–5. A more recent description is in McInnes 2013: 18–20.

Chapter 11: Add. MS 5666 77

one paper leaves (albeit with a parchment frontispiece, fol. 1), measuring only 13 × 10 cm. The paper is thick and seems uniform throughout. The contents may be summarized as follows:

A Poems and songs, mostly with music, fols. 2–8v (with an unfoliated stub between fol. 4 and fol. 5 and an unfoliated blank leaf after fol. 8), all apparently written by a single copyist. All the music is written 'landscape', on very roughly drawn staves.
B Grammatical treatise in Latin, fols. 9–13v, apparently without beginning or end. All in a single hand, possibly the same hand that wrote the song texts in section A.
C Financial accounts, fols. 14–17v, 19v–20 and 21v, concerning the expenses of John White, dated 12 Henry IV (= 1411); his name also appears on fols. 6v, 7, 7v and 8. Fols. 18v–9 and 21 are blank; fols. 18 and 20v contain designs of a heart with an arrow through it.
D Fragment of French love poetry on fol. 22v. (Fol. 22 is blank.) Two blank unnumbered leaves after fol. 22 seem to be of the same paper.

The materials in section A break down as follows:

nos. 1–4   fols. 2–3   *Lullay, my child and wepe no more* (*MC* 2^A; *EEC* 151B), with monophonic music for the burden only

According to John Stevens (*MC*: 123), there are four copies of this song here: 'versions of the first 10 measures are written on fol. 2 over faded writing; the last of these three versions is inverted'. The version published as *MC* 2^A is on fols. 2v–3, with 6 stanzas, though there is music only for the burden. Cambridge, University Library, MS Add. 5943, has the burden and stanzas 1, 2 and 4; OxEng has the burden and stanzas 1, 2 and 4–6, with 3 more; stanza 3 of Add. MS 5666 seems to be unique.

no. 5   fol. 3 (bottom)   *Now has Mary born a flour* (ed. Westrup 1932: 339) with monophonic music

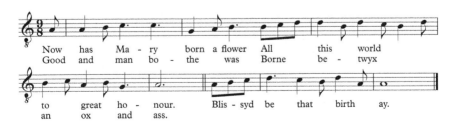

Example 11.1 Now has Mary born a flower (Add. MS 5666). Complete

Chapter 11: Add. MS 5666

no. 6	fol. 3v	*I have loved so many a day* (*MC* 3[A]; *EEC* App. VIII; also printed in Joseph Ritson, *Ancient songs* (1790): xxxviii), with monophonic music
	fol. 4 is blank	
no. 7	fols. 4v–5	*Lullay, lullow: I saw* (*MC* 1; *EEC* 144; also printed in Ritson, *Ancient songs* (1790): xxxviii–xl), with music in two voices
	fols. 5v–8 have scattered bits of writing	
no. 8	fol. 8v	*Puer natus in Betlehem*, with monophonic music

Example 11.2 Puer natus in Betlehem (Add. MS 5666). Complete

This last comes with eight lines of text, lines that are familiar from several other sources, going back at least to the thirteenth century: among those are the Ritson carol *Parit virgo filium* (*MC* 73), the mid-fifteenth-century Glastonbury poetry manuscript, Trinity College, Cambridge, MS O. 9. 38, and the printed book of *Piæ cantiones* (1582). Those four versions of the poem align as follows:

BL, Add. MS 5666		*MC* 73	*PC*	Tr
Puer natus in Betlehem,	unde gaude Jerussalem.	2	1	1
Assumpsit carnem Filii	Dei Patris altissimi.	4	2	3
Per Gabrielem nuncium	virgo concepit Filium.	3	3	2
Sicut sponsus de talamo	processit [matris] utero.	1	7	4
Congnovit bos et assinus	quod puer erat dominus.	5	9	5
Intrantes domum invicem	nomen salutant hominem.	6	12	
Benedicamus Domino	uno deo sempiterno.	?7	13	

It should be added here that there are various other inscriptions in the manuscript, most of them apparently either irrelevant or mendacious. As Greene reports (1935: 331–2):

> The note written on fol. 1v is certainly erroneous. It states that the volume is in the hand of Friar John Brackley of Norwich, the friend and adviser of the Paston family. None of the hands, however, is that of Brackley as represented in his preserved holograph letters (British Library, Add. MS 34888).

While the entire look of the manuscript is decidedly scruffy, as though perhaps indeed intended as a kind of pocket-book with a variety of bits and pieces, that very circumstance makes it hard to date anything here, at least from the viewpoint of script. What can be said is that there is a certain communality of style between the polyphonic carol and three of the monophonic songs, and that style shares nothing with the remaining polyphonic carols of the fifteenth century. To say that there is a certain stylistic similarity in the music of *MC* 1[A], from the Cambridge University Library MS Add. 5943, perhaps from *c*. 1400, is probably pushing the evidence too far, since all the melodies concerned are so short. Nothing here changes the picture already painted of the surviving monophonic music for carol poetry, namely that there is no coherent picture to be drawn: the surviving poetic repertory, particularly of Sloane, makes it almost certain that there was a flourishing tradition of monophonic carols, but not enough music survives to permit any confident statement about it.

12 Awareness of the carol, 1: 1600–1890

This chapter is the first of three *entractes*, following the awareness of the English medieval carol through the years. One side theme of these three chapters is that of the commentators before World War I only Sir John Stainer seems to have recognized the true value of the music but that he died just too soon to say so properly.

An irony in the story is that the carol first made its way into the secondary literature not through any of the fifteenth-century music sources discussed so far but from a much later copy. The earliest printed references – by Bishop Percy (1765), John Stafford Smith (1779) and Charles Burney (1782) – are all based on a strange document in the Pepys Library at Magdalene College, Cambridge. Placed proudly at the front of the first of five magnificent volumes of printed broadside ballads owned by Samuel Pepys is a handwritten copy of the Agincourt carol (Figure 5). That it was copied after 1659 seems clear from the inscription on the other side of the leaf: 'Ex Biblioth. Bodleianâ. Arch. B. Seld. 10.' – for Selden's library did not reach the Bodleian until that year.[1] But it could have been added at any point up to the early years of the eighteenth century[2] – a consideration that makes it all the more significant that the copy is in fact done on parchment, still being used for legal documents and deeds, therefore easily available to Pepys in the Admiralty.

How did Pepys know of the carol? There seems to be no earlier printed reference to it or indeed to any other carol. The guess at first seemed easy enough: Pepys plainly knew John Selden (1584–1654), who was, alongside much else, a

---

[1] The earlier shelf-mark 'Arch. B. Seld. 10' rather than '26' was the original number, as reported in, for example, Edward Bernard, *Catalogi librorum manuscriptorum Angliæ et Hiberniæ* (Oxford: E Theatro Sheldoniano, 1697): Tom. I part 1, p. 262, no. 3340; I am grateful to Dr B.C. Barker-Benfield of the Bodleian for drawing my attention to this entry and also to the remark in the *Summary catalogue*, vol. II part 1 (Oxford: At the Clarendon Press, 1922): 595, stating that the renumbering took place 'early in the 18th century'.

[2] *Catalogue of the Pepys Library at Magdalene College, Cambridge*, ed. Robert Latham, vol. 1: *Ballads*, part 1: *Catalogue* by Helen Weinstein (Woodbridge: Boydell and Brewer, 1992): xvi, states that the 'original binding of the ballad volumes must have taken place about 1702 or soon after, because the portrait title of Volume I dates the collection as having been "continued to the year 1700" and the latest ballads to which dates can be assigned with confidence are a group of seven ballades from 1702 announcing the death of William III'.

major authority on maritime law, which was of central importance to Pepys.[3] It was Selden who began the collection of broadside ballads that now survives in the Pepys Library at Cambridge; so presumably it was Selden who alerted Pepys to the existence of the Agincourt carol among his manuscripts.

But the truth turns out to be quite different. Pepys learned about it from the young Humfrey Wanley (1672–1726), who would have come across in the course of preparing Edward Bernard's *Catalogi librorum manuscriptorum Angliæ et Hiberniæ* (1697). The correspondence between Pepys and Wanley seems to have begun on 7 April 1701; but already in a letter of 10 April Pepys wrote:[4]

> You won't forget my request about Froissart; and if you could prompt me to any means for my coming to more knowledge of the volume of ballads you mentioned yesterday, wherein was that of the battle of Agincourt, I should gladly look after it.

It is clear that the Selden manuscript (Figure 3) was the exemplar for the Pepys copy, not just from the musical details but particularly because the copy omits the top line in that manuscript, containing bars 1–11 of the discantus, apparently because the copyist thought it was just the end of the preceding piece and that the highest texted line on the page was the first line of the Agincourt carol.

That is how it is interpreted in Thomas Percy's *Reliques of ancient English poetry* (London: J. Dodsley, 1765). In vol. 2, pp. 24–5, he printed the text, prefaced by the disarming remarks:

> That our plain and martial ancestors could wield their swords much better than their pens will appear from the following homely Rhymes, which were drawn up by some poet laureat of those days to celebrate the immortal victory gained at Agincourt, Oct. 25, 1415. This song or hymn is given merely as a curiosity, and is printed from a MS copy in the Pepys collection, vol. I. folio. It is there accompanied with the musical notes, which are copied in a small plate at the end of this volume.

In that plate it is clear that Percy's engraver had no idea what he was reproducing. It just happens that for most of the page the music is in two voices, so there is text below every alternate line of the music. Bishop Percy's engraver concluded that the texted lines were the vocal lines and that the untexted lines below them were the accompaniment, so he added braces that are all between the wrong staves. Needless to say, the engraver's misunderstanding led to further errors, with a result that is complete musical nonsense.[5]

---

3 *The diary of Samuel Pepys*, ed. Robert Latham and William Matthews, 11 vols. (London: G. Bell and Sons Ltd, 1970–83): ii.222–3 and vi.81.

4 *The life, journals, and correspondence of Samuel Pepys*, ed. John Smith, 2 vols. (London: Richard Bentley, 1841): ii.264.

5 The same was reprinted in Nicholas Harris Nicolas, *The history of the battle of Agincourt* (London: Johnson, 1827): 130.

82   Chapter 12: Awareness of the carol, 1

That is why Charles Burney felt it necessary to travel to Cambridge and check the manuscript. In his *A general history of music*, vol. 2 (1782: 383), he wrote:

> The transcribers of ancient MSS. seem in general to have been utterly ignorant of music, and so indifferent as to the place and form of Notes as to have made them unintelligible; and indeed, though I made a journey to Cambridge, in order to see the original Music of the song which had been transcribed for the *Reliques of Ancient Poetry*, it was not till after I had tried to write it many different ways that I was able to disentangle the parts, and form it into a score.

But three years before Burney's edition (1782: 384–7) appeared in print, John Stafford Smith (1750–1836) had published it in his *A collection of English songs, in score for three and four voices composed about the years 1500 and taken from MSS of the same age, revised and digested by J S Smith* (London: J. Bland, 1779): 2–3. This is a most remarkable book for the twenty-nine-year-old son of a west country cathedral organist, the man who was later to compose the music for *The star-spangled banner*. It includes not only a complete English translation of the substantial patent placed at the beginning of Petrucci's Third Book of Josquin masses (Fossombrone, 1514), which he found in the British Museum, and no fewer than fourteen complete (and mainly accurate) transcriptions of those marvellous florid songs that appear in the Fayrfax book from around 1500. His commentary shows that he also had a good knowledge of the Pepys MS 1236 and the British Library Harley MS 978. But his opening piece was the Agincourt carol, presented first in careful pseudo-facsimile of the Pepys Library copy (p. 1) and then in an excellent transcription (p. 2) – of course, omitting the discantus of the first 11 bars, overlooked by the Pepys copyist.[6]

Burney's transcription has annotations that go into considerable detail about particular notes and progressions in the piece: that is to say that he made a serious effort to come to terms with what seemed to him an exceptionally rare document. He had after all written earlier (1782: 383–4, note *m*):

> Indeed, specimens of Musical Compositions at such an early period, are so scarce, and this in particular seems so much to belong to my subject, that a History of English Music would be deficient without it.

---

6   John Stafford Smith's heavily annotated copy of Burney's *General history* survives as Royal College of Music, 61776.a.2: the annotations are extremely critical of Burney's ignorant copying of material already presented in Hawkins's *History*, for which the young Stafford Smith was apparently a co-worker. Several of his vituperative comments are published in Elizabeth Cole, 'Stafford Smith's Burney', *Music and letters* 40 (1959): 35–8. Sadly, though, his copy contains no pertinent annotations on the Agincourt carol.

And, in view of its importance, he had a few more details to add about the Pepys manuscript (1782: 384):

> The Copy in the Pepysian Collection is written upon Vellum in Gregorian Notes, and can be little less ancient than the event which it recorded. There is with it a paper which shews that an attempt was made in the last century to give it a modern dress; but too many liberties have been taken with the melody, and the drone base which has been set to it for Lute is mere jargon. I shall therefore present my reader with a faithful copy of this venerable relic of our nation's prowess and glory, in the beginning of the fifteenth century, from which we are perhaps entitled to more honour than from the poetry and Music with which they were then celebrated.

John Stafford Smith had also described the later Pepys version in the following words (p. vi):

> The next Leaf contains *the same in moderne Dresse*, but so very imperfect that it can hardly be called *the same*. An Ear which can judge from Nature will find it pleasing.

That next leaf is indeed a most surprising document, an arrangement of the Agincourt carol for bass voice and five-course plectrum guitar (Figure 6, transcribed in Example 12.1). That Burney was wrong in thinking it for lute is clear enough not only from the continual use of all five strings but particularly from the tuning, which must be *a d' g b e'* – the system given in Luis de Briçeño's *Metodo mui facilissimo para aprender tañer la guitarra a lo español* (Paris: Pierre Ballard, 1626): fol. 5,[7] and in Marin Mersenne's *Harmonie universelle* (Paris: various printers, 1636), ii: *Livre second des instrumens a chordes*, p. 95;[8] it is reported later in England by Richard Toward (1660) and James Talbot (1690s).[9] Moreover, it is well known that Pepys was an avid guitar player, as particularly witnessed by the five books of music for guitar and voice assembled for him by his servant Cesare Morelli.[10]

---

7 James Tyler, *The early guitar: a history and a handbook* (London: Oxford University Press, 1980): 40–41. José Castro Escudero and Daniel Devoto, 'La méthode pour la guitare de Luis Briçeño', *Revue de musicologie* 51 (1965): 131–48, based on a study of the only known copy, Paris, Bibliothèque nationale de France, Rés. Vm⁸. u. 1, where the author's name is misprinted 'Briçño'.
8 Facsimile with introduction by François Lesure (Paris: Éditions du Centre National de la Recherche Scientifique, 1986).
9 Christopher Page, *The guitar in Stuart England: a social and musical history* (Cambridge: Cambridge University Press, 2017): 11.
10 *Catalogue of the Pepys Library at Magdalene College Cambridge*, ed. Robert Latham, vol. iv: *Music, maps and calligraphy* (Woodbridge: Boydell and Brewer, 1989). Biographical material on Morelli is available in *Oxford dictionary of national biography* (Oxford: Oxford University Press, 2004 and online), s.v. 'Servants of Samuel Pepys'.

Here the tenor is transposed down a second (with an appropriate key-signature of two flats) in line with Pepys's own preferred vocal range.[11] In burden II at the word 'red-de' the arranger misinterprets the ligature, thereby losing a bar in the regular four-bar phrasing of the carol. The reason, though, is clear: although there are two earlier *cum opposita proprietate* ligatures, which he had interpreted correctly, this one also entails *alteratio*, of which the arranger evidently knew nothing, so he grasped at the nearest likely solution. And just before that he had interpreted a dot of division as a dot of augmentation. Those are surely permissible slips at the time. That the guitar accompaniment is apparently written in a regular pattern of three strums a bar (two down, one up: denoted by minims in the manuscript and by downward and upward arrows in example 12.1) adds to the folksy impression the arrangement seems intended to portray.

Most interesting, though, is the way some of the texting is changed, and I am inclined to think that these changes were made consciously by Pepys. Now that we can see how he changed it, it should be clear that the original stress, 'De-ó gra-tí-as' is unfortunate, or at least seemed inappropriate to a sensitive musician in c. 1700. Also intriguing is the way the rhythm of the penultimate bar of the first burden is changed to match all the other lines but the last: this change contradicts the two known fifteenth-century manuscripts of the carol, but it seems a very good solution.

That information, incidentally, enables us to date the copy and the arrangement with some precision. Plainly the arrangement was made for Pepys. Since he first heard of the Selden manuscript from Wanley in April 1701 and died in May 1703, both documents must have been produced in that two-year gap.

Many readers may be disappointed that the first revival of the carol should be the xenophobic Agincourt carol; and they may be happier to know that the picture looks a lot more rounded in the next decades. Joseph Ritson's *Ancient songs* (1790) included several carol texts, among them *Lullay: I saw a sweet* (*MC* 1, from his own manuscript, now British Library, Add. MS 5666), Audelay's *Welcome yule: Welcome be thou, Heaven king* (*EEC* 7), and the 1521 printed carol *The boar's head in hand bear I* (*EEC* 132); but it also included two carol texts from another manuscript of his own, the one we still call Ritson's manuscript: *Nowell, nowell: The boarës head* (*MC* 79) and *Nowell, nowell: who is there* (*MC* 80). Even more impressive is that John Stafford Smith, over thirty years after his pioneering transcription of the Agincourt carol, printed the music of four carols from Ritson's manuscript in his *Musica antiqua* (London: Preston, 1812).[12] These

---

11 Alana Mailes, 'Teaching in exile: Cesare Morelli's transcriptions in Pepys Library mss. 2803–4', *Early music* 45 (2017): 267–82, at p. 274, and citing Steve Race, 'Samuel Pepys, music lover', *The consort* 39 (1983): 498–501, at p. 499.

12 Full title: *Musica antiqua: a selection of music of this and other countries, from the commencement of the twelfth to the beginning of the eighteenth century; comprizing some of the earliest & most curious motetts, madrigals, hymns, anthems, songs, lessons & dance tunes, some of them now first published from manuscripts and printed works of great rarity & value, the whole calculated to shew the original sources of the melody & harmony of this country & to exhibit the different*

Example 12.1 *Deo gracias, Anglia* (Pepys arrangement). Complete

Example 12.1 (Continued)

are *Sing we to this merry company: Benign lady blessëd mote thou be* (*MC* 76, of which he printed only the two burdens, at p. 21, but the verse on p. 23, as though a different piece), *Nowell, nowell: The boarës head* (*MC* 79, at p. 22), *Nowell, nowell: who is there* (*MC* 80, burden only, at p. 26), and *Marvel not, Joseph* (*MC* 81, pp. 24–5).

But these appear to have had little impact. By and large the English music historians of the nineteenth century ignored the earlier English music – understandably, in view of its transcription difficulties. The three highly successful volumes of Henry Ramsden Bramley and John Stainer, *Christmas carols new and old* (London: Novello, 1871–80) included some sixteenth-century pieces but nothing earlier than that; and the real breakthrough came from two surprising quarters, to be discussed in chapter 17.

All the same, it would be wrong to leave this chapter without saluting the publications of Thomas Wright (1810–77), antiquarian, polymath and prolific writer.[13] One of his earliest publications (1836) had included a group of carols from Sloane; but in 1848 he printed the entire contents of the Oxford carol manuscript, OxEng; and in 1856 he printed the entire contents of Sloane. (He had also in 1842 printed for the first time the entire contents of the famous fourteenth-century poetry manuscript Harley 2253.) Apart from John Stafford Smith, he seems to have been the only person before Stainer to have really relished these poems.

---

styles & degrees of improvement of the several periods. Selected and arranged by John Stafford Smith, Organist to His Majesty. Intriguingly, this book was published one year before the auction of John Parker's library at which John Stafford Smith bought the Old Hall manuscript for £1 2s.

13 Details of his life are in the excellent article in *Oxford dictionary of national biography* (Oxford: Oxford University Press, 2004 and online), by Michael Welman Thompson. The British Library catalogue has over 180 entries for books and pamphlets by him.

13 Composers

One hindrance to appreciating early carol music is its anonymity. That should not be a problem, certainly not now that we have been long accustomed to talk of the 'death of the author'. But this may in any case just be down to chance. Of the famous continental songbooks from the second half of the fifteenth century, several have no ascriptions: the Wolfenbüttel chansonnier, with fifty-six songs; the Copenhagen chansonnier 291, with thirty-three songs; the gorgeous Chansonnier Cordiforme of Jean de Montchenu, with forty-three songs; the Paris chansonnier f. fr. 1597, with sixty-seven songs; the Bologna manuscript Q16, with 131; the recently discovered Leuven chansonnier, with fifty. Nothing in these famous manuscripts names a composer. In addition, the Pavia manuscript Aldini 362 has but a single ascription among its forty-four songs; the Glogauer Liederbuch has five ascriptions among its 294 pieces; the Cape Town manuscript has two ascriptions among eighty-five pieces; the 'second' Riccardiana chansonnier has two ascriptions among seventy-three pieces. Which is a way of saying that without the heavily ascribed chansonniers (Mellon, Casanatense, Pixérécourt) we would have almost nothing.[1] The present anonymity of the carol music could well be entirely different if we just happened to have one manuscript with ascriptions.

More than that, the grammatical literacy of all the carol music stands in startling contrast to the apparently informal and 'low-style' musical repertories as they are known from Italy and Germany, for example. Certainly, most of the earliest carols are in a simple style, and there is evidence of aural transmission in places; but they are always musically literate. Everything about these carols appears to say that they are composed by actual composers, people as musically sophisticated as Power, Dunstable or Bedyngham. It is just bad luck that the three musical manuscripts that happen to survive for the earliest layer of this repertory transmit their music anonymously, just as do countless manuscripts from the same

---

1 Matters explored a little further in David Fallows, 'Dunstable, Bedyngham and *O rosa bella*', *The journal of musicology* 12 (1994): 287–305, at p. 287. Details of these manuscripts are in David Fallows, *A catalogue of polyphonic songs, 1415–1480* (Oxford: Oxford University Press, 1999), to which must now be added David J. Burn, *Leuven chansonnier* = Leuven library of music in facsimile 1 (Antwerp: Davidsfonds, 2017).

years on the continental mainland: the only difference is that for the continental mainland sources we happen to have parallel sources that contain large numbers of ascriptions.

For the entire carol repertory, there is just one clear ascription, 'Childe' for the carol *Y-blessed be that Lord* in Selden (fol. 28v: *MC* 40). The only proposed identification of that man is a William Childe who was an assistant master at Eton College in 1446–9 and died in 1487.[2] But since I believe that Selden manuscript is unlikely to date after 1440 (to be argued in due course) and the carol itself no later than 1430, he seems too young to be a likely contender; and there is nothing at all in his biography to suggest any connection with music. A bit more promising would be either the 'Willelmus Child clericus' who died in 1457 according to the register of London parish clerks or the 'Iohannes Chylde' who appears on the first list of its members in 1449.[3] But in the circumstances we have almost nothing to go on. Small wonder that several people have even questioned whether this is really an ascription,[4] though it is clearly placed at the top of the page in the middle, just like nearly all ascriptions from those years.

Another inscription in Selden has been misleadingly reported over the years. The carol *I pray you all* (*MC* 15: Example 15.2; Figure 7) has the letters 'qd JD' at the end of the text *residuum*. John Stevens (*MC*: 117) wrote: 'There is no evidence for or against the ascription of this carol to Dunstable; but it is at least possible that the initials J D refer to their most famous owner'. To which one must remark: (a) that the ascription is not where a musical ascription would normally be, namely at the head of the music, or just conceivably immediately after the music; and (b) that John and its cognates is the most common name anywhere in medieval Europe. Similarly, Greene (1977: 315, but not in either of his earlier collections, both of which include the poem) wrote of the initials: 'These may refer to the great composer John Dunstable, as the music is in a style used by him, but there

---

2 Harrison 1958: 456. His identification is endorsed by John Caldwell (*Die Musik in Geschichte und Gegenwart*, ed. Friedrich Blume: *Supplement*, 1973) and David Greer, *The new Grove dictionary of music and musicians*, ed. Stanley Sadie (London: Macmillan, 1980) and in *The new Grove dictionary of music and musicians: revised edition*, ed. Stanley Sadie and John Tyrrell (London: Macmillan, 2001). His will, including bequests to New College, Oxford, as well as Winchester and Eton, is reported in Wyn K. Ford, 'Some wills of English musicians of the fifteenth and sixteenth centuries', *R. M. A. Research Chronicle* 5 (1965): 80–4, at p. 83.

3 N. W. James and V. A. James, *The bede roll of the Fraternity of St Nicholas* = London Record Society Publications 39 (London: London Record Society, 2004): 48, 50 and 5.

4 Harrison 1958: 420n3. Greene, on the other hand (1962: 178; 1977: 315), wrote that 'Since composers' names in general are not given by this MS., it is more probably a note of ownership'. That seems impossible: fol. 28v is an absurd place for a note of ownership when the manuscript runs from fol. 3 to fol. 33; and while there is indeed no other ascription in this short manuscript, this ascription is precisely where almost all other musical ascriptions appear in manuscripts of the fifteenth century, namely above the music and centred. Greene may be right in his assertion that the name is in a different hand, though it seems to be in the same colour as the text underlaid to the music (as against the much darker colour of the ink for the additional verses, which are quite definitely in a different hand); but that too is often the case with musical ascriptions. I see absolutely no case for viewing this as anything other than an ascription for the music.

is no further evidence'.[5] In both cases this is the wildest guesswork. It is almost certainly not an ascription for the music. It could just be an ascription for the text; but it is more likely to identify the copyist of the lines (who appears nowhere else in Selden).[6]

I shall in fact argue later in favour of the possibility that Dunstable was the composer of at least some of the surviving carols, but absolutely not on the basis of that Selden annotation.

Finally, we must confront Richard Smert and John Trouluffe. In the first layer of Ritson, their names are scattered across the pages in large letters below or around fifteen of the carols plus three settings of *Nesciens mater*, often with both names together, usually near the bottom of the page (see Figure 8). The positioning of those names is unlike that of any ascription known from the fifteenth century. Harrison (1958: 421) treated them as joint ascriptions, though without saying whether he thereby meant that one wrote the text, the other the music. But that, at least, is unlikely, since both names appear on fols. 57v–58 below a setting of the well-known Latin text *Nesciens mater*:

Soghfte and esely Sayde Trouluffe. Well fare yeure hertys Sayde Smert.

This is characteristic of the bantering tone that appears throughout those mysterious inscriptions.

At least we have some dates for Smert.[7] He was ordained deacon and priest in 1427, so in view of the normal ordination age for a priest being twenty-five, he is likely to have been born in about 1402. He served as a vicar choral at Exeter Cathedral between 1427 and about 1430 and again from 1449–78; from 1435 until 1477 he was rector of Plymtree, a tiny village ten miles from Exeter. Since one of the entries in the Ritson manuscript names him as 'Smert Ricard de Plymptre' (fols. 17v–18), this portion of the manuscript must have been copied after 1435. But it cannot have been much later, for reasons to be explored in chapter 18.

The earliest reference at all to John Trouluffe is from 1448, when Edmund Lacy, Bishop of Exeter from 1420 to 1455, appointed him to a canonry and prebend in the collegiate of Probus in Cornwall; and Nicholas Orme judges that Trouluffe

---

5 The proposal first crops up in E. W. B. Nicholson's report on the manuscript in Stainer 1901: i.xxii. He remarks that J. F. R. Stainer had drawn his attention to the inscription, 'which I conjectured to indicate Dunstable's authorship; but I am told that such of his known works as are signed by him have a different form' – which is true but irrelevant.
6 It is perhaps worth mentioning – if only in a footnote – that Fuller Maitland ([1891]: v) describes the carols in the Trinity manuscript as 'almost without a doubt the work of one composer', whom he later identifies as Dunstable (vi, viii) on the basis of a similarity he discerns between *O Rosa bella* and the carols *MC* 2, 8 and 10. It needs to be borne in mind that there was almost no music of the fifteenth century then available in modern edition. Most authorities now agree that *O Rosa bella* was by Bedyngham and composed in the 1440s; and it seems to me that none would be happy to agree on any common ground between that piece and the Trinity carols.
7 Orme 1978: 401–2 and 410.

could have been in Lacy's private chapel.[8] But whereas Smert simply disappears from the record in 1479 (at which point he would have been almost 80), we do know that Trouluffe died in the winter of 1473–4. The available documentation does not allow us to judge which of the two was older.

But it seems impossible to discern whether they were composers (and, if so, how they divided their work), or whether they were somehow jointly involved in adapting and arranging music received from elsewhere, or perhaps jointly involved in copying the music (unlikely since all the Ritson carols look as though they were copied by a single hand). What can be said is that the Ritson carols are distinctly different in style from the remainder of the carol repertory: still recognizably carols and still quite different from what we otherwise know of polyphony in the fifteenth century, but far less direct and incisive than the main carol repertory we know from the other three sources.

8 Orme 1978: 402–3 and 410.

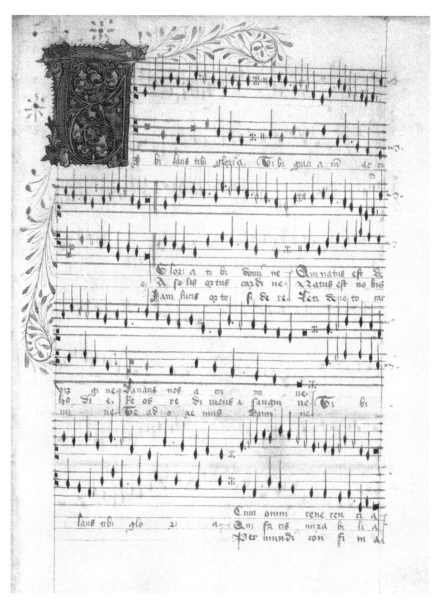

Figure 1 British Library, Egerton MS 3307, fol. 49: *Tibi laus* (*MC* 44) with the decorated initial that opens the carol section of the manuscript

© The British Library Board

Figure 2 Cambridge choirbook fragment: University Library, MS Ll. 1. 11, fol. 32, containing *Nowell, nowell: Out of your sleep* (*MC* 14A)

Reproduced by kind permission of the Syndics of Cambridge University Library

Figure 3 Agincourt carol (*MC* 29), from Oxford, Bodleian Library, MS Arch. Selden B. 26, fol. 17v

By permission of The Bodleian Library, University of Oxford

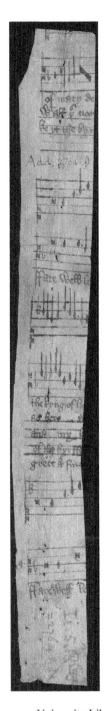

Figure 4 Cambridge fauxbourdon page: University Library, MS Add. 2764 (1)
Reproduced by kind permission of the Syndics of Cambridge University Library

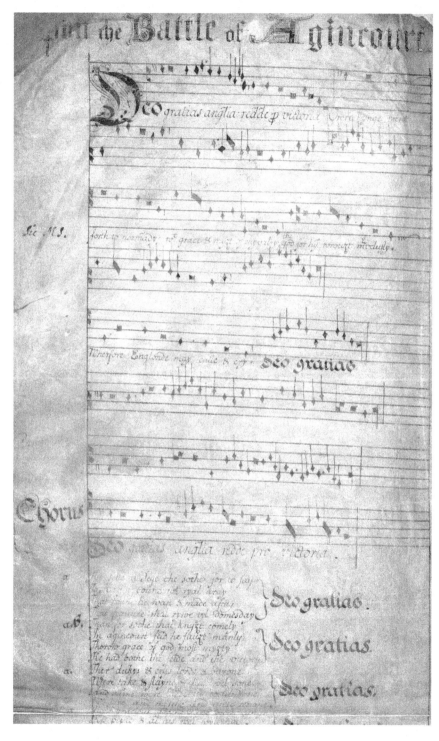

Figure 5 Cambridge, Magdalene College, Pepys fol. 1 (copy of Agincourt carol) 'PL Ballads 1.4'

By permission of the Pepys Library, Magdalene College, Cambridge

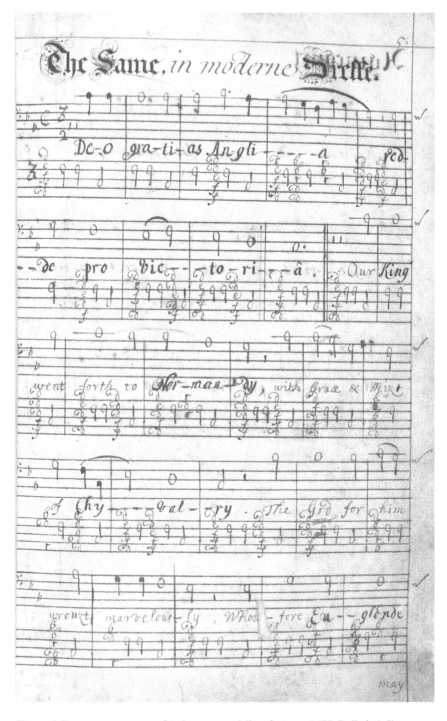

Figure 6 Pepys: arrangement of Agincourt carol (just first page) 'PL Ballads 1.5'
By permission of the Pepys Library, Magdalene College, Cambridge

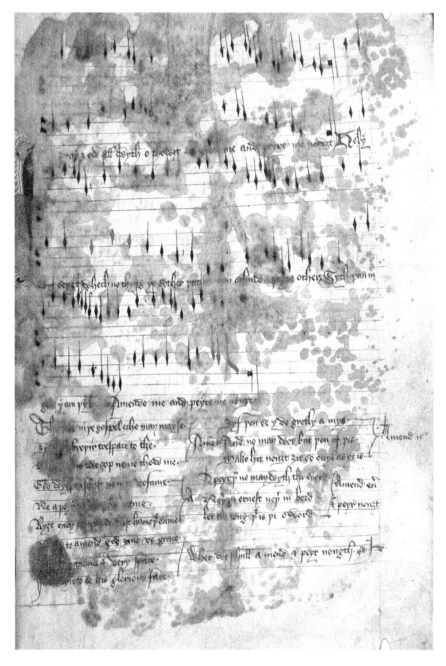

Figure 7 Oxford, Bodleian Library, MS Arch. Selden B. 26, fol. 5 with original ruling and quod j.d.

By permission of The Bodleian Library, University of Oxford

Figure 8 Ritson (British Library, Add. MS 5665), fol. 16v, with apparent ascriptions to Smert and Trouluffe
© The British Library Board

14 Social context, 1: The Royal Court and Political Propaganda

Nowhere are the 1920s roots of received thought on the carol more clearly seen than in Greene's opinion that they were composed by the elite but intended for consumption by the common people. His verdict that they were 'popular by destination'[1] has been quoted in almost every statement on the carol since 1935. Perhaps it is time to question this when the repertory includes twenty-six texts entirely in Latin, some of them fairly complicated.

Greene's view needs to be seen in the context of the search for indigenous popular song in many countries during the nineteenth century.[2] Folksongs were extracted from all kinds of manuscripts and inevitably also from polyphonic sources. With the 1950s came a more nuanced approach to this quest. But in 1935 Greene was saying simply that these catchy compositions ought not to be quarried for potential folksongs (and in chapter 25 we shall see a distinguished musician doing precisely that only three years earlier).

This was all the same one of those comments that was worth more in 1935 than it has been since the emergence of the Egerton manuscript in 1946, containing nineteen carols entirely in Latin – along with several more in which half the text is in Latin. For schools, for ecclesiastical establishments, for universities, but not for popular gatherings. And in this context it is perhaps doubly important to repeat that the poetic form of the Egerton Latin carols, like their music, is absolutely that of the English carols studied by Greene just as it is entirely different from any known form among continental music.

So recent writers have tended to reject Greene's view. John Caldwell wrote:[3]

> The polyphonic carol is nearly always a high-minded genre; the musical settings of satirical, amorous, or erotic songs in this form have mostly disappeared. These will have been the province of a lower class musician, for production at a more advanced stage of an evening's entertainment.

---

1 Greene 1935: xciii; 1977: cxviii.
2 A persuasive description of this in France is in Jane Alden, *Songs, scribes, and society* (New York: Oxford University Press, 2010): 1–38.
3 *The Oxford history of English music: Volume 1: From the beginnings to c.1715* (Oxford: Oxford University Press, 1991): 164.

Similarly, Roger Bowers was surely right to say (2001: 191n94) that they were 'music of elevation and refinement, created by learned composers for the entertainment and the diversion of the educated, both performer and listener'.[4]

In fact Greene himself outlined a much-needed new view of the carol in his 1962 book *A selection of English carols*, where the fifty-page introduction includes the following statement (1962: 27; reprinted exactly in 1977: xxxviii):

> Beyond all question the principal use of the kind of carol which predominates in this collection was at celebrations involving feasting or social dining. The chief habitat of the manuscript carol was the hall, whether of a castle or major house or of a monastery or cathedral. This was the place above all others where religious and laity, men and women, and, within limits, great and humble most frequently met to form a common audience, and to indulge a taste in lyric entertainment that varied less from group to group than is often thought.

That this remark stands in stark contradiction with what he said elsewhere in both books is just one symptom of the way his later thinking on the matter was never incorporated into his original ideas: I have said already that particularly the 1977 revision of his 1935 book was a cut-and-paste job, simply adding bits to his original statement and rarely even deleting anything. (But, then, who would be so cavalier as to cut out the beautiful prose of his original achievement, particularly comments like 'popular by destination' which had become part of the entire rhetoric surrounding the carol? I have also said earlier, but must repeat, that his gathering of new material over the intervening forty years demonstrates the most extraordinary concentration and stamina, just as it yields a priceless legacy of lifelong erudition from a seriously devoted scholar.)

But I would like to go considerably further than any of these writers and focus for a few pages on the carol as a royal court entertainment and as a political statement. We can begin with *Benedicite Deo Domino* (*MC* 57):

B

Benedicite Deo Domino;   Bless the Lord God;
Laudate eum in secula.   praise him in all generations.

1

Angeli et ethera,   Angels and heavens,
Virtutes et maria,   powers and seas
Omnia et opera: and all works:
Benedicite Deo Domino;   *Bless the Lord God;*
Laudate eum in secula.   *praise him in all generations.*

---

4 Perhaps the most sustained criticism is in Catherwood 1996: 350–68.

2

Sol, luna et sydera,	Sun, moon and stars,
Ros, ignis et frigora,	dew, fire and cold things,
Tenebre et fulgura:	shadows and lightnings:
Benedicite Deo Domino;	*Bless the Lord God;*
Laudate eum in secula.	*praise him in all generations.*

3

Omnia mobilia	All moving things
In mundo vivencia	living in the world
(Per) debita servicia:	owed services:
Benedicite Deo Domino;	*Bless the Lord God;*
Laudate eum in secula.	*praise him in all generations.*

4

Anglia et Francia,	England and France,
Cunctaque imperia	and all empires
Orbis intra climata:	within the cardinal points of the world:
Benedicite Deo Domino;	*Bless the Lord God;*
Laudate eum in secula.	*praise him in all generations.*

The last stanza absolutely assumes that England and France had common aims: that could be applicable from the Treaty of Troyes (May 1420) until perhaps a few years into Henry VI's reign, but never again in the fifteenth century.[5] More particularly, it could be between the Treaty of Troyes, when Charles VI of France officially made Henry V his heir, and the deaths of Henry V and Charles VI late in 1422.

The background here was the murder on 10 September 1419 of John the Fearless, Duke of Burgundy, by attendants of the Dauphin, who three years later was to become Charles VII of France. This was the culmination of a series of problems as a result of which Charles VI disinherited his son, gave his final blessing to the marriage of his daughter Catherine to Henry V (concerning which negotiations stretched back almost ten years) and designated Henry V his regent and successor. For the previous five years, Charles VI had faced a double threat, internally from his cousin Burgundy and externally from Henry V, who had during most of that

---

5 A twelve-month peace between England and France was signed on 24 January 1414 and ratified in Paris on 10 March 1414, see Wylie 1914–29: i.156–7; but it was a low-profile affair, and it is plain that Henry V was actively preparing for a French invasion already within a few weeks of a his coronation: on 10 May 1413 he issued an order 'that no bows, arrows or artilleries were to be sold to the Scots or other foreign enemies', quoted from Wylie: i.161, where it is followed by a substantial lists of similar orders over the next months.

time been steadily conquering large portions of northern France. An additional problem was that of Charles VI's twelve children, only six were male and only four of the six lived past infancy. The last three Dauphins were Louis, who died at the age of eighteen in 1415, Jean, who died at the same age in 1417, and the future Charles VII, who was himself just fourteen years old when he inherited the title on 5 April 1417. From the summer of 1418 the Dauphin had set up household in Bourges, publicly declared his father incapable of ruling (which had been the case for over twenty years) and proclaimed himself official regent of France. The murder of John the Fearless tipped the balance: by the end of October 1419 there was agreement in principle that the Dauphin had shown himself unfit to rule and that Henry V would be the regent and successor to Charles VI.

Three possible occasions for the carol present themselves in this context. The first is Christmas of 1419, when the agreement was in place and Henry V celebrated Christmas at Rouen;[6] the second is on the occasion of the Treaty of Troyes, signed on 21 May 1420, the same day that Henry was formally betrothed to Catherine de Valois (after which twelve days of celebrations and feasts led to the actual wedding in the cathedral); the third is Christmas 1420, which Henry and his new wife celebrated with the court in Paris – in fact in the Louvre, while Charles VI and his queen celebrated with far less ceremony in their normal Paris residence, the Hôtel Saint-Pol.[7]

Of these three, the Treaty of Troyes is the most likely occasion for *Benedicite Deo Domino*, particularly bearing in mind that the carol includes absolutely no seasonal references. And that would explain why the text is in Latin. The music is decidedly English in style, but the audience was international. I would remind the reader at this point that the date proposed here is twenty years earlier than the received date for the Egerton manuscript and that Gwynn McPeek (1963: 15) was inclined to associate the carol with Henry VI's marriage to Marguerite d'Anjou in 1445;[8] but there are very few later dates at which the

---

6 Grattan Flood 'The English Chapel Royal under Henry V and Henry VI', *Sammelbände der Internationalen Musik-Gesellschaft* 10 (1909): 564, states that the Chapel Royal joined Henry in time for Easter Day, 1418; this information is already present in Henry Davey, *History of English music* (London: J. Curwen, 1895): 55.
7 Wylie 1914–29: iii.232; Jonathan Sumption, *The hundred years war* 4 (London: Faber & Faber, 2015): 717.
8 On the face of it, this is marginally possible as an occasion for the carol. The betrothal coincided with the Treaty of Tours, signed on 28 May 1444. It was 'the first general truce to be concluded in the war since 1420' according to Ralph A. Griffiths, *The reign of King Henry VI* (London: Ernest Benn, 1981): 486. After the wedding itself, celebrated at Tichfield Abbey on 22 April 1445, the queen entered London on 28 May to the most elaborate celebrations. John Lydgate's poems for the occasion – printed in Carleton Brown, 'Lydgate's verses on Queen Margaret's entry into London', *The modern language review* 7 (1912): 225–324 – include the lines:

   So trusteth your people with affiance
   Through your grace and high benignity
   Twixt the realms two, England and France,
   Peace shall approach, rest and unity,
   Mars set aside with all his cruelty

96   *Chapter 14: Social context, 1*

unity of France and England could so confidently be asserted. Moreover, the music, in major prolation without any three-voice burden and closely resembling the style of the earliest Trinity carols, could well date from the years around 1420.

With that possibility in mind, it begins to look as though the same kind of date is appropriate for *Princeps serenissime* (*MC* 62). This is almost certainly addressed to Henry V: earlier suggestions that it could be addressed to Henry VI seem so stretched as to be virtually impossible.[9] Of course 'princeps' could refer to any prince or duke, and it would be unwise to discard the possibility that the carol is far later and addressed, for example, to one of Henry V's brothers. But every detail of the text makes the most sense when it is associated with Henry V, perhaps at Christmas 1420 in the Louvre or – reading the text more literally – at New Year 1421 in Rouen.

The burden is to some extent ambiguous: it could refer to a living prince or to the Prince of Peace. But the second stanza holds the clue here, the wish that he who is born of a virgin (i.e. Christ) should give 'to you' (singular) the Light of Light. The carol is addressed to a single person, who is a 'serene prince'. The references to his 'good rule' in stanza 1 and to 'the palm of victory, a crown of justice and the love of England' in stanza 3 seem hard to construe unless in reference to Henry V, particularly since the music is again in major prolation.[10]

B

Princeps serenissime,	O most serene prince,
Te laudamus carmine.	we praise you in song.

   Which too long hath troubled the realms twain,
   Bidding you comfort in this adversity,
Most Christian princess, our lady sovereign. On the other hand, it is hard to believe that a carol for that occasion would have its text in Latin, whereas Latin would obviously be appropriate for the Treaty of Troyes; moreover the simple two-voice counterpoint in major prolation seems hardly likely for an occasion as late as 1445.

9 So far as I can see, the earliest suggestion that this really concerns Henry V, rather than Henry VI or some other prince, is in Anne Curry, *The battle of Agincourt: sources and interpretations* (Woodbridge: The Boydell Press, 2000): 286.

10 Greene (1954: 6–7) disputed this conclusion. He challenged Stevens's translation (forgetting that it had the benefited from the generous help of Frederick Raby, not just a professional Latinist, which Greene was not, but at the time the leading scholar in the world on the matter of medieval Latin poetry). He suggested that the 'peerless prince' in the first line may be the Prince of Peace rather than a living prince, though the second stanza confirms Stevens's reading. And he suggested that the New Year's gift is not 'something tangible brought in the King's presence rather than to be prayed for from Christ'. This last assertion is valid but irrelevant to the topic. Small wonder that Stevens did not change his translation in the 1958 revision of *MC*. Harrison (1964: 407) queried the use of 'princeps' for a king and suggested perhaps Duke Humfrey of Gloucester, to whom, it seems to me, the text would also be inappropriate – though obviously neither he nor Henry VI was immune to flattery.

1

Anni donum, domine,
Pro bono regimine
Mereris mirifice,
Princeps serenissime,
Te laudamus carmine.

The year's gift, O lord,
because of your good rule
you wonderfully deserve,
O most serene prince,
we praise you in song.

2

Quod Lumen de Lumine
Donet tibi hodie,
Qui natus (est) de virgine;
Princeps serenissime,
Te laudamus carmine.

Which [gift] may the Light of Light
give to you today,
He who was born of a virgin;
O most serene prince,
we praise you in song.

3

In palma victorie,
Corona justicie,
Et amore Anglie:
Princeps serenissime,
Te laudamus carmine.

With a palm of victory,
a crown of justice
and the love of England:
O most serene prince,
we praise you in song.

4

Et in fine patrie

Sine [fine] vivere
Cum celesti agmine.
Princeps serenissime,
Te laudamus carmine.

And within the bounds of the
    [heavenly] country
to live perpetually
with the celestial host.
O most serene prince,
we praise you in song.

If it is indeed addressed to him, it is hard to see a performance context without the king's presence. Once again, the Latin text helps make the carol appropriate for an international audience; and the major prolation without a three-voice burden, as well as the musical style in general, makes a date around 1420 distinctly possible. Given that Henry V's Chapel Royal was with him in France from the Spring of 1418, it could have been on any occasion over the next couple of years. But on New Year's Eve, 1420, after celebrating Christmas in Paris, Henry and his new wife entered Rouen,[11] where they celebrated the feast of Epiphany in

---

11 Wylie 1914–29: iii.234.

98 Chapter 14: Social context, 1

Example 14.1 Princeps serenissime, MC 62. Complete

some style; although Henry stayed in Rouen until at least 18 January, his chapel had left nine days earlier.[12] The only seasonal reference is in the words 'anni donum' in stanza 1: the rest is pure political propaganda. The date may be only a plausible guess, but the main point here is that both *Benedicite Deo Domino* (*MC* 57) and *Princeps serenissime* (*MC* 62) are effectively incomprehensible without being seen in the context of a royal court and without being considered important components of the propaganda machine. It must be clear that the fairly simple two-voice polyphony of Example 14.1 is a mere hint of the magnificence that would have been expected to celebrate Henry V's new circumstances in France.

More tentatively (though I find it hard to think of any better suggestion), the same group of occasions seems appropriate for another Egerton carol, *Princeps pacis strenue* (*MC* 45):

B

Princeps pacis strenue, O mighty prince of peace,
Pacem nobis tribue. give peace to us.

---

12 Wylie 1914–29: iii.266, citing Sir Harris Nicolas, ed., *Proceedings and ordinances of the privy council of England* 2 (London: The Commissioners of the Public Records, 1834): 326. The preceding footnote goes into some detail about whether Henry himself left Rouen on the 18th or the 19th: that's what I particularly value about this kind of book; it's also the reason why I so often cite Wylie as documentation rather than more modern histories.

1

Amores amplifica,
Majestas mirifica
Deitatis preclue;
Manu sub munifica
Pacem nobis tribue.

Increase our loves,
O wonderful Majesty
of glorious Godhead;
under thy generous hand
give peace to us.

2

Pax pollescat florida,
Lis labescat marcida,
Discordias dilue;
Summi proles provida,
Pacem nobis tribue.

Let flowery peace grow strong,
let withered strife decay;
wash away our discords.
O fore-seeing offspring of the Most High,
give peace to us.

3

Lex lucescat regia,
Expulsit elegia,
Plebs plaudat melliflue;
Lux lucis egregia,
Pacem nobis tribue.

Let royal law shine out;
it has expelled miserable things;
let the people clap in a honey-flowing way.
O excellent Light of Lights,
give peace to us.

4

Jugi cum memoria
Tibi laus et gloria,
Christe, rex ingenue;
Veram cum victoria
Pacem nobis tribue.

In perpetual memory
be praise and glory to thee,
O Christ, true-born King.
With victory,
give true peace to us.

Here, the 'princeps pacis' is indeed Christ. But there is absolutely no seasonal reference: it is political, mentioning the 'royal law' and 'victory' that lead to true peace. Certainly there is no specific reference to England and France: it could concern any peace treaty, and there were many over the years. But the references to 'our loves' and particularly to 'let withered strife decay; wash away our discords' seem far more appropriate to either the Treaty of Troyes in May 1420 or the Christmas of 1420 than to any other time. This, it should be emphasized, is less obviously true from the music, which is in perfect time, with a three-voice burden and a three-voice insert into the verses as well as a far more expansive style; but there were few occasions in the sad life of Henry VI when such optimism would have seemed appropriate.

All three carols, if I have construed them correctly, are: (a) for performance in the presence of Henry V and addressing particular events of the years 1419–21; (b) plainly political in intent; and (c) not by any stretch of the imagination 'popular by destination', despite the relatively simple written form of their music.

If these carols are accepted as royal and political, perhaps it is worth just adding a few words on three other carols that could be seen in a similar context, particularly the Agincourt carol. Since it tells the whole story of Agincourt, including the king's return to London in November 1415, but makes no mention of his far more successful second French campaign, started August 1417, let alone of his marriage, regency of France or his death, it seems reasonable to conclude that the carol was composed within those two years.[13] The scornful reference to the French in stanza two makes it almost impossible to think that it was composed after it became almost inevitable that Henry V would become regent and heir of France, namely December 1419.

Moreover, the fifth stanza gives the clearest sense of an eyewitness report:

There lordës, earlës and baron
Were slain and taken and that full soon,
And some were led into London
With joy and bliss and great renown:
Deo gracias.

Those lines were surely written very soon after Henry's triumphal entry into London. That much seems certain. More of a guess, but in my view permissible, is that – given the royal associations already proposed for those three Egerton carols – the carol was composed specifically for Henry V, and in particular for his Christmas celebrations in 1415, which took place in Lambeth Palace 'where all went mad with music and revelry'[14] in praise of their *gloriosissimo et victoriosissimo principe.*[15]

What is absolutely clear is that the text conforms to Henry V's directive, reported in the *Vita et gesta Henrici Quinti,* that no song in celebration of Agincourt should be made unless it credited the victory to God.[16] Moreover, given that the Agincourt

---

13 A point already made by Nicholson in Stainer 1901: i.xxi.
14 Wylie 1914–29: ii.275.
15 Pier Candido Decembrio, quoted in Wylie 1914–29: ii.275. Deeming 2007 proposes that the carol was composed for Henry's London entry in November 1415, though admitting that there is no direct reference to it among the copious descriptions of that event: she counters the clear statement in the fifth stanza, just cited, which is a *post facto* description of the prisoners arriving in London, by suggesting (2007: 30) that the lines 'could have been added to an earlier version of the carol'. She also claims (2007: 23) that earlier writers had suggested that it was composed and sung on the battlefield of Agincourt, but I have seen no such suggestion (apart from Laurence Olivier's 1944 film) and she cites no source; and in fact it is hard to think how anybody could reach that conclusion.
16 *Thomæ de Elmham vita & gesta Henrici Quinti, Anglorum regis,* ed. Thomas Hearne (Oxford: E Theatro Sheldoniano, 1727): 72, in the context of the description of his entry into London on 23 November 1415: Rex vero, mundanis pompis inaniter gloriari renuens, devota cordis humilitate omnem istam gloriam, & consimilia quæcumque, offert Deo, nec aliquantulum sibi, sed soli omnipotenti Deo se velle victoriam imputari, omnibus plane refert, in tantum, quod cantu de suo triumpho fieri, seu per citharistas, vel alios quoscumque cantari penitus prohibebat.

carol includes a three-voice burden and survives in Selden in perfect time, that date helps us to accept the 1420 date just proposed for *Princeps pacis*.

In this context it is as well to remember a comment of Anne Curry:[17]

> Every parliament from the victory until October 1419 includes mention of the battle in the chancellor's opening speech . . . Significantly, however, the battle is not mentioned at all in parliamentary texts after Henry became heir and regent by the Treaty of Troyes.

Two further carols contain insulting remarks about the French and seem to me not only plain political propaganda but in that context almost certainly written before December 1419.[18] One is the carol in honour of St George, *Enforce we us with all our might* (*MC* 60): it describes the apparent vision of St George at the battle of Agincourt, but it also includes in its last stanza the lines:

> In his virtue he will us lead
> Against the fiend, the foul wight.

There seems an almost overwhelming case for placing the carol between 1415 and 1419. The other is the next carol in Egerton, *Exultavit cor in Domino* (*MC* 61), all in major prolation and all in two voices. This is the one with an incomplete text describing Henry V's valour in battle. Its third stanza includes the lines:

> Superborum confusio   The confusion of the proud
> Piorum est proteccio.   is the protection of the faithful.

Given that Agincourt was the last actual battle that Henry V fought, this must be the reference; and the reference to the French as arrogant and the British as 'faithful', namely fighting with divine aid, is not only fully in line with Henry V's political propaganda in preparation for this second French campaign of 1417 but very hard to contemplate at any point after December 1419.

Finally, if there is any merit in my view that the new form and style came early in the reign of Henry V and began as part of a propaganda effort in favour of English nationalism and the retrieval of England's legally attested possessions in France, it may be relevant that one of the earliest known carols, without surviving music, and with the heading 'A carolle for Crystynmesse', is the following (*EEC* 427):

---

17 Anne Curry, *Agincourt* (Oxford: Oxford University Press, 2015): 52. Details are in *The parliament rolls of medieval England*, ed. Chris Given-Wilson, 16 vols. (Woodbridge: Boydell, 2005), vol. 9: *Henry V, 1413–1422*, ed. Chris Given-Wilson.
18 In that context, it is hard to avoid noting the consistent references to the French as devious and evil in the *Gesta Henrici Quinti: the deeds of Henry the Fifth*, translated and ed. Frank Taylor and John S. Roskell (Oxford: At the Clarendon Press, 1975). The editors point out that the book was plainly a propaganda publication to encourage support for Henry's second French campaign, beginning in the summer of 1417.

B

The rose is the fairest flower of all
That evermore was or evermore shall,
The rose of ryse; *on branch*
Of all these flowers the rose bears prize.

1

The rose it is the fairest flower;
The rose is sweetest of odour;
The rose, in care it is comforter;
The rose, in sickness it is saviour,
The rose so bright;
In medicines it is most of might.

2

Witness these clerks that been wise:
The rose is the flower most holden in price;
Therefore me think the flour-de-lyce
Should worship the rose of ryse *on branch*
    And been his thrall
And so should other flowers all.

3

Many a knight with spear and lance
Followed that rose to his pleasance;
When the rose betide a chance,
Then faded all the flowers of France
    And changed hue
In pleasance of the rose so true.

Sadly, the manuscript (British Library, Add. MS 31042, Robert Thornton's manuscript, in which this is the only carol) lacks the next two leaves, so we cannot know if there were further stanzas.[19] But only in the third stanza does it become clear that the rose is Henry V and that the reference is to his first French campaign of 1415, when 'all the flowers of France' faded and – as in the second

---

19 That is Greene's view (1977: 475). Phillipa Hardman, 'Compiling the nation: fifteenth-century miscellany manuscripts', in *Nation, court and culture: new essays on fifteenth-century English poetry*, ed. Helen Cooney (Dublin: Four Courts Press, 2001): 50–69, at p. 57n20, argues that the layout of the page concerned speaks strongly in favour of the poem being complete.

stanza – the *fleur-de-lis* should owe obeisance to him. Both the burden and the verses are rather longer than was normal at this stage in the form's history. But there must be room for thinking that this, too, was composed for Henry V's 1415 Christmas celebrations at Lambeth Palace – already at that point the Archbishop of Canterbury's official residence.

15 Social context, 2: Orality and the Polyphonic Carol

To say that certain carols make no sense unless they are seen in the context of Henry V's royal court in the years 1415–20 is by no means to state that all carols are intended for such circles. Particularly among such text sources as Sloane and OxEng there are plenty of poems that would have no place at court. We must consider also the possibility of noble and episcopal households, of university colleges and of more humble gatherings. But, to repeat, the surviving polyphony for carols is all highly literate, a far cry from some of the supposedly popular polyphony known from Italian and central European sources. Little of it is easy to sing; and almost none of it looks improvised. But there are details in the transmission that raise questions.

Pray for us, thou Prince of Peace, Amice Christi Johannes

With six known sources (*EEC* 103), Greene described this poem as 'found in more different sources (as a carol) than any other' (1977: 366 and cxxx). But a comprehensible version of the first line appears only in the latest source, Richard Hill's commonplace-book of the early sixteenth century, with the reading 'Pray for us to the Prince of Peace' (though British Library, Harley MS 4294 comes close to the mark, with the reading 'Pray we all to the Prince of Peace'). That is to say that the carol addresses Saint John the apostle and invites him to intercede with the Prince of Peace. All the earlier sources (Trinity, OxEng, and two settings in Ritson) address St John as though he were himself the Prince of Peace – a notion that makes no sense at all.

Moreover, given that each stanza ends with the words 'Amice Christi, Johannes', each must be addressed to St John.[1] That situation obtains only for the Trinity carol roll. OxEng and the two Ritson copies address him in the first stanza but otherwise keep him in the third person. Hill and Harley have all the stanzas in the third person. Plainly the poem was originally all addressed to St John and all

---

[1] For the writers of carols, St John the evangelist was identified with St John the apostle (described in St John's gospel as 'the disciple whom Jesus loved') and St John 'of Patmos', author of the Book of Revelation.

the other versions are corruptions. Interestingly enough, those differences more or less reflect the received chronology of the sources, with the sole exception that only the two latest sources have the crucial word 'to' in the first line of the burden. Given that no commentator has yet drawn attention to the absurd situation in the sources, perhaps readers will share my joy at having the complete poem as it may have originated (albeit with modern orthography). The references in each stanza to John as a maiden, that is, sexually pure, build up to the last stanza, describing how Christ entrusted the care of his maiden mother to his maiden bosom friend.

B

Pray for us to the Prince of Peace,
Amice Christi, Johannes.

1

To thee now, Christës dear darling,
That were a may both old and ying, *maiden; young*
Mine heart is set to thee to sing,
Amice Christi, Johannes.

2

For thou were so clean a may, *maiden*
The prophettes of heaven forsooth thou say,
When on Christës breast thou lay,
Amice Christi, Johannes.

3

When Christ beforn Pilate was brought,
Thou cleanë maid forsook him nought;
To die with him was all thy thought,
Amice Christi, Johannes.

4

Christës mother was thee betake,
A maiden to be another's make;
Thou be our help we be not forsake,
Amice Christi, Johannes.

In the circumstances, it is odd to read (Greene 1935: cv–cvi; 1977: cxxx) that this belongs to the class of carols whose 'versions agree so closely as to show without question that they derive from written copies with no dependence on oral transmission and its consequent lapses of memory and perversion of meaning'. The variants would seem to me plain evidence that the poem was in all cases copied more or less from memory, and not very good memory at that. Such a conclusion obviously concerns only the text: the three copies with music all have entirely different music.

Omnes una gaudeamus

Another piece that has received less than its fair share of attention is the Christmas song *Omnes una gaudeamus* (*MC* 15[A]), ignored largely because it is not actually in carol form, even though its mood and style are entirely in line with the earliest polyphonic carol repertory. It survives in both Selden and Egerton, here superposed to show some of the ways in which they differ. It almost looks as if one or other version was written down from memory, or perhaps as though both were the results of fairly informed improvisation. Both in fact have notational details that smack of little thought: that there are two *similis ante similem* infractions in Selden should surprise nobody, since that is common in that manuscript; but more surprising is the missing dot in the Egerton tenor at bar 3.[2]

Here there can be no disputing that they are the same piece, with the same length, the same cadences and broadly the same melodic outlines. But the differences particularly at the start of the last line seem incompatible with written transmission unless one were to argue for a compositional revision, that somebody at some stage found the last few bars of the Selden version a touch weak and substituted the decidedly stronger Egerton version. (The structure entirely in five-bar phrases, on the other hand, points to a carefully devised basis.)

There are also issues with the text. The two manuscripts begin with the same two stanzas (though line 2 is missing in Selden):

1

Omnes una gaudeamus;   Let us rejoice together;
Christo laudes referamus.   let us give praises to Christ:
    Qui natus est de virgine   the one born of the virgin
    Illuxit nobis hodie   has shone on us today.

2

Christus volens incarnari   Christ, wishing to be made flesh
Nosque sibi copulari: and to join us to himself,
    Qui natus est *etc*   the one born *etc*

---

2 Detailed collation. Selden: 1 i 1: has a superfluous point of division; 8 ii 5: erroneous *semibrevis* (which would be perfect) for *minima* (which would be altered). Egerton: 3 ii 3: lacks point of division; word 'est' wrongly written every single time as 'es' – which is a very odd mistake. I am also more or less certain that 3 i 1 should be g' (as in Selden), not e'.

Chapter 15: Social context, 2   107

Example 15.1 Omnes una gaudeamus, MC 15^A. Complete

But then the two remaining stanzas of Egerton are unique:

3

In presepi inclinatur   He is laid down in a manger
Qui cunctorum dominator.   he who is lord of all:
  Qui natus est *etc*   the one born *etc*

4

Hec est spes redempcionis;   This is the hope of redemption;
Iram non vult ulcionis: he does not wish the wrath of
                                    revenge:
  Qui natus est *etc*   the one born *etc*

This is a neat kind of poem, all in eight-syllable lines, with paroxytones in the stanza but oxytones in the refrain – or, to put it in more musical terms, with upbeats to the refrain lines. Certainly, the second stanza seems to lack a main verb and the third has a slightly rough rhyme, but this is enormously more skilled than Selden, which continues with the following unique stanzas where hardly a single line matches the eight-syllable paroxytones of Egerton. More specifically, only the second of these couplets matches the metre of Egerton.

3

Carnem sumpsit virginis　　　　　　He took the flesh of the virgin
Et habitavit in nobis.　　　　　　　　and lived among us.
　　Qui natus est *etc*

4

Collaudemus venerantes　　　　　　Let us praise together, worshipping,
Nosque simul exultantes　　　　　　and exulting at the same time.
　　Qui natus est *etc*

5

Ut in suo clarissimo　　　　　　　　so that he may give us a place
Nos ordinet palacio.　　　　　　　　in his fairest dwelling.
　　Qui natus est *etc*

6

Laudemus Christum mente pia　　　Let us praise with a devout mind
Qui natus est de Maria　　　　　　　Christ, who is born of Mary.
　　Qui natus est *etc*

7

Venit nos redimere　　　　　　　　　He came to redeem us,
Qui passus fuit in cruce　　　　　　he who suffered on the cross.
　　Qui natus est *etc*.

That is to say that comparison of their texts has a clear upshot: the Egerton text is mandarin and controlled, with every syllable in place, whereas the Selden text looks as though it were jammed together without any particular logic or metre.

The central question here is one of form and genre. In terms of genre it seems absolutely characteristic of the carol style and – to repeat – quite unlike anything we otherwise know of music in the early fifteenth century. In terms of form, it is a strophic song with a refrain at the end of each stanza, not the beginning. But

Chapter 15: Social context, 2   109

Example 15.2 *I pray you all with one thought*, MC 65. Complete

actually one could turn it round and say that it differs from the other carols only in lacking a refrain at the start. Of course it would be quite easy to put the refrain at the start, were it not that these two quite different copies both lay out the music in the same way and were it not that the refrain music begins in a way quite untypical of carol settings.

What does seem to be essential in the form, though, and quite different from the known carol repertory, is that the music of the verse is repeated; and in this it goes alongside the virelai forms of fourteenth-century France, particularly Guillaume de Machaut's virelai no. 13, the monophonic *Quant je suis mis au retour*.

But in the context of the present chapter we must assert that the variants between the two copies of the music point strongly towards an oral transmission and that the variants between the two copies of the text similarly point at an oral transmission in which the Selden text is just a jumble of half-remembered liturgical phrases.[3]

I pray you all with one thought

Also on the matter of form, it is worth glancing at *I pray you all with one thought, Amendeth me and payre me nought* (*MC* 15/65), which also appears in both Selden and Egerton. The two manuscripts agree on their texts, down to the detail of a single word (though the orthographies are of course different). They also more or less agree on the music and particularly on the text underlay. It should be apparent that the matching of words and music in the burden is very loose: the music really looks as though it were composed for an entirely different text with longer lines. But it seems odder still when the words 'Amendeth me and payre me nought' recur as a refrain at the end of each of the six stanzas: they appear with the music that was originally used for the first half of the burden, 'I pray you all with one thought'.

Also odd is the way the verse opens with the same music as the burden, though to different words. As a result, the verse has the musical design a b c a' for a rhyme scheme *aaar*. That the mere fourteen bars of written music include the same two bars of music three times hints that there may be a past history of which we know little. As it stands, the carol may give those bars more importance than they can bear.

So there is an apparent paradox here. Within a repertory that includes works plainly intended for the royal court there are others with details that border on the unwritten tradition. Two resolutions may be proposed. First, that the four musical sources contain a wider range of materials than has been supposed. Second, that not all music-making at even the highest court of the realm was fastidiously written down in all its details.

---

3 This may seem an ungraceful moment to refer to the doctoral dissertation of Beth Ann Zamzow (2002) or indeed the commentaries on Ryman's poems by Julius Zupitza (1894–7). But both show to a remarkable degree the extent to which the carol poetry of the fifteenth century relies on bits of liturgical and biblical writing.

16 Social context, 3: The Notion of Communal Song

There is another aspect of the social context here. As an example of what can be misunderstood, Kathleen Palti (2008: 247) noted Daniel Wakelin's description (2006: 37) of the 'we' imperatives in carols as making them sound 'not only like a voice of the people but also like a written diktat'.[1] She continued:

> Wakelin's judgement here is balanced, but the second half repeats a tendency in criticism on the carols to present them as though they were religious propaganda, implicit in Greene's widely accepted argument that they were 'popular by destination', but not in origin.

As readers will know by now, I firmly accept the notion of propaganda to describe many of these carols (though I am not so certain that it is implicit in Greene's remark); and I firmly accept the view that many of the carols are addressed to a community.

Palti came up with the term 'communal', which is far more to the point than 'popular' – even though she conceded that there is no source authority for that word. She illustrated the point with various lines from the three poetry manuscripts that were her main focus. But the point seems more powerfully made with quotes from the carols that survive with polyphonic music. Perhaps I should apologize for the extent of the following list, but it seems remarkable that almost half of the surviving polyphonic carols have such appeals to a community embedded within their burdens. Besides, a quick read-through of these quotes gives another hint of the sheer condensed power of the texts (which is of course another of my main themes):

> Now may we singen as it is,
> Quod puer natus est nobis. (*MC* 5: burden)

> Be merry, be merry, I pray you everychon. (*MC* 6: burden)

> Nowell sing we now all and some,
> For rex pacificus is come. (*MC* 7/16: burden)

---

1 Similar comments in Palti 2011: 146.

Chapter 16: Social context, 3

Now make we mirthë all and some,
For Christëmassë now is y-come
That hath no peer,
Sing we all in fere,
Now joy and bliss
They shall not miss
That maketh good cheer. (*MC* 9: burden)

Pray for us [to] the Prince of Peace,
Amice Christi, Johannes. (*MC* 13/106/115: burden)

Of a rosë singë we,
Misterium mirabile. (*MC* 19: burden)

Sing we to this merry company,
Regina celi, letare. (*MC* 21: burden)

Deo gracias
Persolvamus alacriter. (*MC* 22: burden)

Make we joy now in this fest,
In quo Christus natus est;
Eya. (*MC* 26: burden; *MC* 97: burden)

Novo profusi gaudio,
Benedicamus Domino. (*MC* 47: burden)

The holy martyr, Stephen, we
Pray to be our succour both night and day. (*MC* 50: burden)

Saint Thomas honour we
Through whose blood Holy Church is made free. (*MC* 59: burden)

Enforce we us with all our might
To love Saint George, our lady['s] knight. (*MC* 60: burden)

Princeps serenissime,
Te laudamus carmine. (*MC* 62: burden)

Gaudeamus pariter
Et laudemus Dominum. (*MC* 72: burden)

Sing we to this merry company
Regina celi, letare. (*MC* 76: burden)

Make us merry this New Year
Thanking God with heartly cheer. (*MC* 83: burden)

Regi canamus glorie,
Qui natus est de virgine. (*MC* 89: burden)

Psallite gaudentes,
Infantum festa colentes. (*MC* 93: burden)

Worship we this holy day,
That all innocentës for us pray. (*MC* 94: burden)

Jesu fili virginis,
Miserere nobis. (*MC* 111: burden)

Since this book is mainly about the music of the carols it is worth noting that some of the carols are fairly easy to sing (mainly those in the Trinity and Selden manuscripts) but that many (particularly those in Ritson) are extremely challenging, both for singers and for listeners. And I should repeat that Greene's discussions all exclude the carols that are entirely in Latin.

Moreover, we have just seen that a surprisingly large proportion of the earliest carols can be associated with the court and circle of Henry V, of whom E. F. Jacob wrote:[2]

> He supervised in closest detail the services of his chapel and took special pains over the choice of his confessors and, most of all, of his bishops. His liturgical interests can be seen in his request to convocation for the increased devotion to be paid to St. George of Cappadocia and in the choice of psalms and responses after the procession and litany which, after his return to England in November 1415, preceded his daily Mass.

In the intervening years various different viewpoints have been espoused, ranging from the view that reading and literacy were far more widely cultivated in the 'traditional religion' than has previously been considered the case to the view that the mystery plays, for example, were not for the general public at all but were performed to an elite group of the mayor and council.[3] Either way, though, it needs to be clear that the two ends of the fifteenth century saw contrasts that can hardly be paralleled in any other century. The rise of printing, the growth of vernacular religion, the rise of popular preaching and much else meant that the changes were cataclysmic.

---

2 *The fifteenth century 1399–1485* = The Oxford history of England 6 (Oxford: At the Clarendon Press, 1961): 126.
3 Eamon Duffy, *The stripping of the altars: traditional religion in England, c.1400–c.1580* (New Haven and London: Yale University Press, 1992); Alan H. Nelson, *The medieval English stage: Corpus Christi pageants and plays* (Chicago: Chicago University Press, 1974).

17 Awareness of the carol, 2: 1891–1901

We left the story of the carol's return to public consciousness at the end of the life of Thomas Wright (1877). At that point, the Agincourt carol had been published several times (all disastrously, because taken from the faulty copy in the Pepys Library), John Stafford Smith had published a few carols from the Ritson manuscript and Thomas Wright had, heroically, published the entire contents of the two poetic miscellanies of the fifteenth century containing carols. Then in the 1890s, there were three major developments.

The first of these was J.A. Fuller Maitland's *English carols of the fifteenth century from a ms. roll in the library of Trinity College, Cambridge* [1891]. This is not just the first publication of an entire English musical manuscript of the fifteenth century but the very earliest publication of an entire fifteenth-century song collection from anywhere in Europe.[1] It is a magnificent book, made finer by a full-colour frontispiece of the Agincourt carol. Even so, its first bizarre detail is how little enthusiasm the future chief music critic of *The Times* showed for the music. Fuller Maitland wrote (p. v):

> The series of carols contained in this volume shows the science of counterpoint in a very early and rudimentary condition, and from many passages it is clear that the influence of the 'organum' was still strongly felt by the composer.

In the preceding paragraph, he had referred to organum as 'hideous'; and one may wonder why he bothered at all. Much later, in his autobiography, *A doorkeeper of music*, he mentioned his edition almost in passing (1929: 223–5, in the chapter 'Old and new music'), mainly as an opportunity to tell a feeble anecdote about the Pepys copy of the Agincourt carol.

The explanation for the book's existence probably lies with Stanford and Rockstro. When Fuller Maitland (b. 1856) went up to Trinity College, Cambridge he

---

[1] The next is Hugo Riemann's edition of a little fragment in the Bavarian State Library, *Sechs bisher nicht gedruckte dreistimmige Chansons (für Tenor, Diskant und Kontratenor) von Gilles Binchois (c. 1425) aus dem Codex Mus. Ms. 3192 der Münchner Hof- und Staatsbibliothek* (Wiesbaden: [no named publisher], 1892). One year earlier than Fuller Maitland is Francisco Asenjo Barbieri's magnificent and enormous edition of the Cancionero de Palacio in Madrid, *Cancionero musical des los siglos XV y XVI* (Madrid: Real Academia de Bellas Artes de San Fernando, 1890); but the manuscript was actually copied early in the sixteenth century.

quickly became a close friend of the professor of music, Charles Villiers Stanford, also of Trinity College. Later, he became particularly close to W.S. Rockstro (1823–95), of whom he wrote: 'At the time I suppose that he was the only Englishman who had mastered the principles of ancient music' (1929: 107); and Rockstro added four-voice arrangements of all the pieces in the Trinity roll. Fuller Maitland provided diplomatic transcriptions of the music (though in his Appendix, pp. 60–61, he provided a very good modern transcription of the Agincourt carol as it appears in Selden); opposite each piece he placed the text in black-letter type and original spelling. Rockstro's four-voice arrangements mainly include the original voices as he understood them, but his understanding of the notation seems to have been less than Fuller Maitland showed in his Oxford transcription. At least the texts were printed alongside Rockstro's arrangements with modernised orthography and punctuation. It is easy enough to imagine that Sir John Stainer – who had himself published three volumes of Christmas carols from later generations – would have been able to conclude that this was a repertory of some power. He may well also have registered, from Fuller Maitland's Appendix, that there was a manuscript in the Bodleian containing carol music. The book is beautiful; but the transcriptions and general presentation are so absolutely gruesome that it is a relief to turn from there to the sheer professionalism and musical insight of the transcriptions produced by the Stainer family only a few years later.

Here there are marvellous editions as well as a sadly missed opportunity, because it looks very much as though Stainer recognized the significance of the repertory, to some extent provoked by Maitland's edition, but that he would have contributed far more, and far more definitively, if he had lived just a few more years. To see this, we need a small detour about Stainer and his activities in the last six years of his life.

Stainer had become Heather Professor of Music at Oxford in 1889, partly because failing eyesight forced him to relinquish his position as organist of St Paul's Cathedral at the age of fifty. He had been knighted in 1888 and was nationally famous primarily for his educational work. Soon after his installation as Heather Professor he was approached by Bodley's Librarian – as the Oxford University librarian has been proudly titled since the sixteenth century and still is today. E.W.B. Nicholson, had been Bodley's Librarian for fourteen years: born in 1849, he had achieved the position as one of the senior librarians in the country in his early thirties.

Nicholson was now in his mid-forties when he seems to have conceived a series of facsimiles and transcriptions of early Bodleian music manuscripts in 1895. In the 'Introduction' to the first of these publications, *Dufay and his contemporaries* (1898), he wrote:[2]

> In the summer of 1895, when I suggested to our Professor of Music to undertake the publication of facsimiles of early Bodleian manuscript music, all the MSS. were put before him which I had noted as containing secular compositions earlier than the sixteenth century.

---

2 In *Sacred & secular songs*, J.F.R. Stainer also states that the design was 'formed by my father in the autumn of 1895'.

But then he added:

> Mr. C. L. Stainer then examined the indices of all our catalogues of MSS., under such heads as I suggested to him, and in doing so almost immediately came across the mention of MS. Canonici misc. 213. . . . I myself must have opened it in 1887, but, knowing nothing then as to the rarity of fifteenth century continental secular music, had made no note of it, and had forgotten its existence.

Thus Nicholson announced the discovery of what has become the most famous of all fifteenth-century musical manuscripts. Charles Lewis Stainer was born in 1871, and thus was only twenty-two when he set to work trawling through the Bodleian catalogues. He seems then to have withdrawn from the operation, though he went on to become a distinguished historian, playwright, editor of Oliver Cromwell's speeches, and author of a well-received book on early English coins. Work on the Canonici manuscript was to be done largely by the two eldest Stainer children, as can be seen from the title-page of the Dufay volume, which reads:

> Dufay and his contemporaries: fifty compositions (ranging from about A.D. 1400 to 1440) transcribed from the MS. Canonici misc. 213, in the Bodleian Library, Oxford, by J. F. R. Stainer, B. C. L., M. A. and C. Stainer; with an introduction by E. W. B. Nicholson, M. A., Bodley's Librarian, and a critical analysis of the Music by Sir John Stainer.

John Frederick Randall Stainer was the eldest child of Sir John, born in 1866, thus thirty years old at the time. After Winchester and Magdalen he aided his father in the completion of the *Catalogue of English song books*, published by Novello in 1891. And he seems to have played a major role in the whole Bodleian operation.

Cecie Stainer – actually baptized Elizabeth Cecil and pronounced 'Sessy' (information kindly provided by her great-nephew Gareth Stainer) – was born in the next year, 1867, and had been educated in Germany. Cecie had published a book already in 1896, at the age of twenty-nine: this was her *Dictionary of violin makers compiled from the best authorities*, issued by her father's publisher, Novello, and twice reprinted over the following years. She also went on to publish some distinguished articles and reviews, particularly about fifteenth-century music. That several of her articles and reviews were published in German journals may be less evidence of her international reputation than of the fact that she had been educated in Germany and evidently retained her German contacts. All the same, her record is impressive.

What needs to be stressed here, though, is that Nicholson's original plan was thrown totally off course by the discovery of the Canonici manuscript. This is clear from a letter apparently dated 28 September 1895 in which Sir John Stainer

Chapter 17: Awareness of the carol, 2 117

declared himself too busy to accept a commission from King's College, Cambridge. He wrote:

> How I should like to write an 8-part service for you, but where is the time to come from? I and two of my children are preparing a big 2 vol work: – Vol. I, over a hundred facsimiles of Bodleian music dating from AD 1225 to AD 1400. Vol. II a transcription of all the music! Of course it will only appeal to students and antiquarians – but to them it will be deeply interesting. I am also supervising for the said 2 children 'Dufay and his contemporaries', a collection of 50 compositions between AD 1400 – & 1440! from the canonici M.S.

Jeremy Dibble dates this letter September 1894,[3] but that cannot be right: both Nicholson and J. F. R. Stainer state that the project began in 1895; and from September 1895 there are dated transcriptions from the Canonici manuscript in the British Library, as Add. MS 43736. Folios 12–36 contain careful diplomatic transcriptions of twenty-four Dufay songs, mostly in the hand of J. F. R. Stainer, dated between 28 August and 24 September 1895. And on 12 November 1895 Sir John Stainer presented a paper about the manuscript to the Musical Association (now the Royal Musical Association) of which he was the second president. It looks as though they all worked with a burning intensity during those few months.

But the detail worth focus is that in the Preface to *Dufay and his contemporaries* Stainer states that this volume is the second in the series and in a footnote gives the information that the first volume is called *Facsimiles of early Bodleian music from about A.D. 1175 to about A.D. 1490*. Plainly it was a very late decision to print *Dufay and his contemporaries* first. Plainly, too, the volume eventually called *Sacred & secular songs* was still being called something else at that point.

What that would seem to mean is that the original plan was just for a single volume of facsimiles, including those now in Nicholson's volume (1913). When *Dufay and his contemporaries* went to press it still seemed as though the volume of facsimiles would be published first. It then went through a significant change: several manuscripts from after 1400 were added, and the earliest material was relegated to a third volume. And it is now easy to see how this happened. With their new enthusiasm and skills in transcribing the music of the fifteenth century, J. F. R. and Cecie really wanted to get their teeth into the big manuscript Arch. Selden B. 26, with its large collection of carols, a genre opened up only a few years earlier by Fuller Maitland's transcription of the Trinity carol roll. It is easy to see Sir John being seriously excited about the inclusion of this repertory.

Perhaps the most significant detail of the 1895 letter is the way Stainer describes the two volumes: of the facsimiles and transcriptions of English music he says 'I and two of my children are preparing', whereas for *Dufay and his contemporaries* he says he is just supervising 'said 2 children'. And if we look at the title pages of the two volumes the distinction is clear: that the Dufay volume was mainly the

---

3 Jeremy Dibble, *Sir John Stainer: a life in music* (Woodbridge: The Boydell Press, 2007): 257.

118   *Chapter 17: Awareness of the carol, 2*

work of his children, with his essay on the music, whereas the *Sacred & secular songs* volume was his own, with help from his two children and Nicholson.

Its first volume opens with a preface signed not by Sir John but by J. F. R. That is because Sir John had died unexpectedly on holiday at Verona in March 1901; and the volume, though dated 1901, was actually published in 1902, as reported by Nicholson in the last volume (1913). J. F. R. wrote that all the music was passed for press by his father 'some time before his death'.

The volume of facsimiles is done with great care by Nicholson. His 110 facsimiles are preceded by twenty-five massive folio pages analysing and proposing dates for each fragment, followed by an extraordinarily detailed index before the plates begin. At the end there is a beautiful list of contents and of manuscripts. This is scholarly book-making on a very high level indeed.

When we come to the volume of transcriptions, it is worth reporting that some of the fragments they transcribed are almost illegible: today with the aid of ultraviolet light and digital manipulation it is still not easy to produce transcriptions that are significantly better than those of the Stainers. Beyond that, several of the Selden pieces are in extremely complicated notation: their mainly accurate transcription was unusual before the appearance of Johannes Wolf's *Geschichte der Mensural-Notation von 1250–1460*, 3 vols. (Leipzig: Breitkopf und Härtel, 1904).

There is a long introduction by Sir John, which he did not manage to complete or revise, according to this son. And it contains some astonishingly prescient comments about pitch and about florid singing.

The transcriptions of the liturgical pieces each have a description, which is not clearly credited, but occasionally the writer refers to 'my son' and 'my daughter', and it seems fair to conclude that the comments are all Sir John's. Inevitably they are a lot more interesting than the broad generalizations in the Introduction. More important, whether they were finished or not, they represent the core of the task Sir John set himself. With the Dufay volume he was content with a general essay about the principles of notation and modality – matters that had been described many times before. Here he was talking about actual pieces of music, one at a time; and it is fair to say that this had not happened earlier. Indeed it has happened very rarely since.

Sadly, though, the pieces on which he almost never offers any comment are the carols – the English secular songs that have all the vitality and energy that he had recognized in the French songs of the Canonici manuscript. That is to say that the book is incomplete: Sir John never quite finished the task that seems to have been a major family collaboration during his last years. The man who had spent the majority of his life performing, editing and thinking about much later carols never made the final statement that he evidently had in mind about the earliest carols.

It is clear, though, that this publication was the one that firmly established the English carols of the early fifteenth century among the repertory; and it seems fairly clear that one of the Stainers, or perhaps all of them, recognized immediately from Fuller Maitland's 1891 volume the distinctive and indeed extraordinary qualities that Maitland himself had so signally failed to recognize.

The third major development of the 1890s is the work of the German scholar Julius Zupitza (1844–95), professor in the University of Vienna at the age of twenty-eight (1872) and then in the University of Berlin (1876) until his early death. His astonishingly copious output covered English literature from the Anglo-Saxons to Shakespeare alongside essays on Goldsmith, Lamb and Shelley.[4] Among his last publications was an edition of the entire songbook of James Ryman (Zupitza 1892) followed by an astonishingly detailed song-by-song commentary published in nine sections (Zupitza 1894–7). That seems to have initiated an interest among German-speaking scholars, who published most of the remaining carol texts in articles over the next few years. Among these were Bernhard Fehr, publishing the entire texts of Ritson and Fayrfax (Fehr 1901 and 1901a), and Ewald Flügel with an extended article on Richard Hill's manuscript (Flügel 1903).

---

4 Arthur Napier, 'Julius Zupitza', *Archiv für das Studium der neueren Sprachen und Litteraturen* 95 (1895): 241–55.

18 The date and origin of Ritson

Even today, writers regularly give Ritson's date as *c.* 1510. That is right for the very end of the book; but for the earliest layer, including its carols, I wish now to make the case for a substantially earlier date, not merely the *c.* 1470 proposed in the best musicological publications but perhaps even as early as the 1430s. John Stevens, in his Musica Britannica edition (1952: 125, but also 1958: 125), suggested '*c.* 1500' for the copying; Richard Greene, in his last statement on the matter (1977: 307), proposed 'Cent. XVI (first quarter)', despite his earlier having written 'I am glad to accept the earlier dating of the Ms. (at about 1500) on which musicologists now appear to agree' (1954a: 82). None of those proposals makes any sense.

The reason for this late date is that Ritson contains King Henry VIII's three-voice *Pastime with good company* – copied twice, the second and better copy having the caption 'The kynges balade' (fols. 141v–142). Since this is also one of the thirty-two pieces credited to 'The Kynge . H . VIII' in the manuscript we call 'The Henry VIII book' (British Library, Add. MS 31922), it seems clear that the king mentioned in Ritson is indeed Henry VIII and that the piece must therefore have been copied there after his accession in April 1509.[1] But those two copies of *Pastime with good company* are at the end of Ritson, which is a complicated manuscript.

The manuscript is copied in various different layers, assembled over time.[2] Basically there are three watermarks, one in fols. 3–121 and the other two in fols. 122–48 (which is the section containing Henry VIII). Those two sections of the

---

1 Further details on this piece and its context are offered in *The Henry VIII book*, ed. David Fallows = DIAMM facsimiles 4 (Oxford: DIAMM facsimiles, 2014): 33–7.
2 Musical researchers have accepted that there is material here from the fifteenth century: Catherine Keyes Miller (1948: 10, 40, and 67) placed the first of the five layers she discerned, namely the layer containing the forty-four carols, all copied together in a single copying act by a single copyist, 'at the end of the second third of the fifteenth century'; and proposed *c.* 1470 for the second section (1948: 77). The *Census-catalogue* (1979–88: ii.43–4) proposed 1460–1510 for the entire manuscript, a dating endorsed most recently in Lane and Sandon 2001. Sylvia Kenney (1964:170) mentioned in passing that Ritson was from the first half of the fifteenth century, but without any further discussion.

manuscript are differently preruled, the main body with red vertical lines *c*. 4 cm from the outside edge and *c*. 2 cm from the inside edge, the last twenty-seven leaves with them in brown, *c*. 2 cm from each edge.[3] The first part comprises gatherings on uniform paper always with parchment bifolia in the middle and on the outside, a common enough pattern in the fifteenth century, designed to strengthen the gatherings of a manuscript that was mainly on paper; the remainder is entirely of paper, plainly added later. What concern us here are the two first copying layers, on fols. 4v–73: apart from a few interruptions in obviously much later hands, these are entirely the work of two copyists. 'A' copied all the carols (nos. 4–34, 36–43 and 45–9 = *MC* 76–119)[4] plus three settings of *Nesciens mater* (nos. 52, 55–6);[5] 'B', a far gentler hand, copied the two-voice hymn [*O*] *lux beata trinitas* (no. 59 on fols. 60v–62) and eight songs (nos. 62–9 on fols. 65v–73). There is no reason to think that either copyist had an associate copying the texts: both are uniform.

The carols of hand 'A' each have one absolutely uniform decorated opening letter with the initial itself in blue and the decorative filigree in red.[6] Whatever the internal chronology of the copying of the carols themselves, it seems clear enough that all the decorated letters were done in a single session: there are absolutely no variations in either style or colour. The three non-carol pieces of hand 'A' have no such decorated letters and plainly expected none: presumably they were copied rather later than the others. The pieces of hand 'B' have no decorated letters but plainly did expect them.[7] No other piece in the manuscript either has decorated initials or a gap for them.

My own latest enquiry – and in fact the springboard for this entire book – began with the songs copied by 'B', which Robbins (1961: 86) dated 'about 1470'. These contain not a single song with its contratenor in a range below the tenor; and nothing that looks likely to have been composed after about 1445. John Stevens had published the songs in Musica Britannica 37 (1975); in preparing Musica Britannica 97 (2014), which contains the remainder of the surviving English song repertory of those years, I noted that these songs are definitively in the style of the Bedyngham pieces that we know, from the watermark dates of the

---

3 For what it is worth, the brown ruling begins on fol. 107v, that is, initially with the outside brown ruling added to the existing red ruling and forming the edge of the staves.
4 The numbering here is from the complete inventory of Ritson in Lane and Sandon 2001, their edition of all the Ritson pieces not published in *MC* or Stevens 1975.
5 All three copied in *cantus collateralis* rather than the pseudo-score of the carols, and without the decorated initials of the carols. Whether no. 57, the anonymous four-voice *Ave regina celorum* is really by the same copyist (as asserted in Lane and Sandon 2001: ix) is unclear to me but peripheral to the main discussion.
6 This with the exception of *Man, be joyful* (*MC* 82) – where the copyist had forgotten to indent the opening of the tenor voice to leave room for the initial – and *Proface, welcome* (*MC* 107), where no such explanation offers itself.
7 The two-voice song *O blessed Lord* (fols. 69v–70) has the gap and the small 'indicator' letter at the beginning; at some point, somebody has simply filled in the missing letter in black ink.

122 Chapter 18: The date and origin of Ritson

Trento manuscripts, to have been composed in the 1440s.[8] The sheer uniformity of the nine pieces by hand 'B' suggests that they were all copied together, presumably also in the 1440s or just possibly in the early 1450s. It looks very much as though they were added after hand 'A' had finished. So the question is: how much later?

Making the whole history of this manuscript harder to trace is the sad circumstance that all the paper leaves are now mounted on separate stubs. Only some of the parchment bifolios have been allowed to retain their integrity. So any attempt at a collation must be based on the presence or absence of watermarks. As luck would have it, the collation is fairly easy to reconstruct up to the end of the fourth gathering (fol. 64) but becomes a lot harder thereafter, not least because some leaves have been lost over the centuries. On the other hand, since the watermarks remain uniform from fol. 4 to fol. 121 it makes sense to see those leaves as a planned volume of regular gatherings, all with parchment around the outside and in the middle.

The carols are in the first four gatherings, as follows:[9]

Gathering I (16 leaves): fols. 3–18, of which fols. 3, 10–11 (conjoint) and 18 are parchment. Fols. 3–4v contain later material, and fols. 4v–5 contain the only Ritson carol in void notation (*Sing we to this merry company*, MC 76); fols. 5v–18v contain an uninterrupted sequence of carols (*MC* 77–89). It therefore looks as though copying began at fol. 5v, with the first two openings originally left blank for the later addition of perhaps a list of contents and a decorative title-page.

Gathering II (16 leaves): fols. 19–35, of which fols. 19, 27–8 (conjoint) and 36 are parchment. Fol. 26 is a correction slip pasted on to fol. 25v but now separated. The gathering contains an uninterrupted sequence of carols (*MC* 89–104).

Gathering III (16 leaves plus one added leaf): fols. 36–52, of which fols. 36 and 52 are parchment, as is fol. 44, which looks as though it was added to the otherwise 16-leaf gathering. The gathering contains *MC* 104–106, followed by the much later carol *How shall I please* (fols. 38v–39), then *MC* 107–114, followed by an opening of chant (fols. 47v–48) and then *MC* 115–119. Why those two openings originally remained uncopied is unclear.

---

8 Compare *Fair and discreet* in Ritson (Stevens 1975: no. 9) with Bedyngham's *So ys emprentid* (Fallows 2014: no. 64) first found in the Trento MS 90 (early 1450s) or with his *Gentil madonna* (Fallows 2014: no. 62), first found in Trento MS 93 (early 1450s); or compare *My woeful heart* in Ritson (Stevens 1975: no. 2) with Bedyngham's *Myn hertis lust* (Fallows 2014: no. 63) also first found in Trento 90. One could also compare *O blessed lord* in Ritson (Stevens 1975: no. 6) with Galfridus de Anglia's *Io zemo* (Fallows 2014: no. 55) almost certainly composed in 1444.

9 Although my own reconstruction of the early gatherings goes back to 1976 or 1977, the final presentation here owes much to the unpublished findings (1983) of Paul R. Laird, then a graduate student at the University of North Carolina, and to Dietrich Helms, *Heinrich VIII. und die Musik* = Schriften zur Musikwissenschaft aus Münster 11 (Eisenach: Karl Dieter Wagner, 1998): 449–54.

Chapter 18: The date and origin of Ritson 123

Gathering IV (12 leaves): fols. 53–64, of which fols. 53, 58–9 (no longer conjoint) and 64 are of parchment. The first recto contains the last page of the final carol (*MC* 119); on its verso is the discantus voice only of the much later song *I have been a foster* (printed in Stevens 1975: no. 1); and facing that are portions of two voices of a textless piece (printed in Lane and Sandon 2001: 6–7). The remaining pieces apparently written by hand 'A' are on fols. 54v–55 and fols. 56v–59. Also in this gathering is the two-voice sacred piece *O lux beata trinitas* written by hand 'B'. The rest of the songs written by hand 'B' lead off the next gathering (fols. 65v–73) before the much later 'Packe' portion of the manuscript, which seems to go uninterrupted until fol. 107.[10]

In summary, the carols occupy the 16-leaf gatherings I–III plus the front page of the apparently 12-leaf gathering IV; originally blank, and now filled with other material, are the opening pages of gathering I (fols. 3–5) and two openings in gathering III (fols. 38v–9 and fols. 47v–8). It can be added that the carol pages are almost always ruled with 7 staves on the left-hand page (for the two-voice sections and text *residuum*) and 9 on the right-hand page (for three-voice sections). The staves themselves appear to be freely ruled, ranging between 10 and 15 mm in depth.

Forty years ago, I wrote that the carol manuscripts with polyphony were easy to date and that they provided the framework against which we could look at the scattered fragments of English non-carol song in the fifteenth century.[11] Nobody ever complained about that: as mentioned earlier, nobody much was exploring this music from a historical angle; most felt that the basic details had been tied up by Stevens and Greene. Besides, nobody seems to have noticed that I never even tried to use the supposed information from the carol manuscripts to date the other English secular polyphony. If I had tried, all those years ago, I might have arrived a lot sooner at my present views.

But now I wish to reverse that older position entirely. The English songs of the fifteenth century are fairly easy to date because a fair proportion of them turn up in continental sources. A few of those continental sources can be dated with some precision; and there are enough of these to make the dating of most of the others relatively easy – within perhaps ten years, at the worst within twenty. That is why I feel fairly confident in saying that all the music of Ritson hand 'B' is from the early 1440s and most unlikely to have been copied much after 1450.

When you look at the Ritson carols alongside that information, two perplexing details jump to the eye.

The first is that Ritson contains only two carols with a contratenor in a range below the tenor – *Marvel not, Joseph* (*MC* 81) and *O blessed Lord* (*MC* 116). In continental manuscripts, the introduction of a low contratenor is plausibly datable

---

10 Thomas Packe, plausibly identified in Lane and Sandon (2001: ii) as copyist of many of the pieces in this layer, was ordained priest at Bristol in 1487 and was at Exeter Cathedral between 1489 and 1499.
11 Fallows, 'English song repertories' (1976–7): 61.

to somewhere around 1450. The old system of contratenor in the same range as the tenor did not entirely die out after 1450, but it became increasingly rare.[12] We must return to those two pieces, because both of them are special cases, whose lower voices by no means indicate copying as late as 1450. But the rest of the repertory has a format that was increasingly rare after 1440.

The critical reader may argue that what happens in continental music is not necessarily valid for England; but these were the years when English musicians and composers were constantly on the continental mainland, not just because of the territorial gains in the Hundred Years' War – during many decades of which England held substantial parts of France – but also because of the massive international church councils at Constance (1414–18) and Basel (1431–49) and additionally the search for foreign singers, particularly in the *nouveau riche* courts of Italy. Briefly, there is enough solid information to support the view that in these years the stylistic and notational changes occurred more or less at the same time in England as in the rest of Europe. When the current view is that the carols in Ritson were copied no earlier than 1470, and the ranges of the music, seen from a continental viewpoint, suggest a far earlier date, there is a problem that needs a second glance.

But thinking about that directly raised the second problem. All the two-voice music of the Ritson carol *Pray for us thou Prince of Peace* (*MC* 106) appears in a Credo setting credited to Binchois in the Trento manuscript 92.[13] This was a detail mentioned in passing in Robert Mitchell's doctoral dissertation of 1989.[14] I suppose it would have gone unnoticed – certainly Mitchell never took it any further – had I not reported it in a review of Philip Kaye's edition of Binchois' sacred music a few years later.[15] It was then picked up and discussed at some length in *Binchois studies* (Oxford, 2000) by Andrew Kirkman (pp. 126–8) and Peter Wright (pp. 88–90). Both Kirkman and Wright felt certain that the carol came first and that the Credo is cannibalized from it: their arguments are compact but convincing. Perhaps the most convincing of all is the alignment of the openings of burden and verse with the corresponding passages in Trento 92.[16]

---

12 Sadly, I am unable to send the reader to a single place to confirm this. In some ways the best statement remains that of Heinrich Besseler in *Bourdon und Fauxbourdon* (1950), not least because he stresses that there were earlier cases of a low contratenor, but that they are rare enough to be exceptions. A chronological outline of the song repertory associated with ranges and dates appears in David Fallows, 'The most popular songs of the fifteenth century', in *The Cambridge history of fifteenth-century music*, ed. Anna Maria Busse Berger and Jesse Rodin (Cambridge: Cambridge University Press, 2015): 787–801.

13 At fols. 40–41v (no. 1398; in the new foliation of the online scans, fols. 42–43v). Modern editions in Jeanne Marix, *Les musiciens de la cour de Bourgogne au XVe siècle* (Paris: Éditions de l'Oiseau-lyre, 1937): 176–81, and in Philip Kaye, *The sacred music of Gilles Binchois* (Oxford and New York: Oxford University Press, 1992): 112–18.

14 Robert J. Mitchell, 'The palaeography and repertory of Trent codices 89 and 91, together with analyses and editions of six mass cycles by Franco-Flemish composers from Trent codex 89' (PhD dissertation, University of Exeter, 1989): 223.

15 *Early music* 21 (1993): 282–3.

16 In Examples 18.1 and 18.2 I have texted the carol with the 'revised' version of the poem that I proposed in chapter 15. The text underlaid in Ritson is corrupt in many different ways, and the text proposed here fits the music far better.

Peter Wright pointed out that the use of red coloration (denoted by half-brackets in Example 18.1) at the start in Ritson is obviously necessary for the two imperfected *breves* but that when the notes are subdivided in Trento 92 the red notation is quite unnecessary and can be explained only in terms of the 'carol' version. It could be added that the match between the two versions is otherwise very close indeed, except that the Trento tenor has a b-flat staff-signature, which can

Example 18.1 *Pray for us to the Prince of Peace*, MC 106. Burden I alongside Credo

126 *Chapter 18: The date and origin of Ritson*

be countenanced in this section but is almost certainly a corruption. In addition, the Trento discantus line at 'Christum filium' differs from Ritson and is plainly a textual error.

Equally, the long held note at the beginning of the verse is far more expressive than the repeated notes in the Credo. Once again, here the discantus and the tenor in the two versions are strikingly close in their readings, apart from the b-flat staff-signature in the Trento tenor, which in this case does cause problems at 'secula' and creates something of a surprise before the last cadence. Beyond that, the b-flat staff-signature in the contratenor begins to seem so disruptive that I have simply omitted it from tenor as well as contratenor in both Example 18.1 and Example 18.2.

But in fact the contratenor in that Credo setting is dismal throughout. Even in the few bars presented here, the parallel 5ths at 'Deum' and the parallel 2nds at 'Deo' give pause for thought; and later in the setting the line is well below the standards of the feeblest composer of the time. It seems clear that the deviser of

Example 18.2 *Pray for us to the Prince of Peace, MC* 106. Verse alongside Credo

Chapter 18: The date and origin of Ritson 127

Example 18.2 (Continued)

this Credo setting took the Ritson carol, adapted it to fit the Credo text, and added a perfectly dreadful contratenor line.

Now the point here is that the various portions of Trento 92 can be dated with some precision, not least because it contains a wide variety of different watermarks. That Credo setting was definitely copied there in the mid-1430s – according to good watermark evidence published by Suparmi Saunders in 1989 and unchallenged since.[17] There is nothing wrong with people copying pieces that are thirty years old; but the style of *Pray for us* is more or less that of all the other carols in Ritson, hence the wish to reconsider a copying date of 1470 for the carol layer of Ritson.[18]

A sub-text in the statements of both Peter Wright and Andrew Kirkman is that the Credo is probably not by Binchois. The Credo appears only in Trento 92, and its ascription to Binchois is only in the two indexes that survive at the front of that manuscript. Wright stated (2000: 89n10): 'The hand which entered the composer's name (Tr 92–1 index, column 3, line 10) is apparently not found elsewhere in the index and may well be unique to the entire manuscript'. A single word is not enough for confidence in such an assertion; but the ink is different, as is the orthography 'bi*n*soys'. In the other index, perhaps a bit later, the entry reads quite normally 'Patrem Binchois 40'. Even so, it seems impossible to imagine Binchois purloining two voices from an existing carol and adding the miserable contratenor here. The piece cannot have anything to do with him.

With those considerations in mind, it is time to turn to the two carols that seem to have a low contratenor, as was normal in continental music after about 1450. In *Marvel not, Joseph* (*MC* 81), the lowest voice is beyond any shadow of doubt the tenor. Example 18.3 is its second burden.

Here it is easy to see that the two lower voices do not in any way function as tenor and contratenor function in later music: the middle voice has 4ths below the discantus in bars 3, 5, 6, 8, 9 and 10: this is absolutely not a tenor. By contrast the lowest voice, besides never having a 4th below the discantus, actually ends on the octave below the discantus. Besides, the range of the lowest voice is less than an octave lower than the range of the discantus. The carol has a marvellously

---

17 Suparmi Elizabeth Saunders, *The dating of the Trent codices from their watermarks, with a study of the local liturgy of Trent in the fifteenth century* (New York and London: Garland Publishing, 1989): 159, giving watermark dates of 1435 and 1437 with a total date range of 1429 to 1437 for the watermarks in that portion of the manuscript (fols. 2–145). These findings are fully supported – thirty years later – in the website www.trentinocultura.net, with its full online scans and detailed descriptions of all seven Trento codices, associated with a full set of watermark beta-radiographs (not online, but available on request).

18 There is a further problem: a glance at the Ritson carol *Pray for us* shows that the three-voice burden (namely the bit that is not in Trento) is entirely different in style from the rest of the carol: moreover, it cadences on D, whereas burden I cadences on C and the verse cadences on G. That there be absolutely no musical relation between the two burdens is not otherwise found in the English carol repertory. An unusual copying procedure is a further hint of problems. The normal pattern in this manuscript is to fill the left-hand page (pre-ruled with seven staves) with two systems of two-voice burden plus one system of three-voice burden; then the right-hand page (pre-ruled with nine staves) began with the remainder of the three-voice burden, after which the last six staves would contain three systems of the two-voice verse; the decorated initial letter was therefore on the second stave of the left-hand page; and the text residuum was at the bottom of the left-hand page. But in the case of *MC* 106 the anomalous three-voice burden is on the left-hand page, whereas all the two-voice music (burden I and verse) is crammed onto the right-hand page.

Chapter 18: The date and origin of Ritson 129

Example 18.3 Marvel not, Joseph, MC 81. Burden II only

inventive texture, but its basic structure is closer to fauxbourdon than to the low-contratenor practices of the later fifteenth century.

More complicated is the case of *O blessed Lord* (*MC* 116) and its four-voice second burden.

Here the third voice is plainly the tenor, following the outlines of the discantus in almost painstaking detail. And the fourth voice is in a range a 4th below the tenor. The question that must confront the reader is whether this brief passage can stand against the entire remaining body of carols in Ritson to argue for the received date of *c.* 1470. In my view there is nothing strange about this passage in a piece composed in the 1430s.

That inevitably brings us back to the matter of Smert and Trouluffe, outlined in chapter 13, associating them with the west country and particularly with Exeter Cathedral. It is easy enough to read those documents as they have always been read in the past and to say that the elderly Smert and the possibly younger Trouluffe assembled the 'A' section of the manuscript in the 1470s (shortly before they died). But in view of the musical style and the business with the 'Binchois' Credo, we can read them differently, namely that in the late 1430s the newly installed Smert compiled this material with his colleague Trouluffe. The mention of Plymtree ('Smert Ricard de Plymptre': fols. 17v–18) means that the section must have been copied after 1435, when Richard Smert became rector of that village.

130   Chapter 18: The date and origin of Ritson

Example 18.4 O blessed Lord, MC 116. Burden II only

A copying date in the 1430s for most of this 'A' section looks thoroughly plausible, just as a copying date in the mid-1440s looks attractive for the 'B' section. Obviously the music could have been copied up to thirty years after it had been composed; but the relatively consistent style of the Ritson carols makes that seem unlikely.

What that means is that Ritson's manuscript has a copying life of perhaps eighty years, from the carols in the 1430s to Henry VIII's *Pastime with good company* copied after April 1509.[19] That may at first glance look implausible, not

---

19 Stevens (1952: notes to *MC* 96 and *MC* 109), drew attention to erasure of the name of St Thomas that 'suggests that the MS, if not necessarily this part of it, was therefore still in use at the time of

least because it is hard to think of any other manuscript with a documentable copying range of more than twenty years. But it is hard to read the evidence otherwise.

It might be mentioned here that various writers have based their dates on the watermarks. Lane and Sandon (2001: i) align the first watermark with Briquet nos. 15069 and 15082, with a date of 1462–9. But the *tête de boeuf* watermark here is one of the most common in the entire fifteenth century. The massive Piccard online collection of watermarks (https://piccard-online.de) had, on 2 February 2012,[20] 1,003 watermarks that vaguely match, from all parts of Germany and Switzerland, dated from 1409 to 1538 but principally spread between 1425 and 1465, none quite seeming absolutely to match the watermark in Ritson. On 28 June 2012 I found 423 matches ranging from 1419 to 1489, though those earlier than 1431 all have the eyes slightly inset with a thread holding them in place. The earliest really good match is from Gelderland, 1433. But putting the tolerance down to 2 mm reduced the number to 140, still ranging from 1419 to 1475 and from most parts of Germany and the Low Countries. (The first known papermill in England was that of John Tate near Hertford, in about 1490; Caxton, for example, imported all his paper from France via Holland.) I conclude that watermarks cannot at this point help us at all.

Almost none of the music in Ritson is known from elsewhere: those sections of *Pray for us*, a heavily adjusted version of a *Salve regina* elsewhere ascribed to Power and Dunstable, the tenor of the Binchois rondeau setting *Vostre tresdouce regard* (with a newly added voice) and – last if not least – Henry VIII's *Pastime with good company*. In that respect, the book looks like a parochial west-country collection, even one specifically to be associated with Exeter Cathedral.

On the other hand, nine of the texts in the Ritson carols had already been set in the earlier sources, Trinity, Egerton and Selden. Some of those also appear in poetry sources, but none of them appears in poetry sources only. That could suggest that the composers of the Ritson music knew the musical repertory in the other three sources.

At the same time there is a major stylistic gap between the carols in the other three sources and those in Ritson. If we are contemplating a copying date of the mid-1430s for the Ritson carols, we need to be thinking about something at least a decade earlier for the others.

---

the Reformation'. *MC* 96 (fols. 27v–28) is on parchment, easily scratched out with a knife; but the three words 'Thome' can still be read with the plain eye. *MC* 109 (fols. 41v–42) is on paper: there's staining, there's scratching, and there's plain crossing out: somebody has made a fair mess of the texts on this opening. That would indeed mean that the manuscript remained available for over a century.

20 Under the headings: Ochsenkopf; Mit Augen und Nasenlöchern; Darüber einkonturiger Stern; chains 38–9 mm apart; head with star 65 mm high, breadth 35 mm. Of course I had the enormous privilege, not available to an earlier researchers, of sitting in a carrell in the British Library with Ritson, an ultraviolet lamp, and online access to the Piccard catalogue. I am deeply grateful to Nicolas Bell for making that possible.

132   Chapter 18: The date and origin of Ritson

It should be mentioned here that some of the non-carol music of hand 'A' does have a low contratenor, in particular the three *Nesciens mater* settings, two of them marked for Trouluffe and one of them marked for Smert and Trouluffe (Lane and Sandon 2001: nos. 52 and 55–6). Nos. 55–6 function exactly like *Marvel not, Joseph*, with a tenor that happens to occupy a range slightly lower than the contratenor. No. 52 carries the borrowed chant in equal *semibreves* in the tenor, with the contratenor occupying a lower register, much in the manner of various Old Hall chant settings. As already mentioned, however, these pieces were copied later than the carols: there are no decorated initials and no space for them. For the carols I cannot imagine a copying date later than about 1445, and my inclination is towards the late 1430s.

And that is the point that became clear to me only after loving and exploring the music for forty-five years, as mentioned in chapter 1. In assembling the English songs of the fifteenth century for Fallows 2014, I realised that the layer 'B' songs in Ritson had really to have been copied in the 1440s at the latest, and I registered that the evidence of the Credo ascribed to Binchois in Trento yielded absolute certainty that the carol *MC* 106 was composed in the 1430s and the high likelihood that the remaining Ritson carols have a similar date.

Exeter Cathedral changed somewhat under the bishopric of Edmund Lacy, one of Henry V's close confidantes, appointed dean of the Chapel Royal in 1414, present at the battle of Agincourt (1415),[21] who had in earlier years been a canon at St George's, Windsor. While Bishop of Hereford (1417–20), he had appointed a John Dunstable to a canonry in 1419.[22] While at Exeter (1420–55) he appointed the Old Hall composer Nicholas Sturgeon to two canonries. And he certainly had a private chapel at Exeter, probably including John Trouluffe.[23] Under Lacy, Richard Smert was ordained priest in 1427; and the documents specifically state that Bishop Lacy appointed him a vicar-choral of the cathedral on 20 September 1427.[24]

It therefore seems most likely that the distinctive style of the Ritson carols arose from Bishop Lacy's patronage. His appointment as Bishop of Hereford in 1417 was evidently a special favour granted by Henry V, as was his promotion to Exeter in 1420. In May 1421, Lacy preached before Henry V at Windsor; in the next year he was an executor of Henry V's will. Plainly he was well placed to

---

21 Nicholas Orme, 'Lacy, Edmund', in *Oxford dictionary of national biography* (Oxford: Oxford University Press, 2004 and online).
22 R. L. Greene, 'John Dunstable: a quincentenary supplement', *The musical quarterly* 40 (1954): 360–63, citing Joseph H. Parry and Arthur Thomas Bannister, *Registrum Edmundi Lacy episcopi Herefordensis* (London: Canterbury and York Society, 1918): 115. Obviously the name was common enough, but Greene makes a strong case for identification with the composer, including the observation that Lacy's consecration as Bishop of Hereford was 'an unusually brilliant ceremony in the lower chapel of Windsor Castle on April 18, 1417, to attend which the King made one of his infrequent visits to Windsor'. Further on Dunstable and Henry V, see chapter 22.
23 Orme 1978: 401.
24 Orme 1978: 402; documentation in G. R. Dunstan, *The register of Edmund Lacy, Bishop of Exeter, 1420–1455*, 5 vols. (Torquay: Devonshire Press, 1963–72).

encourage the continuation of Henry V's musical traditions in Exeter. Associating the first layer of Ritson with Exeter Cathedral in the 1430s, at the height of Bishop Lacy's time there, fits well with what we otherwise know. But it raises questions about some of the other carol manuscripts, to which we must now turn.

19 The date and origin of Egerton

As long as the Egerton manuscript has been known, scholars have disagreed about its geographical origin: some favoured St George's, Windsor (Schofield 1946, Stevens 1952, McPeek 1963, Bowers 2001) and others favoured Meaux Abbey in Yorkshire (Bukofzer 1950, Greene 1954, Greene 1977, Zec 1997: 41–2, Zamzow 2000: 8–10, Reichl 2005: 160). Recently, it has also been proposed that the manuscript could have been prepared at Hythe in Kent, more specifically, the nearby Saltwood Castle, at the time the main residence of the archbishops of Canterbury (McInnes 2013: 204–8).[1] A further proposal was Syon Abbey (Harrison 1964: 407). The startlingly different characters of these establishments, many hundreds of miles away from one another, merit a closer look.

For the first published description of the manuscript, Bertram Schofield (1946) boldly included the words 'of the English Chapel Royal' in his title, though the body of his article, which covers many details of the source and has a full descriptive inventory of its contents, argued – very briefly, just on p. 514 – for origin in Windsor. The only reason he offered was that the hymn *Salve, festa dies* appears here with five different textual continuations,[2] the last of which 'does not, as do the other four, occur in the Sarum Processional'. He added:

> its appearance here is convincing proof that the manuscript was written for a religious establishment of some importance dedicated to St. George and with a strong musical tradition. The one center in England that above all others fulfilled these qualifications in the 15th century was the Chapel Royal of St. George, Windsor.

A year later, Manfred Bukofzer published his continuation of Schofield's article (Bukofzer 1947) without any comment on the manuscript's origins, limiting himself to a brief description and complete publication of two pieces. But three

---

1 Incidentally, the castle was purchased in 1955 by the art historian Sir Kenneth Clark, and it remains in his family at the time of writing.
2 At fols. 37v–42, edited by McPeek (1963: 78–83) and Hughes (1967: 117–25). As mentioned earlier, the original hymn, credited to Venantius Fortunatus, is a rare earlier manifestation of the carol form, though its music in Egerton is not at all in the carol style.

years after that, in his famous book *Studies in medieval and renaissance music*, he included a substantial chapter on the manuscript with the correspondingly bold title 'Holy week music and carols at Meaux Abbey' (Bukofzer 1950: 113–75), repeatedly in the course of the article calling it the 'Meaux Abbey manuscript', without any qualifications. And, like Schofield, he devoted only a few lines – twelve, in fact, on p. 114 – to discussion of its geographical origin. He first noted that the stanza Schofield had mentioned does actually appear in a Sarum Processional[3] written a few years earlier 'for a London church', then stated that Richard L. Greene – in as yet unpublished research communicated privately – 'has established that the dialect of the English carols points in the direction of York', and added that Greene had also 'discovered that the Ivy carol [*MC* 55] refers to the village Hye (Hyth) which formerly belonged to Meaux Abbey in Yorkshire'.

With Greene's own statement on the matter not yet published, John Stevens offered a brief description in his Musica Britannica edition of the carols (Stevens 1952: 125). He followed Schofield in favouring the 'Chapel Royal of St George at Windsor' and added that the carol *Princeps serenissime* (*MC* 62) was 'particularly appropriate to the king's own household'.[4]

When it eventually appeared, Greene's publication (Greene 1954) provided for the first time an extended and detailed consideration of the manuscript's origin. He was quick to assert (pp. 6–7) that *Princeps serenissime* almost certainly addresses no earthly prince but the Prince of Peace – which is of some importance and, as I showed in chapter 14, definitely wrong. He also explained, quite correctly (pp. 2–3), that the Chapel Royal was a peripatetic body serving the king whereas St George's, Windsor, was a fixed college serving the Order of the Garter and the residents of Windsor Castle. That Schofield (and, following him, Stevens) amalgamated the two may be embarrassing, but it is not in itself enough to dismiss their view that it could be for one or the other. Broadly speaking, those who support the Schofield view have since then considered the book to belong to St George's, Windsor.

The case for Meaux

Greene's argument for origin in Meaux begins (1954: 15–19) with his best evidence: two mottos written within the initials on fol. 15, 'Mieulx en de cy' (at the beginning of the St Luke passion, for Palm Sunday), and on fol. 20, 'De cy en mieulx' (at the beginning of the St Matthew passion, for Wednesday in Holy Week). Sadly, somebody has carefully cut out the five opening leaves of the manuscript, which might be expected to have included the clearest sign of ownership; and it must be added that the two initials on fols. 15 and 20 are distinctly feeble efforts, particularly when compared with the magnificent decorated initials for

---

3 Oxford, Bodleian Library, MS Lat. liturg. e. 7, more fully described in this context in Greene 1954: 4–5.
4 The 1958 revision retained the entire description, though adding Greene's 1954 article to the bibliographical references.

O potores exquisiti near the end. Greene (1977: 301, recasting and clarifying his longer original statement in Greene 1954) remarked:

> Though the motto has not been found elsewhere (after much laborious search), puns in such use were ubiquitous, and 'Meaux' was pronounced then as now, exactly like 'mieulx', i.e. 'mews'.[5]

He also offered the view that the motto on fol. 15 could be translated as 'Meaux over here', to distinguish the English abbey from 'the town and abbey of that name in France'.

By contrast, Frank Harrison (1964: 407) after proposing 'the new and fashionable Brigittine house of Syon (founded by Henry V in 1415)', added:

> Some might see support for this speculation in the fact that the motto 'Mieulx en de cy' also appears in the manuscript in the form 'De cy en [=Syon?] mieulx'.[6]

In addition, Greene noted (1954: 18) that these two pages also each contain a 'cross patonce', which also appears in the arms of Meaux, alongside several other religious houses.

> The source of the cross patonce in the case of Meaux Abbey is the coat of its founder, William le Gros, Earl of Albemarle . . . The cross patonce of William is recorded by Dugdale in the arms of Meaux Abbey both between four martlets (footless heraldic swallows) and between two cinquefoils.

He was, though, quick to concede that the two crosses 'patonce' in Egerton are undecorated and far simpler than those described by Dugdale. I can add that whoever drew those two crosses was plainly not otherwise involved in the manuscript; moreover, as one is in the open space at the bottom and the other is in the open space at the top of the page, there might be a good case for suggesting that they were both added substantially later, as noted by McPeek (1963: 13).

From here, Greene passed to the linguistic evidence (1954: 19–21). He was understandably cautious in evaluating this. There are only twelve poems here that

---

5 I am not sure that this is right. Without getting involved on the tricky topic of French pronunciation in various parts of England in the fifteenth century, I would simply note that the Wikipedia article on the village states that it is now pronounced /mjus/ 'mewss', citing as authority the widely-respected G. M. Miller, *BBC pronouncing dictionary of British names* (London: Oxford University Press, 1971).

6 This was in a review of McPeek 1963, a review mainly drawing attention to the major shortcomings in the volume. He did not stop to mention the volume's virtues, but proposed Syon origin as another way of explaining McPeek's point (1963: 10–11, 14) that one of the initials portrays women drinking, that *Comedentes convenite* (*MC* 71) expressly invites women to take part in the celebrations and that the text of the motet *Cantemus socie Domino* is traditionally associated with women. McPeek used that evidence to suggest that the book was for St George's, Windsor; Harrison merely countered that Syon would be a better choice. Neither argument seems particularly firmly grounded.

include English words. Most of the examples he quotes are from two carols, *Ivy is good* (*MC* 55) and *Saint Thomas honour we* (*MC* 59). But he stated that 'the following instances seem to show definite influence of the speech and writing habits of the area north of the River Humber':

> *Novus sol de virgine* (*MC* 48: fol. 53), st 3: abown ilkon (above each one)
> *The holy martyr Stephen* (*MC* 50: fol. 54v), st 4: band (bound)
> *Ivy is good* (*MC* 55: fols. 59v–60), st 3: treyss (trees), snaw (snow); st 5: qwy (why)
> *Saint Thomas honour we* (*MC* 59: fols. 62v–63), st 3: to (till), awen (own); st 5: swaryd (squared): st 6: law (low), overthraw (overthrown), saw (sown)
> *I pray you all* (*MC* 65: fol. 66v), last line: qwer (where)

In response to my enquiry, Prof. Michael Benskin read the evidence rather differently as containing a few details that could point to Norfolk or Lincolnshire or Yorkshire but mostly pointing towards the Home Counties and particularly suggesting 'a northerner whose language had been heavily southernised' (e-mail of 6 March 2016) but occasionally slipped up. He drew attention to the Yorkshire preference for the letter 'y' rather than the otherwise ubiquitous letter 'thorn', noting that the English poems in Egerton contain over forty examples of 'thorn' against two of 'y' and two examples of 'th' (both on fol. 65v). He also drew attention to fifteen appearances of 'wh' against two of 'qw' (which is the Yorkshire preference).

Given the extent to which musicians travelled in the fifteenth century, there seems no difficulty in concluding that the Egerton copyist could conceivably have been born in the north but that his main area of activity was in the Home Counties. I see nothing in Benskin's analysis to support copying of the manuscript in Yorkshire.

Greene's next piece of evidence (1954: 23–5) is perhaps the strangest and weakest of all, though several times cited in his support. The carol *Ivy is good* (*MC* 55) contains in its fifth and last stanza the following lines in praise of ivy:

> Where it taketh hold it keepeth fast
> And strenketh it that is him by;   *makes strong*
> It keepeth wall from cost and waste,
> As men may see all day at hye.

The key, for Greene, was the word 'hye', which he construed as referring to a village called Hythe on the Holderness coast, the property of Meaux abbey but 'washed away by the sea about 1400' (1954: 24). Greene conceded that the place name is very common indeed, meaning just 'harbour': others have suggested identifying the word with Eye in Suffolk or Hythe in Kent.[7] Greene also later conceded that John Stevens's gloss 'at eye, at first sight' 'makes good sense, of

---

7 McPeek (1963: 12), taken up also by McInnes (2013: 204–8).

Chapter 19: The date and origin of Egerton

course' (1977: 384). One component of Greene's view that the word refers to the former Yorkshire village was the line in stanza 3 referring to 'great storms of snow and hail' which first made him 'think of a North-of-England background for it'. But it is hard to imagine how a poem set to music in the fifteenth century could refer to anything in a village washed away in 1400 as visible 'all day' and kept free 'from cost and waste'. That part of the argument therefore seems to me entirely groundless.[8]

The last piece of evidence that Greene brought[9] (1954: 25–7) is the almost untranslatable *Comedentes convenite* (*MC* 71). For him, it was evidence of a broad-minded house that admitted women for the Christmas celebrations. But that hardly limits the potential public to Meaux.

In any case, it is hard to disagree with Frank Harrison's verdict about Egerton (1958: 275), based not on the carols but on the liturgical pieces in the manuscript:

> For liturgical reasons, the theory that [Egerton] belonged to the Cistercian Abbey of Meaux seems untenable. The Cistercian rite was a twice 'reformed' version and conflation of those of Metz and Rome, first under the direction of Stephen Harding and then under that of St Bernard. The uniformity of its texts and music was rigorously imposed, and while some monasteries may have allowed secular rites and customs in the votive services sung out of choir, it is difficult to believe that in a Cistercian abbey the ritual of Holy Week could have been carried out according to a secular Ordinal.

Gwynn McPeek (1963: 13) quoted those same lines, enthusiastically endorsing them. Roger Bowers also endorsed them (2001: 189–92, at 190n91), noting that Greene's most recent statement (1977: 299–301)

> has no response to [Harrison's] apparently indefeasible point that liturgy and chant of the secular Salisbury Use could have had no place in the observance of a Cistercian monastery, least of all in Holy Week.

---

8 And I would argue that the slender philological evidence more or less dismisses Hythe in Kent, though McInnes (2013: 208) carefully frames her tentative proposal by adding that 'Whether Saltwood could have indeed been a possible location for the manuscript or not, the point here is that it is imperative that scholars look to provincial locations for extant manuscripts as well as royal courts, abbeys and cathedrals'. Amen to that, though the quality of the parchment preparation points towards a fairly prominent institution.

9 This is not quite true. Greene brought three further points in favour of Meaux, all of which seem to me irrelevant to the main argument: (a) that the viciously anti-royal carol *Saint Thomas honour we* (*MC* 59) could well have been used at Meaux, which documentably revered St Thomas (1954: 27), a matter I shall take up below; (b) that there is evidence elsewhere for the use of sophisticated polyphony at Meaux *c*. 1300 (1954: 27–30); and (c) that the Old Hall composer John Burrell was a corrodian of Meaux, 1416–37 (1954: 31–4).

That is not entirely fair, since Greene did add the comment (first in 1962: 171, again in 1977: 300), albeit without documentation:

> But Meaux cheerfully ignored other Cistercian regulations against luxury, the presence of women, and church decoration.

And in 1954: 26–7 he had impressively documented this with details of how Meaux made special arrangements to admit women to see their relics. But with the linguistic evidence thoroughly neutral, and with the 'Hye' evidence applicable to dozens of coastline towns in various parts of Britain and in any case plausibly glossed as meaning just 'easily seen', we are left with the two inscrutable mottos on fol. 15 and fol. 20, together with the crosses 'patonce' on those two pages.

The case against Windsor

Greene challenged the 'royal household' theory on various fronts: that the stanza for St George in *Salve, festa dies* was indeed found elsewhere (following Bukofzer), and that there were 126 churches in England dedicated to him;[10] that the carol *Princeps serenissime* (*MC* 62) is addressed not to a worldly prince but to the Prince of Peace (wrong, as explained on pp. 96); that the line 'At Agincourt the chronicle ye read' in the carol *Enforce we us with all our might* (*MC* 60) would be out of place at St George's Windsor, where several veterans of the Battle of Agincourt were present, but acceptable in a monastic house; that the missing name of the king in *Exultavit cor in domino* (*MC* 61) is extraordinary for a manuscript from a royal institution; that the carol *Saint Thomas honour we* (*MC* 59) is virulently anti-royal, and would be ill placed in a manuscript for royal use; that the goliardic drinking-song *O potores exquisiti* would be entirely inappropriate for a royal manuscript, particularly for Henry VI, and that its two elaborate initials depicting drinking and partying – by far the most elaborate in the manuscript – are unsuitable to a royal environment; and that the two crosses on fol. 15 and fol. 20 are found in many arms but certainly not that of St George's, Windsor. In addition, he saw the carol *Comedentes convenite* as inappropriate for St George's Chapel, inviting, as it does, women to take part in the festivities.

As concerns *Enforce we us with all our might* (*MC* 60), referring to St George and his reputed appearance at the Battle of Agincourt, it is easy to dispute Greene's view that the words 'the chronicle ye read' meant that the writers knew of it only from chronicles, not from those who were present at the battle, which would be the case if it was to be performed in royal circles.[11] I would be reluctant

---

10 Greene 1954: 5; citing Francis Bond, *Dedications and patron saints of English churches* (London: Oxford University Press, 1914): 17.
11 For what it may be worth, the earliest surviving chronicle that fully reports the French seeing St George at Agincourt seems to be the version of *Brut* copied in 1478–9, Lambeth Palace Library, MS 84, see Anne Curry, *The battle of Agincourt: sources and interpretations* (Woodbridge: Boydell Press, 2000): 95. But there is an earlier passing mention, far less specific, in Thomas

to allow such weight to be attached to four words inserted into a rhymed poem, partly so formulated because they rhyme.[12] Moreover, the phrase concerns quite specifically the information that the French at Agincourt were frightened to see St George leading the English in battle: it is perfectly possible that none of the English forces had this hallucination. The argument must fall.

B

Enforce we us with all our might
To love Saint George our lady['s] knight.

1

Worship of virtue is the meed	*Honour is the reward of virtue*
And sueth him ay of right;	*And follows him*
To worship George then have we need,	
Which is our sov'reign lady's knight.	

2

He kept the maid from dragon's dread,
And fraid all France and put to flight
At Agincourt, the chronicle ye read:
The French him see formost in fight.

3

In his virtue he will us lead
Againes the fiend, the foul wight,
And with his banner us overspread,
If we him love with all our might.

This is in fact the only surviving carol text dedicated to St George.[13] Greene (1977: 418) softened the impact of this by mentioning five other carols that refer to St George (all of them surviving as texts only): three mention him only in

---

Elmham's *Liber metricus de Henrico Quinto* (*c.* 1418), ed. in Charles Augustus Cole, *Memorials of Henry the Fifth, king of England* (London: Longman, 1858): 123: 'Cernitur in campo sacer ille Georgius armis,/ Anglorum parte, bella parare suis'.

12 McPeek (1963: 11) rightly argued that these words could be interpreted either way and cannot reasonably be used to locate the origin of the manuscript.

13 Nevertheless, there is of course a famous pair of motets to St George in the second layer of the Old Hall manuscript, Thomas Damett's *Salvatoris mater pia/ O Georgi/ Benedictus Marie filius qui ve-* (no. 111) and John Cooke's *Alma proles/ Christi miles inclite/ Ab inimicis nostris defende nos Christe* (no. 112), discussed in chapter 22.

Example 19.1 *Enforce we us with all our might*, MC 60. Complete

passing, alongside many other saints; *EEC* 431.1 is a long narrative concerning Henry VI later in his life, mentioning St George in only the nineteenth of its twenty stanzas; *EEC* 433.1 is a carol in honour of Henry VII, again mentioning St George as national patron saint and giving him a certain prominence. That the Egerton manuscript contains the single carol that is entirely about St George must be considered a relevant detail in assessing its origins.[14]

As mentioned earlier, the opening words of the third stanza, 'In his virtue he will us lead/ Againes the fiend, the foul wight', are most unlikely to have been written after December 1419, when the Treaty of Troyes seemed inevitable. In fact the wording, if taken at all literally, refers to Agincourt and in stanza 3 to the next encounter with the 'foul' French: that would again put this poem among the propaganda items in preparation for the 1417 invasion.

This may seem at first glance worlds away from the Agincourt carol. It does indeed have different features: the 'rhyming' cadences in the last five bars of burden and verse belong to a different rhetorical strategy. Beyond that, the matching of words and music seems a lot laxer: the main aim of the composer is apparently to create musical glory with these relatively simple means. More important, though, there is no mention of any season or of Christianity in general (apart from an indirect allusion to Mary). But the metrical structure tends to align it rather more with the Agincourt carol: the burden has a six-bar phrase answered by one of eight bars; and the verse opens with a five-bar phrase, but then continues with a four-bar line and two eight-bar lines.

As concerns the carol *Exultavit cor in Domino* (*MC* 61) and its apparently missing text, Greene referred (1954: 6) to the words in verse one 'Pro divino auxilio rege' after which there is a blank followed by 'dato potentissimo'; he added that no king's name was mentioned until the next stanza, which then has nothing else.

B

Exultavit cor (in) Domino;   My heart has rejoiced in the Lord;
Nunc concinat hec concio.   Now let this assembly sing together.

1

Pro divino auxilio,   For divine help,
Rege dato [in prelio]   given to the king [in battle]
[rubore] potentissimo.   with most powerful [strength]

---

14 It may be relevant that the feast of St George (23 April) was promoted to a Greater Double feast after Agincourt, celebrated with a national holiday, as noted by Greene (1954: 5, citing Wylie 1914–29: ii.239). On the other hand, the royal free chapel of St George, Windsor, had that title from its foundation by Edward III in 1348; already in the second year of his reign Henry V had a major celebration on St George's day in Windsor, see Wylie: i. 316–19; and the mustering of an army for the 1415 invasion included the 'requirement that all men should wear the cross of St George on their front and back', see Anne Curry, *Agincourt* (Oxford: Oxford University Press, 2015): 11.

Chapter 19: The date and origin of Egerton

2

Henrico Quinto prelio   Henry V in battle...
[   ]
[   ]

3

Superborum confusio,   The confusion of the proud
Piorum est proteccio,   is the protection of the faithful,
Jesu, nostra redempcio.   O Jesus, our redemption.

4

Nunc [in] cantu organico   Now with harmonious music
Cantemus bono animo   let us sing with a good spirit
Pro vero testimonio.   for true witness.

5

Benedicamus Domino,   Let us bless the Lord
Qui [in] celi palacio   who in the palace of the sky
Regnat sine principio.   reigns without beginning.

He concluded by asking:

> Would a manuscript written for use in or before the court be allowed to stand long with blanks at just these points, where the praise of Henry V – to be sung, it is suggested, in the presence of his son – comes to a focus? It is hard to believe.

A response to his question would be on three fronts. First, the entire manuscript is written by a single copyist, showing no corrections by any other hand: the relevant question would be why no other hand is involved. Second, the problem is not that Henry V's name is omitted, for it is there in the second stanza: the problem is just that the poem has missing words in both the first and the second stanzas. Third, it is perfectly possible to sing the carol without the missing words: the careful listener would perhaps be disturbed to note that those two stanzas did not match the form of the later stanzas, but everything that is necessary is actually present in the text, including the name of the king. The missing text therefore seems irrelevant to the question of whether this manuscript was for a royal household or a royal foundation.

The carol *Saint Thomas honour we* (*MC* 59) may seem inappropriate for a royal manuscript, since it blames the king specifically for Thomas's murder, as Greene noted (1954: 7–8). On the other hand, the shrine of St Thomas continued to be revered, and one of the new Henry V's greatest expenses at the funeral of

144 *Chapter 19: The date and origin of Egerton*

his father was the massive sum of £160 for 'a golden bejewelled head to be given as an offering at the shrine of Thomas Becket';[15] moreover, his father's coronation had been graced with a special oil devoutly believed to have been presented to St Thomas by the Virgin Mary, thereafter hidden in Poitiers and rescued by Henry's great-grandfather.[16] And, famously, the English delegation at the Council of Constance had particular impact when it celebrated the feast of St Thomas with special panoply on 29 December 1415 and again in 1416.[17]

So the only compelling case in Greene's argument against St George's, Windsor is the drinking-song *O potores exquisiti*, added after the carols. This famous poem, already found two hundred years earlier in the Carmina Burana manuscript, is unashamedly licentious, praising excess of all kinds. Greene pointed out that it was incompatible with everything that is known of Henry VI, which seems fair enough. He also drew attention to the two decorated initials on its first opening, beautifully painted with a quality far beyond any other decoration in the book, showing male and female courtiers alongside monks or friars.[18] One cannot but agree with Greene's conclusion (1954: 9):

> There is no suggestion of anything courtly or of any suitability to either Chapel Royal or St. George's, Windsor, in either of these skillfully executed and mildly satirical paintings.

---

15 Anne Curry, *Henry V: playboy prince to warrior king* (London: Allen Lane, 2015): 42, citing The [British] National Archives, Kew, E 403/612 (payments enrolled on 31 May and 4 July); see also Wylie 1914–29: i.49.
16 Peter Earle, *The life and times of Henry V* (London: Weidenfeld and Nicolson, 1972): 23; Christopher Allmand, *Henry V* (London: Methuen, 1992): 65, argues the possibility that the same oil was used for Henry V's coronation. On the likelihood that also Henry VI used the same oil, see J. W. McKenna, 'The coronation oil of the Yorkist kings', *The English historical review* 82 (1967): 102–104, who adds the likelihood that Edward IV and Richard III also used it for their coronations. More caution about the matter is expressed in T. A. Sandquist, 'The holy oil of St Thomas of Canterbury', in *Essays in mediaeval history presented to Bertie Wilkinson*, ed. T. A. Sandquist and M. R. Powicke (Toronto: University of Toronto Press, 1969): 330–44.
17 Fuller details in chapter 24. McPeek (1963: 11) added that 'I can find no evidence that the story of St. Thomas of Canterbury, who was popular all over England, was in any way frowned upon at any time or place during the reign of Henry VI'.
18 The two initials differ in some important respects. The smaller, on fol. 73, shows courtiers: two ladies with triangular headdresses, two men with turban-like headdresses, one kneeling man with what one would term a 'Henry V style' haircut and an expensive blue robe, apparently offering a golden goblet to a standing man with what one would term a 'King Wenceslas' hat and hip-belt with sword; and apparently one man in a full black hooded habit is supporting the kneeling man. That on fol. 72v shows at least eighteen figures, all apparently men, plus a large barrel, two dogs and a monkey: two of the men, both with 'Henry V style' haircuts and with expensive gowns (green and red), kneel and offer golden goblets to the main man, who is wearing a square black cap and appears to be refusing the goblets; the rest of the men, four of whom have tonsures, are standing around or conversing.

On the other hand, it is far harder to accept his view that this would be possible only in a monastic context.[19]

Some possible dates

Sylvia Kenney (1965) supported McPeek's dating 1430–44 for Egerton 'suggesting that textual references to war concern the war with France rather than the War of the Roses' – though the references are in all but one case to peace, not war;[20] and peace was a scarce phenomenon in those years. Roger Bowers (2001: 190) says it is 'generally dated to the decade 1440–50'. More specifically, Bowers points to a payment at St George's in 1449–50 to a certain Richard Prideaux for the copying and notating of 'unius libri vocati le Organboke . . . ad usum Collegii';[21] but the description of the book continues by saying it has twelve gatherings, each of six leaves, whereas Egerton's gatherings are all of eight leaves, apart from the second and third (though it does indeed have twelve gatherings).

It may be easier to begin where my own latest exploration of Egerton began, namely that the style of one of its last and most glamorous pieces, the isorhythmic Latin song *O potores exquisiti*,[22] is very much that of Dunstable's two motets *Veni sancte Spiritus/ Veni creator* and *Preco preheminencie/ Precursor premittitur/ Inter natos mulierum*, both generally dated to 1416.[23] From a quite different angle, I concluded (pp. 93–8) that the carol *Benedicite Deo Domino* (*MC* 57) is almost incomprehensible if not related to the peace treaty of 1420 and that *Princeps serenissime* (*MC* 62) needs to be from around the same time; further to that, I argued that *Princeps pacis strenue* (*MC* 45) most plausibly dates from 1420.

Egerton also contains the only surviving polyphonic carols with direct political references – that is, apart from the Agincourt carol.[24] Again, their texts entirely in Latin might just imply that they were aimed at an international audience (though there are also Latin carol texts in Ritson, which seems firmly associated with the

---

19 Greene additionally devoted considerable space (1954: 10–12) to an absorbing and erudite discussion of the strange motet *Cantemus socie Domino*, concerning St Dunstan, who had no association with St George's, Windsor. While conceding his last point, I fail to see how this reflects on the question either way. He also had no known association with Meaux Abbey.
20 The same dates appear in Kathleen L. Scott, *An index of images in English manuscripts from the time of Chaucer to Henry VIII c. 1380–c. 1509: British Library I: MSS Additional and Egerton* (London and Turnhout: Harvey Miller Publishers, 2014): 162, no. 363.
21 Bowers (2001: 189n89 and 192n99), where he argues at some length that the difference was probably just the result of a shorthand in the copyist's invoice. The same identification is supported in James M. W. Willoughby, *The libraries of collegiate churches* = Corpus of British medieval library catalogues 15 (London: The British Library, 2013): 925–6.
22 Modern edition in Fallows 2014: no. 40.
23 Bent 1981: 8.
24 McInnes (2013: 203–9) drew attention to the group of political carols on ff. 60v–64v of Egerton, namely *MC* 56–62; but she then moved off in a different direction.

Exeter area and well into the reign of Henry VI). And that would make sense particularly for *Anglia, tibi turbidas* (*MC* 56):

B

| Anglia, tibi turbidas | England, for yourself after turbid |
| Spera lucem post tenebras. | shadows, hope for light. |

1

Jurandi jam nequicia,   Already the wickedness of one
                                swearing
Tirannidis milicia,   and the armed might of a tyrant
Tergula dant per turmulas;   turn their little backs in small groups;
[Nunc] tuta cum fiducia,   [now] with secure confidence,
Spera lucem post tenebras.   hope for light after shadows.

2

Augescat amicicia,   Let friendship increase,
Inolescat justicia,   let justice take root,
Fugiat fraus in foveas;   let false-dealing flee into pits;
Nulla mentis mesticia,   with no sadness of mind,
Spera lucem post tenebras.   hope for light after shadows.

3

Fervida fax cupidinis,   Let the glowing torch of greed,
Fetida fex libidinis   the stinking dregs of lust,
Purgentur et illecebras   be purged as well as the enticements,
Sanans sente formidinis,   sweeping them away with a briar
                                of fear,
Spera lucem post tenebras.   hope for light after shadows.

4

Pauperum populacio,   Let the despoiling of poor persons
Rapine perpetracio,   and perpetration of robbery
Perennes petant latebras;   seek eternal hiding-places;
Et, priscorum solacio,   and, in the solace of old habits,
Spera lucem post tenebras.   hope for light after shadows.

Plainly this commemorates a newly achieved state of peace, if not specifically a peace treaty. All the details mentioned in the text would make sense if seen in terms of the rebellious French Dauphin, disinherited by Charles VI at the Treaty of Troyes, after Henry V had gained control of much of northern France, which welcomed him with open hands.

Thus I am inclined to propose that no fewer than six of the Egerton carols predate 1422, as follows:

Between Agincourt (Oct 1415) and December 1419, because of insulting remarks about the French:

> *Exultavit cor in Domino* (*MC* 61): major prolation; all 2vv
> *Enforce we us with all our might* (*MC* 60): perfect time but only one burden; all 2vv

Treaty of Troyes (May 1420):

> *Benedicite Deo Domino* (*MC* 57): major prolation; all 2vv
> *Anglia tibi turbidas* (*MC* 56): perfect time; double burden and 3vv insert

Between the Treaty of Troyes (May 1420) and Henry V's death (August 1422) but most probably for the Christmas season, 1420:

> *Princeps serenissime* (*MC* 62): major prolation; all 2vv
> *Princeps pacis strenue* (*MC* 45): perfect time; double burden and 3vv insert

That does not of course mean that the entire Egerton manuscript is likely to be from 1420; but it is yet another hint that the broad dating of the entire carol repertory could be reconsidered.

Some conclusions

Greene's proposal that it was copied at and for Meaux Abbey now seems to be without grounding and is incompatible with the use of Sarum Rite in the liturgical pieces. That the manuscript contains the only surviving carol devoted to St George as well as the rare (albeit not unique) St George stanza for *Salve, festa dies* could suggest one of the many establishments associated with St George.

That I have associated no fewer than six of the thirty Egerton carols with Henry V seems a more significant detail: one addresses him directly; one seems appropriate only at his wedding ceremony or at the following Christmas; three more can only make sense between the Treaty of Troyes in 1420 and Henry's death in 1422; and two more (in English) make sense only between the Battle of Agincourt and the Treaty of Troyes. These lay stress on the idea of the carol as a political statement. And their transmission in Egerton surely implies that this was a collection assembled by somebody close to royalty.

In addition, there are six more carols in major prolation and in two voices throughout: *Tibi laus, tibi gloria* (*MC* 44), *The holy martyr Stephen* (*MC* 50), *Ecce, quod Natura* (*MC* 63), *I pray you all* (*MC* 65), *Ave, plena gracia* (*MC* 66),

Alleluia: Diva natalicia (*MC* 69; also in Selden as *MC* 28). For all six a date prior to 1430 seems highly likely; and several could be from before 1420.

Relevant here seems to be the sheer quality of the manuscript. Gwynn McPeek suggested (1963: 12–13) that Egerton was in the same hand as the main layer of the Old Hall manuscript. That seems now out of the question, though the quality of the parchment preparation and the quality of the decoration are definitely comparable.[25] Moreover, both manuscripts appear to be rastrum-ruled throughout, which gives them a unique position among English manuscripts of the fifteenth century.[26] This is beyond question a classy manuscript. If it is right, as currently believed, that the main layer of the Old Hall manuscript was prepared for the chapel of Thomas, Duke of Clarence, then it is perfectly possible that Egerton was for a similar household.

Nevertheless, the broad stylistic profile of the carols in perfect time makes it seem dangerous at this point to date the entire collection much later than about 1430.

---

25 Conclusions reached in Bent (1968: 102–5) after having viewed the manuscripts on two consecutive days; now that the two manuscripts are in the same library, it was possible for me to see them side-by-side and establish the important point (not visible from scans) that the quality of the parchment preparation is comparable in the two sources.

26 Bent (1968: 40–41) sees two rastra in the Old Hall manuscript, one at 15 mm associated mainly with the first layer and the other at 16 mm mainly with the second layer.

20 The date and origin of Trinity

For the Trinity carol roll, most available descriptions propose merely that it is from the first half of the fifteenth century. Only Roger Bowers (1982: 88) chanced his arm with an earlier date of *c.* 1420, later supported by Paulette Catherwood (1996: 10 and 57–71). Earlier writers (among them the great Bukofzer) were more cautious because they thought its void notation was something that happened only after about 1430.[1]

A recent article by Helen Deeming (2007: 31–4) notes that the dialect of the texts points to the border of south Norfolk and even suggests origin in the collegiate church of Mettingham, just two miles into Suffolk from Norfolk. Founded in 1394 in the grounds of Mettingham Castle, the church has considerable documentation from the years 1403–20 to attest polyphonic activity.[2] She also states that by 1535 the choir had fourteen choristers, 'making Mettingham one of the five largest choirs of boys' voices in the country'. There is no proof that Mettingham was the origin of the Trinity roll; and Deeming later slightly withdraws from her position, suggesting that it could have been the personal property of 'a highly trained individual musician with Norfolk roots'. But the uniform decoration of the initials and the regular alternation of red and blue for key letters throughout the document all point towards institutional origin. As mentioned earlier, the presence of liturgical material added much later on the dorse of the roll suggests the same. If this roll was not for Mettingham, it was certainly for somewhere similar and from the same part of England.

Jonathan King noted (1996: 80) that the entire text and music are uniformly written, apparently by a single hand; and he plausibly judged that the same copyist was responsible for both text and music, drawing attention in particular to the semiminim flags and the loops of the letters 'b', 'h, and 'l'. He added (1996:

---

1 Bukofzer 1950: 148. For the record, I should report that Sir Edmund Chambers, *English literature* (1945): 94, says that 'It can be dated fairly closely as of 1415–22, since it contains a carol on the battle of Agincourt, and Henry V is still alive'. But that argument would apply also to Selden, which is not possible.
2 Deeming cites C. R. Manning, 'Extracts from the ancient accounts of Mettingham College, Suffolk', *Archaeological journal* 6 (1849): 62–8. A fuller account appears in James M. W. Willoughby, *The libraries of collegiate churches* = Corpus of British medieval library catalogues 15 (London: The British Library, 2013): 356–67.

80–86) that the copyist routinely entered the text before adding the music: the text is evenly spaced, whereas the notes (for both voices) are added above the syllable they are to carry. This is a procedure quite different from the other carol manuscripts, and rare in general for polyphony after about 1420.

It has already been argued that the Agincourt carol was almost certainly composed immediately after Henry's triumphal return to London in November 1415, since it makes no mention of the far more glorious second French campaign of 1417–21. And that view is endorsed by the comment that the siege of Harfleur 'made a fray/ That France shall rue till Domesday'. But composition date is not necessarily copying date, particularly in a Suffolk collegiate, well away from the royal politics that seem to be portrayed in Egerton. The only useful information this gives is therefore that the Trinity roll was copied after November 1415.

The other important consideration is that Trinity actually omits a stanza of key importance in the Agincourt carol, surviving in Selden:

> Then went our king with all his host
> Through France, for all the Frenchë boast;
> He spared no dread of least ne most
> Till he came to Agincourt coast;
>   *Deo gracias.*

This stanza comes after stanza 2, explaining how Henry moved from Harfleur to Agincourt, and it seems absolutely central to the story. However, in Selden the stanza seems to have been added as an afterthought: it is actually placed at the end of the poem, but clearly indicated as belonging after stanza 2.[3] Since there is no other sign of hesitation or of delay in the copying, and the next carol starts immediately after the end of the text for the Agincourt carol, we must conclude that the Selden copyist transmitted what was in front of him and realised only at the last moment that the stanza written at the end came after the second stanza.

The one perfect-time carol in Trinity is the strange and partly monophonic *Abide, I hope it be the best* (*MC* 10: Example 10.1), which I proposed may contain traces of an earlier monophonic carol tradition: that is to say that there seems a good chance of this work being a lot earlier than its perfect time may suggest. I also drew attention to what seemed to be errors in the transmission of that carol in both Trinity and Selden.

There are other details worth pondering. In the case of *What tidings bringest thou?* (*MC* 11), the readings in Selden (*MC* 27: Example 5.1) reduce the rests between poetic lines so that the phrases come out as four beats long; and they introduce the 'chorus' insertion towards the end of the verse, an insertion that greatly improves the dramatic impact of the carol.

With *Nowell sing we now all and some* (*MC* 7) we have a similar case: the Selden version (*MC* 16) once again reduces the rests between poetic lines so that the phrases are all of four beats with the single exception of the five-beat second line of the verse.

---

3 As recognized already by Fuller Maitland ([1891]: 61).

Chapter 20: The date and origin of Trinity 151

Example 20.1⁴ Nowell sing we both all and some, MC 7/16

On the other hand, in this case the two versions have entirely different sets of verses, both on a nativity theme, and both citing Latin hymn phrases (though Trinity has its Latin quotes at the beginning of the verse and Selden has them as the last line of each verse). To outline the differences, Example 20.1 includes only the first stanza of each. It would be nice to be able to observe that the last line of the Trinity verse fits the music rather better than the last line in Selden. But plainly the main strategy in the Selden version was to retain the pattern of four-beat lines (just once interrupted), so the musical imperative took precedence; moreover, there have been over the preceding pages enough discrepancies between syllable-structure and musical structure to show that this was not always how the composers worked. All we can say is that in the earliest carols there is a much closer correspondence between poetic metre and musical design than in almost any other music of the early fifteenth century.

The reader will also note, incidentally, that this is again a case in which fauxbourdon fits beautifully to the burden but that the unison towards the end means that fauxbourdon fits the verse rather less well.

---

4 It needs to be stressed again that this edition does not adhere strictly to either source, though it is based on Selden.

Chapter 20: The date and origin of Trinity

But it seems to me significant that in both carols the Selden version has more literal four-beat phrases. It would be over-simple to suggest that somebody had seen the power of those four-beat phrases and adjusted the slightly ungainly Trinity carols; but there can be no question that the Selden versions have more energy, as though at the time when they were copied into the Trinity roll such simple four-beat phrases were considered inappropriate for sophisticated music.

There is yet one more case of almost-concordance between Trinity and Selden. The carol *Nowell, nowell: In Bethlem* (*MC* 3/38) has a three-voice second burden in Selden alone. But this three-voice burden is deeply problematic in that it cadences on C rather than the G of the burden and the verse; beyond that, its main outlines appear to be a 4th below those of the first burden. This is not the only such case, but it is at least a hint that something has become mixed up in transmission. Selden seems far less convincing than Trinity in this case.

Let us now look again at my assertion (chapter 5) that carols with two burdens are by and large later than those with just one. The broader picture of the Trinity carols is as follows:

MC 2   *Hail, Mary, full of grace* = *MC* 31 (Selden)
MC 3   *Nowell, nowell: In Bethlem*: appears with problematic extra 3vv burden II as *MC* 38 (Selden)
MC 4   *Alma Redemptoris mater*: unique
MC 5   *Now may we singen*: unique, with a substantial refrain at end of verse
MC 6   *Be merry, be merry*: unique, with a refrain 'be merry' at end of verse
MC 7   *Nowell sing we*: appears with reduced rests (resulting in regular four-beat phrases) and entirely different verse texts as *MC* 16 (Selden)
MC 8   *Deo gracias, Anglia* (2 burdens): appears in doubled note-values and with a different start to burden II (also with the missing third stanza) as *MC* 29 (Selden)
MC 9   *Now make we mirthë*: end of verse repeats end of burden (from bar 10)
MC 10   *Abide, I hope it be the best* (2 burdens and 2 verses): with variants as *MC* 42 (Selden)
MC 11   *What tidings bringest thou* (text by Audelay): with reduced rests (resulting in regular four-beat phrases) and inserted chorus as *MC* 27 (Selden)
MC 12   *Eya, martyr Stephane*: unique
MC 13   *Pray for us [to] the Prince of Peace*: text reset in *MC* 106 and *MC* 115 (both Ritson)
MC 14   *There is no rose*: unique

When the information is aligned in this way, it strikes the eye that Trinity has more than its fair share of anomalies. First, the two different settings of the entire verse for *MC* 10 (a unique case within the repertory, also present in its copy in Selden as *MC* 42), which already showed signs of growing out of an earlier monophonic tradition. Then the way *MC* 9 has a verse that segues into the second half of the burden (found in a few Ritson carols but not otherwise); and, related to that, the substantial refrain at the end of the verse in *MC* 5. All this hints at a form still in the course of evolution, with only the Agincourt carol showing the full-scale design.

On the other hand, all but one of the Trinity carols are in major prolation, all but five invite the addition of a fauxbourdon voice in the burden, and all but two are for the Christmas season. Besides, most have a dominant four-beat structure in the phrases, though *MC* 7 and *MC* 11 have extra rests that are eliminated in the Selden copies – and the unique *MC* 14 has the same extra rests in its burden.

If the Agincourt carol was composed, as I argued, at the very end of 1415, there seem grounds for thinking that most of the other carols here were older. But there is enough unity of musical style (apart from *MC* 10) to suggest a relatively short composition time for all of these pieces: and, to repeat, this is a style unique to the carol repertory. I am tempted to associate the initiation of the style with the beginning of the new reign of Henry V. That cannot be demonstrated, but it fits well with the mood and the style.

What can be said with rather more confidence is that there is nothing in the Trinity roll that needs to have been composed later than 1415. That cannot be used to argue that the manuscript was copied as early as 1415, but it is to say that the later dates proposed seem to me far too cautious.[5] And it is also to say that there is a good chance that it was copied around the time of Henry V's victorious return to London after Agincourt.

---

5 Deeming (2007: 31) seems to have reached the same conclusion.

21 The date and origin of Selden

The case of Selden is particularly puzzling, since E. W. B. Nicholson calculated that eleven music copyists were involved in the preparation of the mere thirty-one leaves; and he also found a large number of different text hands.[1] Over the years, the figures have been discussed and refined, but it is hard to resist the conclusion that this was an institutional manuscript.[2] Nicholson suggested that it could have been for a Franciscan house, perhaps even that at Canterbury in view of the southern dialect of the texts (Stainer 1901: i.xx–xxiii).[3]

By contrast with the apparent multiplicity of copyists, the decorative initials throughout the manuscript are done by a single hand, all with the initial itself in deep blue with the surrounding decoration in red filigree (fols. 13v and 14 seem to have a lighter colour of blue, but that almost certainly goes back to damage at some point in the manuscript's history). It looks as though their drawing was an uninterrupted process, done at a fairly late stage in the manuscript's compilation.[4] These decorations are by no means complicated: almost any reasonably competent copyist could have done them; but the uniformity of the letters, for example, speaks eloquently for their being done by a single hand in a single sitting. Even so, not all the music copying was done with similar expectations of what the decorator would do. All copyists appear to have routinely left out the first letter, but some left large spaces, some almost no space. (For most of the carols, a space was left in only one line, so the 'pseudo-score' arrangement was already wrong from the first notes of the piece.)

1　Stainer 1901: i.xx–xxi. Further refinements are offered in Padelford (1912: 81) and Greene (1935: 336).
2　The most radical revision is that of Paulette Catherwood (1996: 19), who proposed that it 'was copied primarily by one text scribe and two music scribes, with other scribes copying between one and three pieces each. . . . This evidence does not require a large scriptorium'. Whether one accepts her view or not, the point remains that the manuscript contains a large number of scripts and can only have come from a substantial collegiate.
3　Padelford (1912: 79) similarly concluded that the English texts betrayed a southern dialect.
4　Oddly, there is no decorated initial on fol. 26 for the carol *Ave Maria gracia Dei plena*. It is less odd that there is no decorated initial on fol. 30 (for *Eterne rex altissime*) or on fols. 32v–33 (for the two English songs), since these were plainly added to the manuscript rather later.

Chapter 21: The date and origin of Selden

The parchment is of mediocre quality, in which hair and flesh sides are easily distinguished. The enormous unrepaired hole in the middle of fol. 26 looks like evidence that this was not for a particularly grand establishment – even if several of its members were capable of copying complex music.[5]

Selden comprises four eight-leaf gatherings, with a stub after fol. 28. They are uniformly ruled with nine staves per page, vertical frame-rules to left and right, top line of top stave reaching to the edge of the page, and bottom frame-rule below the bottom stave. It was all pre-ruled, including the last page, which otherwise has only a few scribblings from much later. For all the carols but the first, the area for the text residuum is scraped clear of the staves that were previously ruled there. That seems to say that carols were not originally envisaged as part of the collection.

Schofield (1946) associated Selden with the Chapel Royal (by which he probably meant St George's, Windsor) on the basis of the Agincourt carol and 'a song (in Latin) assumed to be in honour of St George' (Greene 1954: 3). This is *Miles Christi*, which is in fact in honour of Thomas, Earl of Lancaster. He was beheaded as a traitor at Pontefract on 22 March 1322, information that Greene used (1954: 4) as evidence that Selden cannot have had anything to do with the Chapel Royal or St George's, Windsor. He pursued this topic no further, though Harrison (1958: 300) added that in 1330 Thomas's brother Henry founded in his memory St Mary Newarke hospital and college at Leicester.[6] That was part of a campaign

> to have him canonized as the martyr of Pontefract. The canonization did not take place, but the devotion continued, and this antiphon is part of a rhymed office in honour of 'Saint' Thomas. Newarke College is a likely place for such an antiphon to have been sung in the fifteenth century, and it is conceivable that the manuscript originated there.[7]

---

5 A similar hole in the parchment is on fol. 8, though it is to the edge and does not affect the writing area.
6 Robbins (1961: 5) and Strohm (1993: 382) both supported this idea.
7 Harrison refers here to A. Hamilton Thompson's magnificent *The history of the hospital and the new college of the annunciation of St Mary in the Newarke, Leicester* (Leicester: E. Backus, 1937), and to the text in Thomas Wright, *The political songs of England* (London: Camden Society, 1839): 268–72. Fuller references in Greene 1954: 3n9, including reference to the text in Analecta Hymnica 28: 321 (from Cologne 28: fol. 146) and further information in Analecta Hymnica 13: 6–8. This follows the musical form of the antiphon in the office for Thomas of Lancaster in British Library, Royal MS 12 C 12, printed in Christopher Page, 'The rhymed office for St Thomas of Lancaster' (1984). The music is published in Hughes 1967: no. 6 (simply citing Greene as evidence that the antiphon is in honour of Thomas of Lancaster). Harrison added (1958: 300n4) that there may be a special significance in the text of the carol *Alleluia: A newë work is come on hand* (*MC* 30); but that seems unlikely both because the hospital was begun at least a hundred years before the probable date of the carol and because the remainder of the text is pure nativity narrative.

156 *Chapter 21: The date and origin of Selden*

Here is the text:[8]

Miles Christi gloriose, laus, spes, tutor Anglie,	8p + 7pp
Fac discordes graciose reduci[9] concordie,	8p + 7pp
Ne sternatur plebs clamose dire mortis vulnere.	8p + 7pp

This is not a carol but an antiphon setting; and its music, like most of the non-carol music in Selden, is more elaborate than that of the carols. Even so, this is far the most complicated piece in Selden, with florid writing in all three voices and such irregular phrasing that Andrew Hughes was compelled to insert two 7/8 bars into his edition.

What Harrison seems not to have known is that St Mary Newarke was a major preoccupation of Henry V during the first years of his reign, since his mother had been buried there (when he was eight): already on 8 November 1414 he set up orders to have the incomplete church finished by the next Lady Day (25 March 1415) and had paid £43 for a portrait of her to be placed on her grave.[10] To associate the manuscript with this house on the basis of only a single composition would be dangerous, particularly since there is no apparent significance in the place of this composition within the manuscript; but the text was otherwise extremely rare. And St Mary Newarke – in fact the largest collegiate in medieval England – fits the description that emerges from study of the Selden manuscript.[11]

Greene, however, moved in a different direction. On fol. 23, containing *Hail, Mary, full of grace*, a much later looking hand (not otherwise known) has scribbled a further four-line stanza that has a different rhyme-scheme but is presumably intended for the same carol, since the last line 'When the angel said Ave' matches the last line of the first stanza, 'While the angel said Ave'. Nearby on the same page is a scribbled cockerel, possibly in the same hand, which Greene says is the symbol of John Alcock, Bishop of Rochester (1472), Worcester (1476) and Ely (1486–1500). Greene added (1962: 177; 1977: 314): 'It could hardly indicate anyone else. The carelessly written stanza has the northern spelling expected of Alcock, a native of Beverley and educated there'. The twenty-two words concerned hardly seem enough for such a judgement; and they stand very weakly as

---

8 Full text for discantus and contra on fols. 8v–9; tenor has only text incipit of line 5.
9 Hughes (1967: 10) reads 'reducas' (without further comment); Analecta hymnica 28:321, reads 'reduci'.
10 Wylie 1914–29: i. 232–3.
11 Though founded in 1330 for just a warden and four chaplains, it was expanded in 1353, with papal permission, to house a dean, twelve canons, thirteen vicars, six choristers, three other clerks and a verger. The college's endowments increased spectacularly with the accession of Henry V's grandfather, John of Gaunt, as Duke of Lancaster (1362–99). All this information from Hamilton Thompson, *op. cit.*, is neatly summarized in *A history of the county of Leicestershire* 2 (London: Victoria County History, 1954): 48–51. A more recent account appears in James M. W. Willoughby, *The libraries of collegiate churches* = Corpus of British medieval library catalogues 15 (London: The British Library, 2013): 272–9.

the first and main piece of evidence that Greene offers for his view that the manuscript 'must be from Worcester'. What is certain is that the manuscript was basically assembled during Alcock's childhood, *c.* 1440, though the new text and the cockerel could have been added up to a century later. It could be noted in passing that the cockerels in Alcock's coat of arms (in All Saints, North Street, in York, for example or above the porch of Jesus College, Cambridge) are of the head alone, not the entire body. The case for associating Selden with Bishop Alcock (let alone with Worcester) seems non-existent.

As concerns the dating of Selden we have a serious problem. It includes what seem to be some of the very earliest carols. But towards the end there is a setting of *Tota pulchra es* which appears in the manuscript ModB[12] (*c.* 1450) with an ascription to 'Polumier'; the music also appears, anonymously, in the Trento manuscript 90 of about the same date. The best evidence we have of the composer John Plummer is that he was in the Chapel Royal by 1438, living until at least 1484; and the music of his *Tota pulchra es* certainly seems compatible with a date of around 1440. This is obviously much later than the majority of the music in Selden.

One way out of this may be to identify 'Polumier' with John Pyamour, clerk in the Chapel Royal between 1416 and 1420, composer of *Quam pulchra es*, also in ModB (ascribed 'Piamor'), the opening of which is printed in Bukofzer 1952: 39. Andrew Wathey states that this Pyamour died in March 1426.[13] That would fit far better with what we otherwise know of Selden.

But a glance at the music of *Tota pulchra es* confirms that a date of around 1440 is logical. Example 21.1 gives the opening of the *secunda pars*. The declamation in all three voices for 'Flores apparuerunt', the imitative patterns for 'odorem' and the expansion to a melisma for 'vox turturis' all endorse that. Moreover, the equal style of the three voices is a feature of all other music credited to Plummer. It is hard to deny that the style of this piece is that of Plummer and that its date is around 1440.[14] Reinhard Strohm seems to have had a similar view. After describing some of the other music in Selden, he adds: 'Almost incompatible with these idioms is John Plummer's *Tota pulchra es* . . . The form and growth of the piece relies entirely on the word-setting with its increasingly dramatic points of imitation'.[15]

---

12 Modena, Biblioteca Estense, alfa X. 1. 11.
13 Wathey 1986: 5.
14 Compare the other pieces presented in *Four motets by John Plummer*, ed. Brian Trowell (Banbury: Plainsong & Mediaeval Music Society, 1968).
15 Strohm 1993: 382–3. I would, incidentally, be inclined to propose a similar date of *c.* 1440 for the copying of the two pieces after *Tota pulchra es*, namely the songs *Tappster, dryngker* and *Welcome be ye when ye goo*, both in C mensuration, like *Tota pulchra es*. The songs are published in Fallows 2014: nos. 83–4.

158 Chapter 21: The date and origin of Selden

Example 21.1[16] 2nda pars of *Tota pulchra es* (Plummer)

Nicholson found that the music hand here is otherwise unknown, but that the text hand is his D*, the writer found throughout the manuscript; in addition, the decorated initial matches all the others in Selden. The only rational conclusion from this is that the entire manuscript was copied perhaps in the years 1435–40,

---

16 In Selden, the tenor from the middle of the second system (after the word 'odorem') to the end is entirely missing, for reasons that are unclear; it has been restored from the concordance in ModB.

even though much of its repertory was up to twenty years old at the time of copying. After all, to propose that the manuscript itself was copied over a period of twenty years would be totally unrealistic: this is absolutely not comparable to Ritson, with its visibly separate copying layers. Despite eleven music copyists, the entire project looks relatively compact. So for once I find myself agreeing with most earlier writers about its date.[17]

On the other hand, with Trinity dated rather earlier than previously, and with so many Egerton carols apparently dating from 1420 or earlier, it does strike the eye that that carol repertory of Selden is nearly all substantially earlier than 1440. If we add to the twenty-eight formal carols the six more that I previously (chapter 2) mentioned as being in the same style though not precisely the same form, we get an intriguing pattern. Out of the thirty-four pieces, there are just ten with a double burden. We can divide them up as follows:

1 Works that are partly monophonic, hinting at an earlier style, as outlined in chapter 10

Alma Redemptoris mater (*MC* 23)
Nowell, nowell: Out of your sleep (*MC* 25)
Alleluia: A newë work (*MC* 30)
Ave Maria: Hail blessëd flower (*MC* 36)
Abide, I hope it be the best (*MC* 42 = *MC* 10)
Gaude terra (Hughes 1967: no. 12)

2 Carols also in Trinity

Abide, I hope it be the best (*MC* 42 = *MC* 10)
Deo gracias, Anglia (*MC* 29 = *MC* 8)
Nowell, nowell: In Bethlem (*MC* 38 = *MC* 3, with only one burden)

3 Other carols

David ex progenie (*MC* 34 = *MC* 46) entirely in Latin
Laus, honor, virtus, gloria (*MC* 39)
Veni, Redemptor gencium (*MC* 41)

In addition, a large majority of these carols are in major prolation. Carols in perfect time are just eleven in number, again divided into two categories:

1 Carols just mentioned as having two burdens

Alma Redemptoris mater (*MC* 23), partly monophonic
Deo gracias, Anglia (*MC* 29; in major prolation as *MC* 8)
Alleluia: A newë werk (*MC* 30), partly monophonic

---

17 Dom Anselm Hughes, *Medieval polyphony in the Bodleian Library* (Oxford: The Bodleian Library, 1951): 48, proposed '1425–40'; Bukofzer (1950: 114) 'about 1450'; Nicholson, in Stainer (1901: i.xxii), cites Sir E. Maunde Thompson, who 'would not admit an earlier date than 1450–55'.

Chapter 21: The date and origin of Selden

> *David ex progenie* (*MC* 34 = *MC* 46), entirely in Latin
> *Ave Maria: Hail, blessëd flower* (*MC* 36), partly monophonic
> *Laus, honor, virtus, gloria* (*MC* 39)
> *Veni, Redemptor gencium* (*MC* 41)
> *Abide, I hope it be the best* (*MC* 42 = *MC* 10), partly monophonic

2   Carols not in the preceding list

> *Of a rose sing we* (*MC* 19)
> *Novus sol de virgine* (*MC* 35 = *MC* 48)
> *Y-blessed be that Lord* (*MC* 40)

Beyond these, there is the intriguing case of *Nowell, nowell: Out of your sleep*, which is in 9/8 and in some other ways resembles the earliest of all polyphonic carols, *Lullay, lullow* (*MC* 1), surviving only in British Library, Add. MS 5666. On balance, I read all this as indicating that most of the carols and carol-like pieces in Selden are likely to have been composed before 1425, whatever the date when the manuscript was copied.

22 Chronology

English and Latin

When I first had revisionist thoughts about the history of the carol, over thirty years ago, my conclusion was that the new poetic form and the new musical style arose out of the wave of nationalist enthusiasm that grew from the victory at Agincourt. What I had seen was that the early history of the carol was almost non-existent before about 1415 (as outlined in chapter 9). What I had not seen was that the double-burden form of the Agincourt carol hints that it was itself not from the earliest surviving layer of carol music. What I had also not seen was that a group of carols can be associated with Henry V's French campaigns and that their style suggested that the 'third layer' of the carol repertory seems to have been established by about 1420.

The use of English in most of the carol texts is also an important marker. Henry V began writing all his official communications in English from the beginning of his second French campaign in August 1417;[1] and his fund-raising efforts in the summer of 1416 included five speeches in English to the people of London.[2] These were just mileposts along the route from the use of French for all official purposes at the Norman conquest in 1066 to the eventual adoption of English even in the law courts in 1731;[3] and major markers along that way had been set

---

1 Malcolm Richardson, 'Henry V, the English chancery, and chancery English', *Speculum* 55 (1980): 726–50, at p. 727.
2 John H. Fisher, 'A language policy for Lancastrian England', *PMLA* 107 (1992): 1168–80, at p. 1171, citing the publication of those proclamations in H.T. Riley, *Memorials of London and London life* (London: Longman, 1868). More recently, qualifications of these conclusions have been proposed, particularly in Michael Benskin, 'Chancery standard', in *New perspectives on English historical linguistics* 2: *Lexis and transmission*, ed. Christian Kay, *et al.* (Amsterdam: John Benjamins Publishing Company, 2004): 1–40, and Gwilym Dodd, 'The rise of English, the decline of French: supplications to the English crown, c. 1420–1450', *Speculum* 86 (2011): 117–50. On the other hand, it seems to me that the evidence of the carols tends to support Fisher's view, as expressed in Malcolm Vale, *Henry V: the conscience of a king* (New Haven and London: Yale University Press, 2016): 122: 'There may not have been any discernible "language policy", but the usages established under Henry V were, in large part, the product of deliberate choice'.
3 The minutes of parliament were normally in French until 1439.

by the poetry of Chaucer and Langland in the late fourteenth century. But from the earliest years of his reign negotiations with the French repeatedly began with arguments about language: Henry V's diplomats refused to negotiate in French and claimed that only Latin was acceptable;[4] in his second French campaign Henry himself even claimed that his envoys could not understand French fully.[5]

At around the same time, at the Council of Constance, there was intensive discussion of nations: in earlier church councils the English were counted as part of the German 'nation', but in March 1417 Thomas Polton, then Dean of York but more importantly Henry V's proctor at the papal curia, argued passionately and successfully for the English to have voting rights as a nation alongside the German, the French, the Italian, and the Spanish nations.[6]

On a purely diplomatic front, it is worth seeing three separate approaches to the French in Henry V's reign: first, defiant opposition, asserting that the French were illegal, that the French throne belonged rightly to Henry V and later that the victory at Agincourt was evidence that God supported the English position; then came a change, particularly in the last months of 1419, when the murder of the Duke of Burgundy suddenly made it almost inevitable that the French king would appoint Henry V his regent and successor, as he eventually did at the Treaty of Troyes in May 1420; after that came the hardest and most delicate stage of all, the need to reassure the English that their king remained independently king of England and that English independence would not be compromised in any way by Henry's roles as regent and heir to the French throne. As outlined earlier, the first phase entailed the increased use of the English language as a political tool, accompanied by open aggression towards the French, the second phase entailed increasing use of the Latin language so as not to exclude the French allies from any negotiation or celebration, and the third phrase entailed a reassertion of Englishness in England.

In that context it may seem relevant that there is very little Latin in the Trinity carol roll: a few hymn-openings in *Alma Redemptoris mater* (*MC* 4), the same in *Nowell sing we* (*MC* 7) and *There is no rose* (*MC* 14), the entire burden in *Deo gracias, Anglia* (*MC* 8), rather more lines in *Eya, martyr Stephane* (*MC* 12), and just the line 'Amice Christi, Johannes' in *Pray for us* (*MC* 13). These are mostly lines that would be easily comprehensible to any moderately educated churchgoer.

---

4 Certainly as early as September 1413, see Wylie 1914–29: i.153; again in February 1414, Wylie 1914–219: i.156.

5 This was in a letter to the pope's cardinal-legate, Giordano Orsini, quoted in Vale, *op. cit.*: 116–19, citing Rymer *Foedera* ix.655–6, dated November–December 1418: 'Gallicum non intelligent, sed nec penitus loqui suavit'. Plainly it was a lie, but it was important to Henry.

6 It could be added that the 'English' nation at Constance included not only Scotland and Ireland but the kingdom of Araby, the kingdoms of the Medes and Persians, the two Indias, the kingdoms of Ethiopia, Egypt and Nineveh and much else, see *Chronik des Konstanzer Konzils 1414–1418 von Ulrich Richental*, ed. Thomas Martin Buck = Konstanzer Geschichts- und Rechtsquellen 41 (Ostfildern: Jan Thorbecke Verlag, 2010): 37 – with the added qualification that only England and Scotland were strictly Christian countries but that the others had Christian residents who merited representation at the council.

More or less the same could be said of the twenty-eight carols in Selden. Four are entirely in Latin, though they are in very simple Latin and one of them (*Ecce, quod Natura, MC* 37) is an internationally known poem; just *David ex progenie* (*MC* 34) has elaborate and complicated Latin throughout. Some have a few Latin tags, so few that it is not of central importance whether they are understood (*Nowell sing we, MC* 16; *Of a rose sing we, MC* 19), others have just a single line of well-known Latin (*Sing we to this merry company, MC* 21; *Alma Redemptoris mater, MC* 23; *Y-blessed be that Lord, MC* 40; *Veni, Redemptor gencium, MC* 41), and one has a few well-known hymn openings (*Alleluia: Now well may we mirthës make, MC* 20). Beyond these there is just one with enough Latin to confuse the ignorant: *Laus, honor, virtus, gloria* (*MC* 39).

So it is only with Egerton and Ritson that we have enough carols entirely in Latin, often fairly complicated, that the carols are plainly directed at a more sophisticated audience – presumably international in the case of the nineteen Egerton carols and presumably Lacy's Exeter Cathedral in the case of the six in Ritson.

Redating Old Hall

Meanwhile, other English music of the time has been dated earlier than hitherto. Ever since 1976, when Roger Bowers (1975–6) revealed that in 1418 Leonel Power was in the household of Thomas, Duke of Clarence, it has been generally believed that the first layer of the Old Hall manuscript (British Library, Add. MS 57950) – with twenty-two pieces credited to Leonel – was for Clarence's household and was therefore left unfinished at the time of his death in 1421. So the various works in the second layer of the manuscript were likely to be from after that date and therefore almost inevitably from the reign of Henry VI.[7] More recent research and reconsideration has led to an agreement that the second layer, including works by Burrell, Cooke, Damett and Sturgeon, needs to have been copied at a time when these four were all together in the Chapel Royal, namely 1416–19, and that the likelihood is that the first layer was completed by about 1415 at the very latest.[8]

Cutting a long and complicated story short, this revised (or rather, restored) dating has four consequences. First, that Dunstable's four-voice motet *Veni sancte*

---

7 One view that perhaps helped fuel the later dating of the main layer of Old Hall was the suggestion that Byttering's motet *En Katerine solennia* (Old Hall, no. 145) could be for the wedding of Henry V and Catherine de Valois in 1420. There is absolutely nothing in the text to encourage such a suggestion; and St Catherine was of course widely worshipped, as noted in Bent 1967–8: 20.

8 Dates first argued in Bent 1968 and Bent 1967–8 but abandoned in several of her later publications, to be reinstated in her paper delivered at the Medieval and Renaissance Music Conference in Prague, July 2017. So far as I can tell, the case for restoring her original dates was first made in David Fallows and Alexandra Buckle, 'Power, Leonel', in *Die Musik in Geschichte und Gegenwart . . . zweite, neubearbeitete Ausgabe*, ed. Ludwig Finscher, *Personenteil* 13 (Kassel, etc.: Bärenreiter and Stuttgart, etc.: J. B. Metzler, 2005): cols. 862–9, at col. 866. I am grateful to Margaret Bent for sharing drafts of her report on returning to her original dates.

Spiritus/ Veni creator, which appears in the second layer of Old Hall, is likely to date from before 1419.[9] Second, that his structurally almost identical motet *Preco preheminencie/ Precursor premittitur/ Inter natos mulierum* must be the work that Henry V included among the music to be sung regularly by his Chapel Royal in response to Bedford's victory at the battle of the Seine in 1416, as described in the *Gesta Henrici Quinti* (finished before 1417) and particularly in Thomas of Elmham's *Liber metricus*:[10] its unusual title surely makes the case almost impregnably and the pairing of the two motets is confirmed not only by their identical length but also by their appearance together in the manuscript Trento 92 (fols. 182v–184 and 184v–186); and in the circumstances it seems more or less inevitable that *Veni/ Veni* is meant by the entry 'Veni sancte Spiritus' in Henry V's 1416 list of music, just mentioned.

Third, there is the famous pair of motets to St George in the second layer of the Old Hall manuscript, Thomas Damett's *Salvatoris mater pia/ O Georgi/ Benedictus Marie filius qui ve-* (no. 111) and John Cooke's *Alma proles/ Christi miles inclite/ Ab inimicis nostris defende nos Christe* (no. 112). Since Cooke left the Chapel Royal in the summer of 1419 (a year before the Treaty of Troyes), it should be no surprise that the tenor of his motet refers to the nation's enemies with such force (and the motetus explicitly prays for victory). Without wishing to propose too precise a date, it seems plausible to suggest that Cooke's motet was composed before either Henry's first French campaign in 1415 or his second in 1417.

The motetus of Damett's work includes the lines:

Sis Henrici nostri regis	Be present at the deliberations
Presens ad consilium.	of Henry our king.

Since Henry VI (b. 1421) took absolutely no part in government, least of all deliberations, until about 1434, and not officially until he was declared of age in 1437, those lines almost certainly refer to Henry V.

Also part of this group, though not mentioning St George, is Sturgeon's *Salve mater Domini/ Salve templum gratie/ -it in nomine Domini* (no. 113).[11] All now seem likely to have been part of the propaganda designed to support Henry V's

---

9 That would, incidentally, rule out the possibility that it was composed for 26 May 1420, between the Treaty of Troyes and the wedding of Henry V and Catherine de Valois, as proposed on the basis of elaborate numerical calculations in Klaus Hortschansky, 'John Dunstables Motette "Veni Sancte Spiritus – Veni Creator": Zur Frage der Konstruktionsprinzipien' (1986): 24–6.

10 *Gesta Henrici Quinti: the deeds of Henry the Fifth*, translated and ed. Frank Taylor and John S. Roskell (Oxford: At the Clarendon Press, 1975): 152–3; *Elmhami liber metricus de Henrici quinto*, ed. in Charles Augustus Cole, *Memorials of Henry the fifth, king of England* (London: Longman, etc, 1858): 140–1. Bent 1981: 8–9, and Nosow 2012: 19–23.

11 The tenor is a continuation of the tenor used in Damett's *Salvatoris mater pia*, except the letter 'n' occurs in neither motet: whether it was lost by mistake or whether there is a deeper significance here, we cannot say. That Cooke's *Alma proles* appears between them in Old Hall only adds to the puzzlement. What is decidedly odd, though, is that Damett puts the 8th mode melody (*Liber usualis*: 27) down a step to start on F, whereas Sturgeon has it at the normal pitch, starting on G.

two French campaigns.[12] And it follows almost inevitably from this that the main body of the carols in the three earliest manuscripts could all date from the reign of Henry V and in any case from before 1430.

We may never know why the copying of the first layer of Old Hall was curtailed; but it was probably by 1415. The large variety of different styles encompassed by the twenty-two works of Leonel Power in that first layer could well spread across twenty years. Since Dunstable is represented in Old Hall only by the motet *Veni sancte Spiritus/ Veni creator* in the second layer (and apparently composed in 1416), it seems likely that Leonel Power was between ten and twenty years older than Dunstable and that his composing career stretches back to around 1395.

That in its turn means that Leonel may well have laid the foundations for the style and the international fame that made Dunstable the most successful English composer of the middle ages. But it also means that Dunstable can be associated with Henry V's royal court far more closely than the objective documents permit.

To recall: there is absolutely no documentation to associate Dunstable with Henry V; but from the astronomy manuscript in St John's College, Cambridge (MS F. 25, fol. 74), we have the information that he was a musician to Henry's brother John, Duke of Bedford;[13] during the years 1427–36 we have payments to him from the dowager Queen Joan (stepmother of Henry V);[14] and after her death in 1437 we have a document associating him with Henry's youngest brother Humfrey, Duke of Gloucester (d. 1447).[15] That is to say that he was associated with Henry's very closest relatives. If the motets *Veni/ Veni* and *Preco preheminencie* are indeed for Henry's foundations of 1416 we have plenty of grounds for thinking he was close to the centre of the court's musical activity.[16] We can also estimate that Dunstable was closer to Henry V's age than the rather older Leonel Power.

---

12 On this group of motets, see Bukofzer 1950: 67–70, Bent 1967–8: 24–6, Bent 1968: 296–310 and Nosow 2012: 7–32.
13 Wathey 1986: 4–6.
14 Stell and Wathey 1981.
15 Wathey 1986: *passim*.
16 Brian Trowell (1960: 54–5), supports the suggestion of Jeremy Noble (1954: 187) that Dunstable's mass *Da gaudiorum premia* was suitable only for a treaty ending a war and that this too may have been for the Treaty of Troyes. At the time only the Credo and Sanctus were known; since then, portions of the Kyrie and Gloria have emerged, as reported in *John Dunstable: complete works*, ed. Manfred F. Bukofzer, revised by Margaret Bent, Ian Bent and Brian Trowell = Musica Britannica 8 (London: Stainer and Bell, 1970): 208–9, where Trowell added that the wedding of Henry V and Catherine de Valois was on Trinity Sunday and that, since the tenor was a Trinity respond, this would be an even more appropriate occasion for the mass. The chant is from the verse of the respond *Gloria patri geniteque*, presented in Bukofzer, *op. cit.*: 158. Its text reads: 'Da gaudiorum premia/ da gratiarum munera/ dissolve litis vincula/ astringe pacis federa'. The spirit of that text plainly resembles the spirit of the carols I have associated with those years. Apparently unaware of Noble's suggestion, Harrison (1958: 244) suggested (without any arguments) that the same mass was in fact composed for the coronation of Henry VI as king of France in Notre Dame de Paris on 16 December 1431, as endorsed in Craig Wright, *Music and ceremony at Notre Dame of Paris 500–1550* (Cambridge: Cambridge University Press, 1989): 206–17, especially pp. 215–16. Bent (1981: 8) preferred the earlier date. Strohm (1993: 228–9) hinted at his preference for the later. I would note that 1420 seems far too early a date for the imitative style of the mass; but there

Redating the carols

Since the prime strategy of this entire book has been to redate the carols and the carol manuscripts, there is no need here for more than a summary: that at least seven of the carols can be dated with some confidence to events within the reign of Henry V; that the Ritson carols must be substantially earlier than suggested in any of the available literature, perhaps as early as the 1430s; that there is a good case for dating all the non-Ritson carol polyphony to before 1430; and that there would be something of a case for dating most of that carol polyphony to the reign of Henry V (1413–22).

Most important, though, is that the carols that seem to carry unwritten fauxbourdon voices are all in major prolation, which in itself makes it seem certain that they predate 1430; but, seeing them alongside the Agincourt carol, apparently from late in 1415, leaves us with a high probability that most of these major-prolation carols are also from the second decade of the century, thus perhaps ten years earlier than the earliest continental pieces that actually have the word 'fauxbourdon' attached to them.

---

is absolutely no perceptible basis for associating the mass with the 1431 coronation. I would be inclined to conclude that the apparent perfect mix of the mass tenor to both the Treaty of Troyes and the Trinity Sunday wedding of 1420 is just one of those tantalizing coincidences that are so often part of musical history as we have it.

23 The later carols

With the time limits of the earlier carol repertory reduced to the years 1410–40, there is a far greater chronological gap than previously thought between these carols and those in the next musical collection, the Fayrfax book, British Library, Add. MS 5465, almost certainly copied in a short space of time early in 1502.[1] This manuscript contains a truly glorious repertory of secular songs, the secular equivalent of the large Marian works that survive in the Eton Choirbook. Of the fifty-one pieces originally copied into the manuscript (a few leaves are missing, so two of the pieces are entirely lost and several others are now incomplete), at least fifteen are in carol form.[2] But there are important differences here from the earlier repertory. First, the carols are stylistically indistinguishable from the other pieces in Fayrfax: that is to say that the highly distinctive style of the earlier carols is no longer present. Second, the texts of the Fayrfax carols do not appear in any of the known carol poetry manuscripts. Third, the texts do not ever imply a gathering, a community: they are just songs, breathtakingly beautiful ones in many cases, but still just songs that happen to have texts in carol form. Fourth, there is a high proportion of carols on the Passion of Christ, a theme never found in the earlier carols with polyphony. And the curiosity of double burdens is nowhere to be found here. At the same time, the Fayrfax book carols, like all the other music in Fayrfax, are entirely unlike anything that the continental composers wrote – in both form and musical techniques.

Quite how fifteenth-century music in England evolved from the Ritson carols of the 1430s or 1440s to the music of the Fayrfax book, copied sixty years

---

1 Roger Bowers 1995a: 194. It was definitely copied before prince Arthur's unexpected death on 2 April 1502, since it contains three songs in his honour (Stevens 1975: nos. 28, 47 and 64) and, as Bowers noted, 'it is inconceivable that the texts delighting in the life of Arthur as Prince of Wales and commending to God his safekeeping can have been copied into a formal manuscript after his untimely decease'. This is at its most explicit in *From stormy wyndis and grevous wethir/ Good Lord, preserve the estrige fether* by Edmund Turges, written specifically for celebrations associated with the wedding of prince Arthur and Catherine of Aragon in November 1501 (including the lines 'This eyre of Brytayne/ Of Castell and Spayne'), in which case the copying of the Fayrfax book can plausibly be located within a four-month window between the wedding and Arthur's death.
2 All the music is published in Stevens 1975; the texts are published in their original orthography in Stevens 1961; they were first edited in Bernhard Fehr 1901a.

later, it seems impossible to guess. There are far too few surviving sources, and it would be rash to pretend to fill the gaps. Only the similar style of the much larger anthems in the Eton Choirbook provides evidence that the Fayrfax book style was current in England by the last thirty years of the century. What is interesting, though, is the way that style seems to have remained in favour. The earliest music book printed in England, the *Book of XX songes*, dated 1530, includes a similar mix of works. Of its twenty pieces, nine are in carol form, and their style is astonishingly close to that of the Fayrfax book carols, in so far as one can tell from the bassus partbook, which is all that survives today.

Other examples of the style also survive, particularly two songs in the 'Henry VIII book' (British Library, Add. MS 31922, perhaps from around 1513),[3] Pygott's *Quid petis of fili?* (no. 105) and the anonymous *Hey trolly lolly lo* (no. 109). Elsewhere in the Henry VIII book, however, there is an entirely different style of carol, with a simple homophonic burden but apparently no music at all for the verses (nos. 31, 33, 35, 41 and 50).

From then onwards, the form continues to crop up occasionally, but again without any distinctive musical style. John Milsom has identified a number of pieces from the mid-sixteenth century in carol form, most of them surviving only as incomplete fragments:[4] the most impressive of these is Robert Johnson's *Benedicam domino*.[5] Perhaps the last, and in many ways the most unforgettable of all, is William Byrd's consort-song *Lullaby, my sweet little baby*.[6]

---

3 Modern edition in John Stevens, *Music at the court of Henry VIII* = Musica Britannica 18 (London: Stainer & Bell for the Royal Musical Association, 1962); a full-colour facsimile edition with extended commentary and proposed dating is in *The Henry VIII book*, ed. David Fallows = DIAMM facsimiles 4 (Oxford: DIAMM facsimiles, 2014).

4 Milsom 1980–81: 36–8. Among the pieces he mentions, there is a single case of an apparent carol that has a double burden: John Sheppard's *Of all strange news*, of which only two of the original six voice parts survive.

5 Modern edition in *The Mulliner book*, ed. John Caldwell = Musica Britannica 1 (London: Stainer and Bell, 2011): 126–9.

6 *Madrigals, songs and canons*, ed. Philip Brett = The Byrd Edition 16 (London: Stainer and Bell, 1976): 138–43; also, in its fully vocal version, *Psalmes, sonets and songs (1588)*, ed. Jeremy Smith = The Byrd Edition 12 (London: Stainer and Bell, 2004): 142–9. It might be added that two pieces appear in Byrd's *Songs of sundrie natures* (London: Thomas East, 1589) with the heading 'A carowle for Christmas day', namely *From virgin's womb* and *An earthly tree*. In both cases, the famous printing problems of Byrd's book leave it unclear as to whether the 'chorus' functions as a burden in the fifteenth-century sense, that is, sung before the first verse, or whether it is simply a coda to each verse. Milsom (1980–81: 38) suggests that they are 'presumably' the former, though without offering any reason; *Songs of sundrie natures (1589)*, ed. David Mateer = The Byrd Edition 13 (London: Stainer and Bell, 2004), prints the chorus sections before the verses, noting (p. xxii) that in the case of *From virgin's womb*, the text was printed in Richard Edwards, *The paradise of daynty devices* (London: Henry Disle, 1576 and many later editions), with an ascription to Francis Kinwelmersh (1538–c. 1580): here the burden 'Rejoice, rejoice with heart and voice' does indeed appear above the main text. Even so, it seems to me that the musical layout of both pieces means that the four-voice chorus section inevitably follows the solo verses, the chorus beginning with a tripla section and then reaching a climax with fast runs in both cases; and I would suggest that the word 'carowle' in these pieces is not used in the sense defined by Greene: it simply means, as in so many other places, 'a song for Christmas'.

24 Binchois, Dufay and the *contenance angloise*

If it is agreed that the polyphonic carol, like its poetic form, appeared for the first time in any quantity in the Trinity roll, soon after 1415, that may contain the answer to one of the oldest questions in the historiography of fifteenth-century music.

Already in 1982 I stated that the only possible occasion for the famous influence of English music on Dufay and Binchois was the Council of Constance, 1414–18.[1] My main consideration at the time was that there was no evidence of a sudden change of style in the music of those two composers, so the influence must have been when they were young. What I did not say was that the earliest known works of both composers are remarkable for their simplicity and direct communication, for the way they seem to have rejected the complexities that so fascinated the previous generation. What I also did not say was what it was about the English music that so profoundly influenced them. I now believe that it was quite specifically the style of the earliest polyphonic carols. What I had not seen back then was either how many of the earliest carols are plainly from the second decade of the century or how many of them can be connected with the court culture of Henry V.

Two famous documents of the fifteenth century witness this influence. Neither document is quite specific enough for our purposes. The composer and theorist Johannes Tinctoris, wrote in 1472 about[2]

> a new art, if I may so call it, whose fount and origin is held to be among the English, of whom Dunstable stood forth as chief. Contemporary with him in France were Dufay and Binchois.

Over thirty years earlier, in 1441–2, the French author Martin Le Franc had written about the perfection of modern music in his long poem *Le champion des*

---

1 Fallows, *Dufay* (1982): 18–19.
2 In the prologue to his *Proportionale musices*, many times printed and translated. The Latin reads: 'ut ita dicam, nove artis fons et origo apud Anglicos quorum caput Dunstaple exstitit fuisse perhibetur. Et huic contemporanei fuerunt in Gallia Dufay et Binchois'.

170 *Chapter 24: Binchois, Dufay and the* contenance angloise

dames: in some ways he is far more specific, in others not.[3] First of all he tells us of the fame in Paris of Tapissier, Carmen and Cesaris, all composers of known surviving music much in the style we know from music around 1400, with hints of *ars subtilior* complexity and hints of what Guillaume de Machaut had been doing forty years earlier.[4] Then, says Martin Le Franc, came Dufay and Binchois, who completely eclipsed the work of those earlier composers. And he explains why: For they have adopted a new technique of making 'frisque concordance' (sprightly consonance), . . . and they have taken the English countenance and followed Dunstable, whereby a marvellous charm makes their music both cheerful and notable.

Readers will know that there is an enormous literature about those few lines of poetry. They will also know that there is to this day no plausible explanation of the words Martin Le Franc uses in the fourth line of that stanza to define their new style, 'en fainte, en pause et en muance'.[5] There is no evidence that Martin Le Franc had any professional knowledge of music though he certainly knew Dufay at the court of Savoy in the 1430s and may have taken these ideas from him. They will also know that in the 1430s and 1440s there is an enormous quantity of English music in continental sacred music manuscripts (the two choirbooks in Bologna and the seven in Trento), twice in specifically English collections within the manuscripts (Aosta and Modena, alfa X. 1. 11), and often with the mere title 'Anglicanus' as an indication that the nationality of the composer was a matter of prime importance. Perhaps fewer know that the continental song repertory of the 1440s and 1450s was flooded with works by English composers, most particularly John Bedyngham, five of whose songs from those years survive in far more copies than anything by Dufay or Binchois, for example.[6] Major English influence on the continental composers in the first half of the fifteenth century is undeniable.

---

3 Martin Le Franc, *Le champion des dames*, ed. Robert Deschaux, 5 vols. (Paris: Honoré Champion, 1999). The musical lines are cited innumerable times in books of music history, going back to F. J. Fétis, *Biographie universelle des musiciens*, vol. 2 (Brussels: Meline, Cans et Compagnie, 1837): 198–9, s.v. 'Binchois'. A fully critical edition of the six relevant stanzas, taking account of the readings in all known sources, appears in Fallows, 'The contenance angloise' (1987: 205–8).
4 Their known music is conveniently assembled in *Early fifteenth-century music*, ed. Gilbert Reaney = Corpus mensurabilis musicae 11 (American Institute of Musicology, 1955–83): i. Perhaps it is worth adding that the double rondeau by Cesaris, *Mon seul voloir/ Certes m'amour* is cast largely in four-bar units. To judge from its sources and style, it could be substantially later than the other known works of those composers and may indeed – like the works mentioned later in this chapter – have been influenced by the English carols.
5 The fullest exploration of those terms is in Fallows 1987; lucid and early interpretations are proposed in Page 1996: 2–4. What I did not know then is that one of the best explanations was offered by Fétis, in his original *Biographie universelle des musiciens*, not in the article on Binchois but in the next volume, in his article on Dufay: 'dans l'harmonie (*la frisque concordance*, et *la feinte*, ou retard de consonance) et dans la notation (*la pause*)'. Subsequent discussions of the topic include Strohm (1993: 127–9); Strohm (2001); Wegman 2003; Bent 2004; Wegman 2010; Sandmeier 2012; Colton, *Angel song* 2017: 133–48, chapter 6, 'Contenance angloise: a reappraisal'.
6 As outlined in Fallows 2014: xxvii–xxviii.

Chapter 24: Binchois, Dufay and the contenance angloise

More seriously, readers will know that those lines of Martin Le Franc have been associated with various events in the fifteenth century. Paul Henry Lang, Frank Harrison and Nino Pirrotta associated it with the arrival of English musicians at the Council of Constance in 1415; André Pirro and Heinrich Besseler with Dufay's now evaporated presence in Paris in 1425; Charles Hamm and Charles van den Borren with the elimination of major prolation in about 1430; Jeanne Marix and Sylvia Kenney with the Peace of Arras in 1435; Manfred Bukofzer with the Caput mass, once thought to be by Dufay and seen as prime evidence for his adoption of the English style in about 1445.[7]

I have already mentioned that there is no major change in the style of either composer. What also needs to be clear is that neither composer ever composed anything in the manner of Tapissier, Carmen and Cesaris: they were from their very first works quite different, from the beginning showing light, open textures, syllabic setting and a complete contrast to the music of the *ars subtilior* generation. Those first works cannot yet be dated with any confidence, but they do seem to be from shortly before 1420.

When I last wrote about the *contenance angloise*, in 1987, it seemed to me that what Martin was describing was a slow process over perhaps a quarter of a century. After pondering the matter for another thirty years, and experiencing a bit more music, I now see it quite differently. I believe that the impact on Dufay of the English musicians in Constance and the impact on Binchois of the English musicians in northern France in the years immediately after were the crucial factors in making their music so much simpler and more tuneful than the music of their predecessors. One way of expressing it may be to say that Dufay and Binchois discovered that simple metrical patterns, tuneful melodies and largely syllabic declamation that led to direct communication were not shameful features in music aimed at the highest social classes. Another would be to say that Henry V and his brothers offered a model for supremely cultivated music that was not necessarily complicated.

Moreover, apart from the incomprehensible line 4 of Martin's stanza, the other details he mentions beautifully fit the early music of Dufay and Binchois: 'frisque concordance' (sprightly concordance),[8] a feature quite absent from the music of the previous generation, 'merveilleuse plaisance' (a marvellous charm), certainly present in the previous generation, but achieved now with much more simplicity of gesture, 'joieux et notable' (cheerful and notable).

Among the various writers who have considered the *contenance angloise* since my 1987 article, Reinhard Strohm (1993: 128) is the only one to propose a date for the English effect, and he puts it in the 1430s, that is to say in the years

---

7 Closer documentation of their statements appears in Fallows 1987: 193.
8 Takeshi Matsumura, *Dictionnaire du français médiéval* (Paris: Les Belles Lettres, 2015), gives for 'frisque' the general meaning as 'frais, nouveau', but adds a citation concerning wine, 'le vin doit estre frisque, c'est a dire estincelant', from Albert Henry, *Contribution à l'étude du langage oenologique en langue d'öil (XIIe–XVe s.)*, 2 vols. (Gilly: Académie royale de Belgique, 1996).

172   *Chapter 24: Binchois, Dufay and the* contenance angloise

immediately before Martin Le Franc wrote *Le champion des dames* and the years when the music of both Dufay and Binchois seems to have moved from predominant major prolation to predominant perfect time – as first proposed by Besseler (1950: 122) and supported by Hamm (1964: 97–100). There are two problems with that proposal. First, that the date of the change proposed by Besseler and Hamm was in or shortly before 1430, not in the mid-1430s; and second that there is nothing in what Martin Le Franc wrote to suggest that it was to do with matters he had himself experienced.[9]

At the Council of Constance, the major group of English clerics and musicians arrived with the bishops of Lichfield and Norwich on 24 September 1416.[10] On their way, they sang at Cologne Cathedral on 8 September:[11]

> In that same year a bishop from England came to Cologne wanting to visit the Council. He had his own singers and sang a service in the cathedral. That was sung by the English as well as anybody had heard in the cathedral in thirty years.

Of the chroniclers at the Council of Constance, Ulrich von Richenthal is most effusive about the highly original contributions of the English musicians when they mounted special ceremonies for the Feast of St Thomas of Canterbury: December 29. In 1415:[12]

> All the English who were at Constance celebrated St Thomas's Day splendidly at the cathedral, with songs of praise, great pomp, all the relics in Constance, and tall burning candles. And all day long, at Matins, Prime, Terce, Sext, Nones, Vespers and Compline, trumpeters rode about the city, with their king's arms on their trumpets, and blew on them continually.

---

9   In a later stanza he states that he himself had seen Binchois and Dufay looked shamed at the brilliance of the court minstrels; but this is plainly a different narrative of a different occasion, though, as I noted in 1987, a wrong version of the text published by Stainer in 1898 and published again by Hamm in 1964 – referring to the minstrels as 'anglois' rather than 'aveugles' – has resulted in some readers still subconsciously thinking that this later stanza referred to the same events described earlier.

10 Manfred Schuler, 'Die Musik in Konstanz während des Konzils 1414–1418', *Acta musicologica* 38 (1966): 150–68, at p. 158.

11 My translation from *Die Chroniken der deutschen Städte vom 14. bis ins 16. Jahrhundert* 13 (Leipzig: G. Hirzel, 1876): 108. The German reads: 'In dem selben Jar quam ein Bischuf zu Kolen, der waz van Engelant, und wolt zu dem Concilium. Der hat sine eigene Singer und sung in dem Dome dat Ampt. Dat wart alz wal van den Engelschen besungen, alz man in 30 Jaren in dem Dome e hort singen'.

12 Translation from *The Council of Constance: the unification of the church*, translated by Louise Ropes Loomis, edited and annotated by J.H. Mundy and K.M. Woody (New York: Columbia University Press, 1961): 138. Original German in *Chronik des Konstanzer Konzils 1414–1418 von Ulrich Richental*, ed. Thomas Martin Buck = Konstanzer Geschichts- und Rechtsquellen 41 (Ostfildern: Jan Thorbecke Verlag, 2010): 72.

Chapter 24: Binchois, Dufay and the contenance angloise   173

A year later, he has more to say:[13]

> On the eve of St Thomas's Day, which was Holy Innocents' Day, the English began the feast of St Thomas of Canterbury. They sent four trumpeters through the city at Vespers time, with their king's arms hanging from the trumpets. They sang Vespers beautifully in the cathedral, with tall candles burning, bells pealing, sweet singing and the organ. In the morning, on St Thomas's Day, they celebrated Mass in the cathedral and the Bishop of Salisbury sang Mass and two other bishops from England assisted him at the altar. All the clergy were present and the trumpeters blew their trumpets through the city. And the patriarchs and all the bishops and scholars were invited to dinner.

Finally, he reports a celebration a few weeks later on 24 January 1417, St Timothy's Day:[14]

> The English bishops, the Bishop of London, the Bishop of Salisbury, and five other English bishops invited all the town councilors and worthy men of Constance to Burkart Walther's house, that was formerly called the House of the Gate near St Lawrence's church but is now called *zu dem gulden Schwert*. They gave them a sumptuous banquet – three courses, one after another, with eight dishes to each course. All dishes were served but once, and four at each course were on platters of gold or silver. During the banquet, there were shows and pantomimes by players in rich and costly raiment. They played Our Lady holding her Son God Our Lord and Joseph standing beside her and the three holy kings bringing their tribute. They had prepared a shining gold star that went before the kings on a fine iron wire. They played also King Herod sending after the three kings and slaying the children. All the players wore most costly garments and broad gold and silver girdles and played their parts with great diligence and modesty.

It is a well-known paradox that we have almost no information about any of the musicians at the Council of Constance. The best we can do is to guess that Dufay must have been there to have made his contacts with the Malatesta family, resulting in some of his finest works of the early 1420s. There is no record of his presence in Cambrai between his reception shortly after 24 June 1414 and his receiving an allotment of wine on 17 November 1417.[15] He could therefore have been at Constance in the train of Cardinal Pierre d'Ailly, Bishop of Cambrai until

---

13 Loomis: 146–7. Original German in Buck: 82.
14 Loomis: 147. Original German in Buck: 82–3.
15 Alejandro Enrique Planchart, 'The early career of Guillaume Du Fay', *Journal of the American Musicological Society* 46 (1993): 341–68, at p. 353 and p. 360.

1412, who arrived there on 17 November 1414, or that of Jean de Lens, the current Bishop, who arrived on 17 January 1415.[16]

If we agree with my earlier suggestion that the English carol style began quite suddenly in the years just before 1415 it should be no surprise that one year later the English musicians should astonish the commentators at the Council of Constance with their novelty and originality. And it should be no surprise that their simple style of 'frisque concordance' should have been heard by Dufay and Binchois as the way forward after the complexities of the *ars subtilior* generation. Their music may not sound like English carols, but it is imbued with the same aesthetic ideals. I wish to suggest, then, that the English carol was the main influence in that change. Certainly no report says that they sang English carols in Constance, but it is hard to believe that they would not do so, particularly in view of their evident importance to Henry V.

That there is now almost no trace of English carol music on the continent should disappoint nobody. Many manuscripts are lost;[17] or, to put it differently, almost no manuscripts survive. And in any case, the basic principles of the style are so simple that they would be instantly clear to any reasonably educated musician: written music is not necessary to show simple 6/3 triads and regular phrase structures. But it seems to me now unavoidable that the music that so profoundly influenced Dufay and Binchois was the English carol, not just not an insular phenomenon but one of the most powerful influences for change in fifteenth-century music. Certainly it is easier to hear the roots of their style in the carols than in anything else that survives from English composers in the early fifteenth century.

A few examples can show this. Perhaps the clearest are not by Dufay or Binchois but appear in one of the manuscripts that contain some of their earliest works, Venice, Biblioteca Nazionale Marciana, MS. Ital. Cl. IX. 145, and particularly the first portion of the manuscript, fols. 1–41.[18] Among these pieces are two anonymous *laude* in major prolation and very much in the four-bar structure of the carols.

---

16 Planchart, *op. cit.*, at p. 342, citing Schuler 1966: 159. Planchart also proposed (pp. 357–60) that the Kyrie, Sanctus and Agnus based around the tenor known as 'Vineux' were composed before Dufay went to Constance. I am not convinced of the strength of his arguments here, but do note that the three movements display none of the details I wish to associate with the *contenance angloise*.

17 Margaret Bent, 'The earliest fifteenth-century transmission of English music on the continent' (2010), identifies two English pieces apparently between 1400 and 1420 in continental sources, namely the Selden *Sancta Maria virgo intercede* (no. 2), also in Aosta, and the *Benedicta es celorum regina* ascribed 'de Anglia' in Trento 92 and Bologna Q15 and found anonymously in an English fragment. She also argues that the motet *Sub Arturo plebs/ Fons citharizancium*, found in both the Chantilly manuscript and Bologna Q15, dates from the second decade of the century (against several scholars who argue that it is substantially earlier). Bearing in mind that Henry V had his full Chapel Royal in France 1417–20 and that there was a massive English attendance at the Council of Constance during those same years, that is not much. Plainly the sources are lost.

18 Description and detailed inventory in Giulio Cattin, *Il manoscritto veneto Marciano Ital. IX 145* = Biblioteca di "Quadrivium": Serie Musicologica 3 (Bologna: 1962); see also RISM B IV[5], ed. Nanie Bridgman (Munich: G. Henle Verlag, 1991): 550–4.

Chapter 24: Binchois, Dufay and the contenance angloise   175

Example 24.1[19] *Qui nos fecit ex nihilo* (Venice 145)

The other *lauda* in major prolation that matches the regular phrase-structure of the carols is *Padre del cielo* on fol. 31;[20] but there are several more in perfect time, not just in the Marciana manuscript but in the two famous Bologna choirbooks. It seems justified to guess that the perfect time pieces are in general later than the major prolation pieces.

Similarly, there are comparable pieces in the earliest works of Dufay and Binchois. Perhaps most famous is the first of Dufay's *Ave regina celorum* settings, which runs for most of its central section in regular four-beat phrases. Example 24.2 on p. 176. That may seem less strikingly borrowed from the carol style; but the broadly homophonic and syllabic declamation is very much of the carol manner and extremely rare in any earlier music.

Yet another example of the possible English influence can be seen in one of the loveliest and saddest of Binchois' early rondeau settings, *Triste plaisir* on a text by Christine de Pizan. Example 24.3 on p. 177. On the face of it, only the four-bar phrases associate this with the carol style, though there are plenty of carols with the gentler manner that we have here. But the balance of the materials and the approximate repeats are also part of the carol style: in fact they are strikingly

---

19 Published in Elisabeth Diederichs, *Die Anfänge der mehrstimmigen Lauda vom Ende des 14. bis zur Mitte des 16. Jahrhunderts* = Münchner Veröffentlichungen zur Musikgeschichte 41 (Tutzing: Hans Schneider, 1986): 391.

20 Published in Giulio Cattin *Laudi Quattrocentesche del Cod. Veneto Marc. It. IX 145* = Biblioteca di "Quadrivium": Serie Paleografica 10 (Bologna: 1958): 9. It is also published in Diederichs, *op. cit.*: 372, here alongside most of the other comparable pieces in the same manuscript; see in particular *O aquila magna* (pp. 374–5) and the perfect-time piece *Verbum caro* (pp. 355–6).

176   *Chapter 24: Binchois, Dufay and the* contenance angloise

Example 24.2 Section from Dufay's first *Ave regina celorum*

similar to the musical repeats noted earlier in the carol *I pray you all with one thought*, Example 15.2.

Various other songs by Binchois and Dufay show similar influence.[21] But the main point must be that before that generation such regular phrase-structures were

---

21 In particular, among the songs of Binchois one could note: *Adieu m'amour et ma maistresse*, regularly in five-bar phrases (each phrase texted for three bars after which there is a two-bar coda); *Adieu ma doulce*, regularly in eight-bar phrases, with added codas at the end of each half; *Bien puist*, regularly in eight-bar phrases; *De plus en plus*, regularly in four-bar phrases; *Marguerite, fleur de valeur*, in which all lines have eight bars apart from the third, which has nine; *Toutes mes joyes*, in which the first two lines have eight bars each, the other two lines ten bars each; *Amours, merchi*, in which the first two lines each last six bars, the next three have three bars each, and the

Example 24.3 Triste plaisir (Binchois). Complete

very rare indeed. What was new in the years just before 1420 was the sudden simplification of style.

If so, where does Dunstable fit into the story? One possibility is that Martin Le Franc, or whoever informed him, was just ignorant, that like so many other musicians of the fifteenth century he used the word 'Dunstable' to mean 'some English composer'. But another possibility is that Dunstable was in fact the composer of some of the most influential carols, particularly in view of his association with so many of Henry V's closest family, as outlined in chapter 22.

To recall: the three earliest sources of the carol repertory contain just one ascription, a single piece credited to 'Childe' in the Selden manuscript – a manuscript that contains no other ascription even though we have other sources to attest that works here are by Power, Dunstable and even Plummer. Anonymity in sources of music from those years is common. A related question would be whether anything in the ascribed works of Dunstable resembles the music of the early carols. The answer would be that there is no close resemblance but that the style is certainly possible for the author of the works we know as Dunstable.[22] In the circumstances, the safe solution would be to allow this music to remain anonymous, though I have a strong suspicion that much of it may indeed be by Dunstable.

---

last two have four bars each. Also in regular eight-bar lines is the anonymous *Adieu ma tres belle maistresse*, for which Dennis Slavin claimed to see a possible trimmed ascription to Binchois in the manuscript Trento 92. Among the songs of Dufay, one could note: the almost homophonic ballade setting *J'ay mis mon cuer et ma pensee*, with phrases of eight beats and six beats, followed by a coda of eight beats; the rondeau *Adieu ces bons vins de Lannoys*, with an introduction of five bars followed by texted lines of four, four and five bars, after which the secunda pars has a five-bar line, with a two-bar coda, followed by a four-bar line and a four-bar coda; the rondeau *Ma belle dame, je vous pri*, in which almost all the lines are of four bars; the rondeau *Pour ce que veoir je ne puis*, in which the first half comprises a four-bar introduction plus two lines of four bars each and the second half comprises two lines of five bars each. Several of his earliest *Kyrie* settings display similarly regular patterns.

22 Interesting analogies between the works of Dunstable and the carol repertory are proposed in Bent 1981: 23–5, with the observation that 'it is highly probable that Dunstaple himself made a substantial contribution' to the carol repertory.

25 Awareness of the carol, 3: 1902–2017

Probably the first writer to pick up on the achievement of the Stainers was H. E. Wooldridge, who included three carols in the second of his two volumes for the *Oxford history of music* (1905). As concerns *Ecce, quod Natura*, he remarked (p. 128) on:

> continuous *faulx bourdon*, a mode of treatment which, notwithstanding its popularity as a form of extempore discant, was never, as we shall see, tolerated in serious composition. In *Ecce quod Natura*, however – our example from the early Ashmole MS – it prevails throughout.

About the Agincourt carol he was more complimentary (p. 134):

> the melody is quite admirable, and again we find the discant also pleasing in itself; but again, also, the combination is often unsatisfactory, producing, as usual at this time, sometimes bare harmony, and sometimes aimless and arbitrary discord like that of Machault and the Italians.

But the achievements of the 1890s took root only slowly. Henry Davey's extensive *History of English music* (London: J. Curwen, 1895) gives enormous room to Dunstable as the 'inventor' of polyphony but devotes only a short paragraph (p. 71) to the Trinity roll, albeit adding that the works are anonymous 'but both words and music are probably by Dunstable or Power'; in the later revised edition (London: J. Curwen, 1921) had adds a brief note (p. 64) on the Selden manuscript as published in Stainer 1901. Similarly, Ernest Walker's *History of music in England* (Oxford: At the Clarendon Press, 1907) refers to Trinity as edited by Fuller Maitland and even quotes portions of the Agincourt carol (p. 23); he also mentions various details in the Selden manuscript.[1] Edmondstoune Duncan's *The story of the*

---

[1] Walker also alludes to Fuller Maitland's hasty theory that all the Trinity pieces could be by Dunstable ('adopted, less hesitatingly, by Eitner') and to Henry Davey's qualification that they could be by Dunstable or Power, adding that 'there is really no evidence for drawing conclusions of any kind' (p. 24). Understandably, there is no allusion to the possibility in Barclay Squire's article on Dunstable in the second edition of *Grove's dictionary of music and musicians*, edited by his

carol (1911) shows no awareness of the Stainers. *Carols: their origin, music and connection with mystery-plays* (London, 1921) by William J. Phillips, 'Mus. Doc., Queen's College, Oxford', and with a foreword by Sir Frederick Bridge, covers the whole history of seasonal songs, starting from 'the angels over the fields of Bethlehem'; but he shows no awareness of the fifteenth-century musical repertory, though he does quote from poems in the Sloane manuscript (edited by Thomas Wright) and the Trinity roll (presumably as edited by Fuller Maitland). Again, the recognition of their quality and individuality seems to have escaped those authors.

More appreciative was Jessie L. Weston (1911), who published an elegant little selection of *Old English carols from the Hill MS* with modernised orthography and liberal departures from the original. She was aware that they had all been published by Flügel (1903) but apparently unaware of their more recent publication for the Early English Text Society by Dyboski (1908), which is perhaps understandable since her preface was signed in Paris. All the poems printed here are indeed in carol form, which offers reason to believe that she was aware of the earliest printed definition of the word 'carol' as understood here, that by Chambers (1907). But the real breath of fresh air here was her patent enthusiasm for the poems, as expressed in her preface.[2]

Even clearer enthusiasm can be seen in Sir Henry Hadow's *English music* (1931: 18–19), a brief outline of only 174 tiny pages but with the following remarkable paragraph:

> For in spite of official reticence there is beginning to emerge from the darkness a new radiance of secular music. We had not in England such splendid organizations as those of the Troubadours and Trouvères in France or the Minnesingers and Mastersingers in Germany: as we were leading their nations in the Church so we fell behind them in the court and the marketplace. But there have come to light a good many "songs and madrigals" of the fifteenth century, not only carols, in which the period is particularly rich, but songs of a more secular character. Good examples are to be found in the Selden manuscript, which is dated by scholars between 1415 and 1455, and which, beside carols and sacred pieces, includes a spirited drinking-song, a lyric in praise of country life, and what may well be regarded as the climax and cynosure of them all, the superb song of thanksgiving for the victory at Agincourt. It is one of the finest popular tunes in the world, a noble Triumphlied in which the patriotism of the nation speaks out with a full heart. George Brandes once said that Shakespeare's *Henry V* was a national anthem in five acts. The Agincourt song is its compendium and quintessence: a core of white heat that burns in the very soul of our people.

Even to my enthusiastic eye, that seems to over-egg the pudding. But it is a relief to see somebody reacting with passion to such passionate music.

---

brother-in-law Fuller Maitland (London: Macmillan, 1904): i.742–4. (The first edition of *Grove* had no article on Dunstable since its title specified that it concerned only music from 1450.)

2 Some of the same enthusiasm can be read a few years later in the article by H. J. L. J. Massé (1921).

As a further – and bizarre – continuation we may cite Sir Richard Runciman Terry's *A medieval carol book* (London: Burns Oates & Washbourne, 1932). Terry (1865–1938, therefore at the time almost seventy years old) was famous as the first director of music at Westminster Cathedral (1901–24) and a major figure in the revival of Tudor church music, most particularly Byrd and Tallis. He was also the original editor of the series *Tudor church music*.[3] But his book of carols is a most curious affair: it includes twenty carols from Selden and eleven from Trinity (omitting the Agincourt carol and *Abide, I hope* as being not carols, by his Christmas-based definition); and it refers to Stainer's publication of the Selden carols, albeit showing no knowledge of the Fuller Maitland edition of Trinity;[4] but in all cases he extracts just the tenor line, puts it up an octave, and adds three lower voices in standard hymn-tune style. His justification (p. i) reads:

> As they stand in the MSS. (in the crude and experimental counterpoint of their period) these carols are of the highest antiquarian and historical value, but only the sheerest preciosity would suggest their public performance in that form, or claim for them any aesthetic appeal to musicians of to-day.
>
> Their unsuitability for performance *in their original form* is not due to their antiquity; the folk-tunes on which they are founded are of even earlier date but are nevertheless grateful to modern ears. It is merely that the folk-tunes of the carols are a finished artistic product, while the crude counterpoint which is woven around them is the first fumbling attempts in search of a technique which did not attain perfection until the sixteenth century.

That such words (or even such arrangements) should have been published as late as 1932 seems hardly credible.

As mentioned earlier, the years 1945–54 saw a massive growth of serious writing about the carol, starting with the masterly summary of the literary side by Sir Edmund Chambers (1945). Although I have expressed unhappiness at the brevity and lack of logic in its conclusions about Egerton's origins, Bertram Schofield's article (1946) did much to put the carol on the map. Bukofzer's magnificent chapter about Egerton (1950) needs to be read alongside his two chapters for the New Oxford History of Music (1960, 1960a), written at about the same time though not published until long after his early death in 1956. 1952 saw the publication of the entire musical repertory by John Stevens (1952; revised edition 1958). And then in 1954 came not just the two massive reviews of the Stevens edition (Bukofzer 1954; Greene 1954a) but Greene's enormous article basically devoted to showing that Egerton came from Meaux Abbey in Yorkshire. That I now entirely disagree with his arguments about its origin should not be read as lack of appreciation for

---

3 For a far from generous view of Terry, see Richard Turbet, 'An affair of honour: "Tudor Church Music", the ousting of Richard Terry, and a trust vindicated', *Music and letters* 76 (1995): 593–600; a more sympathetic account is in Timothy Day, 'Sir Richard Terry and 16th-century polyphony', *Early music* 22 (1994): 296–307.

4 He states that there is no modern edition but adds that 'a complete MS score in modern notation will (I believe) be found in the College Library' (p. i).

the enormous body of carefully assembled scholarship in Greene's article. But that body of scholarship more or less concluded the specific research on the carol. In one sense, the 1977 new edition of Greene's *The early English carols* tied up that phase of carol research.

Literary scholarship has not progressed much since then. I already mentioned a few articles noting new sources and some doctoral dissertations. But more general studies devote distressingly little space to carols. *Nation, court and culture: new essays on fifteenth-century English poetry*, ed. Helen Cooney (Dublin: Four Courts Press, 2001) claims to show that English poetry in the fifteenth century is far better than its reputation but devotes only five pages to the carol (pp. 179–83), with the comment that 'its words on the page seem not susceptible to the intensities of close reading' but at least concedes that the carol covers more social levels than suggested in the available literature.

Even so, it was presumably the view that the carol was an insular phenomenon that limited comments on the repertory in more general histories of music over the following years. Ironically, the years that saw the peak of carol scholarship were also the years that saw the massive burst of scholarly writing about fauxbourdon. As outlined in chapter 6, our earliest examples of fauxbourdon are in the earliest carols, but they were never mentioned in that literature.

Thus in more recent years the carol seems to have disappeared from sight. Gustave Reese's evergreen *Music in the renaissance* (New York: Norton, 1954) gave it two pages (pp. 765–7) but at least refrained from mentioning the Agincourt carol. Allan W. Atlas, in his best-selling *Renaissance music* (New York: Norton, 1998) gave it less than half a page among over 700, referring only to the Agincourt carol; more recently, *The Cambridge history of fifteenth-century music*, ed. Anna Maria Busse Berger and Jesse Rodin (Cambridge: Cambridge University Press, 2015), gave it rather less than a single page (out of some 900). Most surprisingly of all, the 690 pages in volume 1 of John Caldwell's *The Oxford history of English music* (Oxford: Oxford University Press, 1991), gave it only four pages plus two musical examples. In the second volume, *The middle ages*, of Boris Ford's *The Cambridge guide to the arts in Britain* (Cambridge: Cambridge University Press, 1988), the carol is not even mentioned, either as a poetic or as a musical manifestation. Nor is it in the massive *Opening up Middle English manuscripts: literary and visual approaches*, ed. Kathryn Kerby-Fulton, *et al.* (Ithaca and London: Cornell University Press, 2012), running to over 400 jumbo-sized pages. The two-volume *Die Musik des 15. und 16. Jahrhunderts*, ed. Ludwig Finscher = Neues Handbuch der Musikwissenschaft 3 (Laaber: Laaber Verlag, 1989–90) mentions the carol only with a passing dismissal (p. 329: 'laienhaften Carols'); the twenty-four-volume *Handbuch der musikalischen Gattungen*, ed. Siegfried Mauser (Laaber: Laaber-Verlag, 1993–2010), has no entry in its index for either 'carol' or 'carole'. Richard Taruskin's six-volume blockbuster *The Oxford history of western music* (Oxford: Oxford University Press, 2005) gave it four pages, again printing the Agincourt carol with the comment: 'Such songs had probably been sung in England since the Normans arrived in the eleventh century, if not before'.

I am herewith trying to change that.

26 'Blessid Inglond ful of melody'

According to John Capgrave's *Chronicle of England*, when King Sigismund left England in August 1416 he had his servants distribute copies of a leaflet containing the following lines:[1]

> Farewel, with glorious victory,
> Blessid Inglond, ful of melody.
> Thou may be cleped of Angel nature;
> Thou servist God so with bysy cure.
> We leve with the this praising,
> Whech we schul evir sey and sing.

Others report the same story but give a Latin text.[2] On the face of it, Latin may seem the more probable language for such a declaration; but the English version even rhymes and (after a fashion) scans. It is perfectly possible that after a four-month (self-invited) stay in England Sigismund himself had mastered a few elements of the language; but it is more likely that, as a minimum courtesy after the hospitality provided by Henry V, he had taken the precaution of commissioning a statement in English. After all, the use of English was a major plank of Henry V's policy. The point here is that only the English version mentions the 'melody'.

---

1 *The chronicle of England by John Capgrave*, ed. Francis Charles Hingeston (London: Longman, Brown, Green, 1858): 314. Hingeston reports (p. xx) that there are two known manuscripts, both in Cambridge: the author's autograph in the University Library, Gg. 4. 12; and one in Corpus Christi College, MS 167. The chronicle goes down to the year 1417, but it is dedicated to King Edward IV. Since Capgrave was born in 1393, he would have been able to witness the events described as in 1416, so I put much trust in his account, even though no other early source reports it.

2 *Gesta Henrici Quinti: the deeds of Henry the Fifth*, translated and ed. Frank Taylor and John S. Roskell (Oxford: At the Clarendon Press, 1975): 156: Vale et gaude glorioso cum triumpho, O, tu felix Anglia; et benedicta, quia quasi angelica natura gloriosa laude Ihesum adorans [acrostic: ANGLIA] es iure dicta. Hanc tibi do laudem quam recto iure mereris. Taylor and Roskell report similar phrasings in the *Liber metricus* (p. 141), Strecche (Frank Taylor, 'The chronicle of John Strecche for the reign of Henry V (1414–1422)', *Bulletin of the John Rylands Library, Manchester* 16 (1932): 137–87, at p. 155), Adam of Usk (p. 130) and Thomas Walsingham (*The St. Albans chronicle 1406–1420*, ed. V. H. Galbraith (Oxford: At the Clarendon Press, 1937): 101).

It is clear that Henry V used music as part of his charm-offensive against Sigismund's aim to establish peace between England and France. The chronicles mention plenty of music in their descriptions of Sigismund's visit. And these were the months in which Henry's propaganda machine moved into full force: he had his Agincourt victory and now he desperately needed financial support for a second French campaign. How far the carols were part of this we cannot be sure. But the power of their poetry seems part of the strategy, as does the power of their music.

But various new conclusions about the carol have emerged. First, that the poetic form, while related to that of the virelais, *ballate*, and *cantigas*, is utterly distinct from any continental form. Second that the musical style, while having sporadic precursors in the English and continental repertories, was also *sui generis* among the written record, though many details, including the often regular phrase-lengths, must have had their precursors in the unwritten tradition. Third, that the poetic form and the musical style really make their first appearance in the Trinity carol roll, for which I now propose a copying date soon after the Agincourt carol was composed. Fourth, that they contain the earliest surviving examples of fauxbourdon, at least ten years before the Dufay postcommunion hitherto considered the earliest example. Fifth, that they have substantially the earliest specific references to a 'chorus' in polyphonic music. Sixth, that they include the earliest surviving examples of vernacular sacred polyphony in any language. Seventh, that most of the repertory in the three earlier manuscripts was from the reign of Henry V, with the Ritson carols for the most part probably from the 1430s. Eighth, that the earliest carols had a vital place in the court culture of Henry V and his political propaganda. Ninth, that they had a massive effect on European music in the years around 1420.

But the main thrust of this book is to say that the earliest carols are not only an integral part of the English repertory but among the most individual music that survives from the first third of the century. They deserve at the very least an honourable mention in any view of English culture in the fifteenth century.

Bibliography

Margaret BENT 1967–8, 'Sources of the Old Hall music', *Proceedings of the Royal Musical Association* 94: 19–35

Margaret BENT 1968, 'The Old Hall manuscript: a paleographical study' (PhD dissertation, University of Cambridge)

Margaret BENT 1981, *Dunstaple* (London: Oxford University Press)

Margaret BENT 2004, 'The musical stanzas in Martin Le Franc's *Le champion des dames*', in *Music and medieval manuscripts . . . dedicated to Andrew Hughes*, ed. John Haines and Randall Rosenfeld (Aldershot: Ashgate): 91–127

Margaret BENT 2010, 'The earliest fifteenth-century transmission of English music on the continent', in *Essays on the history of English music in honour of John Caldwell*, ed. Emma Hornby and David Maw (Woodbridge: The Boydell Press): 83–96

Heinrich BESSELER 1948, 'Der Ursprung des Fauxbourdons', *Die Musikforschung* 1: 106–112

Heinrich BESSELER 1948a, 'Dufay Schöpfer des Fauxbourdons', *Acta musicologica* 20: 26–45

Heinrich BESSELER 1950, *Bourdon und Fauxbourdon: Studien zum Ursprung der niederländischen Musik* (Leipzig: Breitkopf & Härtel; 2nd, revised edition, ed. Peter Gülke, 1974)

Heinrich BESSELER 1957, 'Das Ergebnis der Diskussion über "Fauxbourdon"', *Acta musicologica* 29: 185–8

Roger BOWERS 1975–6, 'Some observations on the life and career of Lionel Power', *Proceedings of the Royal Musical Association* 102: 37–54, reprinted in Bowers, *English church polyphony: singers and sources from the 14th to the 17th century* (Aldershot: Variorum, 1999): chapter IX

Roger BOWERS 1982, 'Trinity College, MS O. 3. 58', in *Cambridge music manuscripts, 900–1700*, ed. Iain Fenlon (Cambridge: Cambridge University Press): 88–90

Roger BOWERS 1983, 'The performing ensemble for English church polyphony, c. 1320 – c. 1390', in *Studies in the performance of late mediaeval music*, ed. Stanley Boorman (Cambridge: Cambridge University Press): 161–92, reprinted in Bowers, *English church polyphony: singers and sources from the 14th to the 17th century* (Aldershot: Variorum, 1999): chapter I

Roger BOWERS 1995, 'To chorus from quartet: the performing resource for English church polyphony, c.1390–1559', in *English choral practice, 1400–1650*, ed. John Morehen (Cambridge: Cambridge University Press): 1–47, reprinted in Bowers, *English church polyphony: singers and sources from the 14th to the 17th century* (Aldershot: Variorum, 1999): chapter II

Roger Bowers 1995a, 'Early Tudor courtly song: an evaluation of the Fayrfax book (BL, Additional MS 5465)', in *The reign of Henry VII: proceedings of the 1993 Harlaxton symposium*, ed. Benjamin Thompson = Harlaxton medieval studies 5 (Stamford: Paul Watkins): 188–212

Roger Bowers 2001, 'The music and musical establishment of St George's Chapel in the 15th century', in *St George's Chapel, Windsor, in the late middle ages*, ed. Colin Richmond and Eileen Scarff = Historical Monographs relating to St George's Chapel, Windsor Castle 17 (Leeds: Maney Publishing): 171–214

Carleton Brown 1924, *Religious lyrics of the XIVth century* (Oxford: At the Clarendon Press; 2nd edition revised by G. V. Smithers, 1957)

Carleton Brown 1937, review of Greene 1935 in *Modern language notes* 52: 125–9

Carleton Brown 1939, *Religious lyrics of the XVth century* (Oxford: At the Clarendon Press)

Manfred F. Bukofzer 1936, *Geschichte des englischen Diskants und des Fauxbourdons nach den theoretischen Quellen* = Collection d'études musicologiques/ Sammlung musikwissenschaftlicher Abhandlungen 21 (Basel: [no named publisher])

Manfred F. Bukofzer 1947, 'A newly discovered 15th-century manuscript of the English Chapel Royal – part II', *The musical quarterly* 33: 38–51

Manfred F. Bukofzer 1950, *Studies in medieval and renaissance music* (New York: W. W. Norton)

Manfred F. Bukofzer 1952, 'Fauxbourdon revisited', *The musical quarterly* 38: 22–47

Manfred F. Bukofzer 1954, review of Stevens 1952 in *Journal of the American Musicological Society* 7: 63–78

Manfred F. Bukofzer 1960, 'Popular and secular music in England (to *c.* 1470)', in *Ars nova and the renaissance 1300–1540*, ed. Dom Anselm Hughes and Gerald Abraham = New Oxford history of music 3 (London: Oxford University Press): 107–133

Manfred F. Bukofzer 1960a, 'English church music of the fifteenth century', in *Ars nova and the renaissance 1300–1540*, ed. Dom Anselm Hughes and Gerald Abraham = New Oxford history of music 3 (London: Oxford University Press): 165–213

Charles Burney 1782, *A general history of music from the earliest ages to the present period*, vol. 2 (London: Printed for the Author)

John Caldwell 1993, 'Relations between liturgical and vernacular music in medieval England', in *Music in the medieval English liturgy: Plainsong and Medieval Music Society centennial essays*, ed. Susan Rankin and David Hiley (Oxford: Clarendon Press): 285–99

Martin Camargo 1998, 'Two Middle English carols from an Exeter manuscript', *Medium ævum* 67: 104–11

Carolyn Paulette Catherwood 1996, 'English polyphonic carol manuscripts, c. 1420–1450' (DPhil dissertation, University of Oxford)

Census-catalogue 1979–88, *Census-catalogue of manuscript sources of polyphonic music 1400–1550*, 5 vols. = American Institute of Musicology: Renaissance manuscript studies 1 (Neuhausen-Stuttgart: Hänssler-Verlag)

Seeta Chaganti 2008, 'Choreographing *mouvance*: the case of the English carol', *Philological quarterly* 87: 77–103

E. K. Chambers and F. Sidgwick 1907, *Early English lyrics, amorous, divine, moral and trivial* (London: A. H. Bullen)

E. K. Chambers and F. Sidgwick 1910–11, 'Fifteenth century carols by John Audelay', *The modern language review* 5: 473–91, and 6: 68–84

E. K. Chambers 1945, *English literature at the close of the middle ages* = Oxford history of English literature 2 (Oxford: At the Clarendon Press)

Sydney Robinson CHARLES 1976, review of Stevens 1975 in *Notes* 33: 160–62

Heather COLLIER 1997, 'Richard Hill: a London compiler', in *The court and cultural diversity: selected papers from the eighth triennial congress of the International Courtly Literature Society*, ed. Evelyn Mullally and John Thompson (Cambridge: D. S. Brewer, 1997): 319–29

Heather Diane COLLIER 2000, 'Late fifteenth and early sixteenth century manuscript miscellanies: the sources and contexts of MS. Balliol 354' (PhD dissertation, The Queen's University, Belfast)

Lisa COLTON 2017, *Angel song: medieval English music in history* (London and New York: Routledge)

J[ames] COPLEY 1954, 'The 15th-century carol and Christmas', *Notes & queries* 201: 242–3

J[ames] COPLEY 1958, 'John Audelay's carols and music', *English studies* 39: 207–12

J[ames] COPLEY 1958a, 'A second carol of Agincourt', *Notes & queries* 205: 239 [on *Enforce we us*]

J[ames] COPLEY 1958b, 'Carol and cantilena', *Notes & queries* 205: 239–40

J[ames] COPLEY 1959, 'A popular fifteenth-century carol', *Notes & queries* 206: 387–9 [on *What tidings bringest thou*]

Gareth CURTIS and Andrew Wathey 1994, 'Fifteenth-century English liturgical music: a list of the surviving repertory', *Royal Musical Association Research Chronicle* 27: 1–69; revised version available on the website of Early English Church Music

T[hurston] D[ART] 1953, review of Stevens 1952 in *Music and letters* 34: 78–9

Helen DEEMING 2007, 'The sources and origin of the "Agincourt carol"', *Early music* 35: 23–38

E. J. DOBSON and F. Ll. Harrison 1979, *Medieval English songs* (London: Faber and Faber)

Edmondstoune DUNCAN 1911, *The story of the carol* (London: The Walter Scott Publishing Co., and New York: Charles Scribner's Sons; reprint Detroit: Singing Tree, 1969; reprint Detroit: Omnigraphics, 1992)

Roman DYBOSKI 1908, *Songs, carols, and other miscellaneous poems, from the Balliol MS. 354* = Early English Text Society, Extra series 101 (London: Kegan Paul, Trench, Trübner, '1907 (*issued in* 1908)')

A. S. G. EDWARDS and Toshi Takamiya 2001, 'A new Middle English carol', *Medium ævum* 70: 112–15

David FALLOWS 1976, 'The Fayrfax manuscript', *The musical times* 117: 127–30

David FALLOWS 1976–7, 'English song repertories of the mid-fifteenth century', *Proceedings of the Royal Musical Association* 103: 61–79, reprinted in Fallows, *Songs and musicians in the fifteenth century* (Aldershot: Variorum, 1996): chapter I

David FALLOWS 1978, review of Greene 1977 in *Early music* 6: 447–9

David Fallows 1982, *Dufay* = The master musicians (London: J. M. Dent; expanded reprint 1987)

David FALLOWS 1984, 'Oxford, Bodleian Library, MS Bodley 88*', *Early music history* 4: 313–29

David FALLOWS 1987, 'The contenance angloise: English influence on continental composers of the fifteenth century', *Renaissance studies* 1: 189–208, reprinted in Fallows, *Songs and musicians in the fifteenth century* (Aldershot: Variorum, 1996): chapter V

David FALLOWS 2014, *Secular polyphony 1380–1480* = Musica Britannica 97 (London: Stainer and Bell)

Anthony FAULKES 2005, 'A new medieval carol text', *Notes and queries* n.s. 52: 445

Bernhard FEHR 1901, 'Die Lieder der Hs. Add. 5665 (Ritson's Folio-Ms.)', *Archiv für das Studium der neueren Sprachen und Litteraturen* 106: 262–85

Bernhard FEHR 1901a, 'Die Lieder des Fairfax Ms. (Add. 5465 Brit. Mus.)', *Archiv für das Studium der neueren Sprachen und Litteraturen* 106: 48–70

Bernhard FEHR 1902, 'Die Lieder der Hs. Sloane 2593', *Archiv für das Studium der neueren Sprachen und Litteraturen* 109: 33–72.

Susanna FEIN 2009, *John the blind Audelay: poems and carols (Oxford, Bodleian Library MS Douce 302)* (Kalamazoo: Medieval Institute Publications)

Susanna FEIN 2009a, *My wyl and my wryting: essays on John the blind Audelay*, ed. Susanna Fein (Kalamazoo: Medieval Institute Publications)

Susanna FEIN 2013, 'John Audelay and James Ryman', in *A companion to fifteenth century poetry*, ed. Julia Boffey and A. S. G. Edwards (Woodbridge: Boydell and Brewer): 127–41

Ewald FLÜGEL 1889, 'Liedersammlungen des XVI. Jahrhunderts, besonders aus der Zeit Heinrich's VIII.', *Anglia* 12: 225–72 and 585–97 [this latter including '3. Fragment der Christmasse Carolles von Wynkyn de Worde. 1521' (p. 587) and '4. Christmas Carolles newely Inprinted. Ohne Jahr. (Douce Fragments 94.)' (pp. 588–9)]

Ewald FLÜGEL 1903, 'Liedersammlungen des XVI. Jahrhunderts, besonders aus der Zeit Heinrichs VIII.: III', *Anglia* 26: 94–285 [entirely about Balliol 354]

J. A. FULLER MAITLAND [1891], *English carols of the fifteenth century from a ms. roll in the library of Trinity College, Cambridge . . . with added vocal parts by W. S. Rockstro* (London: Novello, and New York: Scribner's)

J. A. FULLER-MAITLAND 1929, *A door-keeper of music* (London: John Murray)

Thrasybulos GEORGIADES 1937, *Englische Diskanttraktate aus der ersten Hälfte des 15. Jahrhunderts: Untersuchungen zur Entwicklung der Mehrstimmigkeit im Mittelalter* = Schriftenreihe des Musikwissenschaftlichen Seminars der Universität München 3 (Munich: [no named publisher])

Alexandra GILLESPIE 2003, 'Balliol MS. 354: histories of the book at the end of the middle ages', *Poetica* 60: 47–63

Otto GOMBOSI 1953, review of Stevens 1952 in *Renaissance news* 6: 6–10 and 32–5

Douglas GRAY 1978, review of Greene 1977 in *Music and letters* 59: 209–11

Douglas GRAY 2001, 'Fifteenth-century lyrics and carols', in *Nation, court, and culture: new essays on fifteenth-century poetry*, ed. Helen Cooney (Dublin: Four Courts Press): 168–83

Richard Leighton GREENE 1929, 'The English carol before 1550' (PhD dissertation, Princeton University)

Richard Leighton GREENE 1935, *The early English carols* (Oxford: At the Clarendon Press) [Reviews in Brown 1937, Greg 1937]

Richard L. GREENE 1954, 'Two medieval musical manuscripts: Egerton 3307 and some University of Chicago fragments', *Journal of the American Musicological Society* 7: 1–34

Richard L. GREENE 1954a, review of Stevens 1952 in *Journal of the American Musicological Society* 7: 78–82

Richard Leighton GREENE 1962, *A selection of English carols, edited with an introduction, notes and glossary* = Clarendon medieval and Tudor series, ed. J. A. W. Bennett (Oxford: At the Clarendon Press) [Review in Robbins 1963]

Richard Leighton GREENE 1962a, review of Robbins 1961 in *Renaissance news* 15: 224–7

Richard Leighton GREENE 1977, *The early English carols: second edition, revised and enlarged* (Oxford: At the Clarendon Press) [Reviews in Fallows 1978, Grey 1978, Wenzel 1979]

Richard Leighton GREENE 1980, 'Carols', in *A manual of the writings in Middle English 1050–1500* 6, ed. Albert E. Hartung (New Haven: Connecticut Academy of Arts and Sciences): 1743–52 and 1940–2018

W. W. GREG 1937, review of Greene 1935 in *The review of English studies* 13: 85–8

Jeremy GRIFFITHS 1995, 'Unrecorded Middle English verse in the library at Holkham Hall, Norfolk', *Medium ævum* 64: 278–84 [Holkham Hall 229: new source of *There is no rose* (*MC* 14; *EEC* 173)]

W. H. HADOW 1931, *English music* (London, New York and Toronto: Longmans, Green and Co.)

J. O. HALLIWELL 1844, *The poems of John Audelay: a specimen of the Shropshire dialect in the fifteenth century* (London: Percy Society)

Charles HAMM 1960, 'A group of anonymous English pieces in Trent 87', *Music and letters* 41: 211–15

Charles E. HAMM 1964, *A chronology of the works of Guillaume Dufay based on a study of mensural practice* = Princeton Studies in Music 1 (Princeton: Princeton University Press)

Phillipa HARDMAN 2000, *The Heege manuscript: a facsimile of National Library of Scotland MS Advocates 19.3.1* = Leeds texts and monographs, New series 16 (Leeds: School of English)

R. A. H[ARMAN] 1953, review of Stevens 1952 in *The musical times* 94: 356–7

Frank Ll. HARRISON 1958, *Music in medieval Britain* (London: Routledge and Kegan Paul)

F[rank] Ll. H[ARRISON] 1964, review of McPeek 1963 in *Music and letters* 45: 405–7

Frank Ll. HARRISON 1965, 'Benedicamus, conductus, carol: a newly-discovered source', *Acta musicologica* 37: 35–48

John C. HIRSH 2012, 'Christian poetics and orthodox practice: meaning and implication in six carols by James Ryman, O. F. M.', in *Medieval poetics and social practice: responding to the work of Penn R. Szittya*, ed. Seeta Chaganti (New York: Fordham University Press): 53–71

Dagmar HOFFMANN-AXTHELM 1972, 'Faburdon / fauxbourdon / falso bordone', in *Handwörterbuch der musikalischen Terminologie* (Wiesbaden: Franz Steiner Verlag)

Klaus HORTSCHANSKY, 'John Dunstables Motette "Veni Sancte Spiritus – Veni Creator": Zur Frage der Konstruktionsprinzipien', in *Festschrift Arno Forchert zum 60. Geburtstag*, ed. Gerhard Allroggen and Detlef Altenburg (Kassel etc: Bärenreiter, 1986): 9–26

Andrew HUGHES 1967, *Fifteenth-century liturgical music: I: Antiphons and music for Holy Week and Easter* = Early English Church Music 8 (London: Stainer & Bell)

Jean JACQUOT 1953, review of Stevens 1952 in *Revue de musicologie* 35: 100–101

M. R. JAMES and G. C. Macaulay 1915, 'Fifteenth century carols and other pieces', *The modern language review* 8: 68–87

David L. JEFFREY 1975, *The early English lyric and Franciscan spirituality* (Lincoln: University of Nebraska Press)

David L. JEFFREY 1984, 'James Ryman and the fifteenth-century carol', in *Fifteenth-century studies: recent essays*, ed. R. F. Yeager (Hamden, CT: Archon Books): 303–20

Sylvia W. KENNEY 1964, *Walter Frye and the contenance angloise* = Yale studies in the history of music 3 (New Haven and London: Yale University Press)

Sylvia W. KENNEY 1965, review of McPeek 1963 in *Journal of the American Musicological Society* 18: 246–50

Jonathan KING 1996, 'Texting in early fifteenth-century sacred polyphony' (DPhil dissertation, University of Oxford)

190 Bibliography

Andrew KIRKMAN 2000, 'Binchois the borrower', in *Binchois studies*, ed. Andrew Kirkman and Dennis Slavin (Oxford: Oxford University Press): 119–35

Eleanor LANE and Nick Sandon with Christine Bayliss 2001, *The Ritson manuscript: liturgical compositions; votive antiphons; Te Deum* (Newton Abbot: Antico Edition)

Timothy McGEE 2012, review of Mullally 2011 in *Music and letters* 93: 399–401

Louise McINNES 2013, 'The social, political and religious contexts of the late medieval carol: 1360–1520' (PhD dissertation, University of Huddersfield)

Louise McINNES 2015, '"That we with merth mowe savely synge": the fifteenth-century carol – a music of the people?', *Early music performer* 36: 4–12

Gwynn S. McPEEK 1963, *The British Museum manuscript Egerton 3307: the music, except for the carols, edited and transcribed, and with a general commentary; texts edited and transcribed by Robert White Linker* (London: Oxford University Press) [Reviews in Harrison 1964, Kenney 1965]

H. J. L. J. MASSÉ 1921, 'Old carols', *Music and letters* 2: 67–76

Sanford B. MEECH 1935, 'Three musical treatises in English from a fifteenth-century manuscript', *Speculum* 10: 235–69

Catherine Keyes MILLER 1948, 'A fifteenth century record of English choir repertory: B. M. Add. Ms. 5665; a transcription and commentary', 2 vols. (PhD dissertation, Yale University)

Catharine K. MILLER 1950, 'The early English carol', *Renaissance news* 3: 61–4

Catharine Keyes MILLER 1953, review of Stevens 1952 in *The musical quarterly* 39: 455–60

Catharine Keyes MILLER 1953a, review of Stevens 1952 in *Notes* 10: 311–12 [entirely different from Miller 1953]

William Ian MILLER 1975, 'The Poetry of MS. Sloane 2593' (PhD dissertation, Yale University)

John MILSOM 1980–81, 'Songs, carols and "contrafacta" in the early history of the Tudor anthem', *Proceedings of the Royal Musical Association* 107: 34–45

Robert MULLALLY 1986, 'Chançon de carole', *Acta musicologica* 58: 224–31

Robert MULLALLY 2011, *The carole: a study of a medieval dance* (Farnham: Ashgate) [Reviews in McGee 2012, Wulstan 2012]

Edward William Byron NICHOLSON 1913, *Introduction to the study of some of the oldest Latin musical manuscripts in the Bodleian Library, Oxford* = Early Bodleian Music [3] (London: Novello)

Jeremy NOBLE (1954), 'John Dunstable: a line of approach and a point of departure', *The musical times* 95: 185–7

Robert NOSOW 2012, *Ritual meanings in the fifteenth-century motet* (Cambridge: Cambridge University Press)

Nicholas ORME 1978, 'The early musicians of Exeter Cathedral', *Music and letters* 59: 395–410

Frederick Morgan PADELFORD 1912, 'English songs in manuscript Selden B. 26', *Anglia* 36: 79–115

Christopher PAGE 1984, 'The rhymed office for St Thomas of Lancaster: poetry, politics and liturgy in fourteenth-century England', *Leeds studies in English* 14: 134–51, reprinted in Page, *Music and instruments in the middle ages: studies on texts and performance* (Aldershot: Variorum, 1997): chapter XIV

Christopher PAGE 1996, 'Reading and reminiscence: Tinctoris on the beauty of music', *Journal of the American Musicological Society* 49: 1–31

Christopher PAGE 2010, 'The carol in Anglo-Saxon Canterbury?', in *Essays in the history of English music in honour of John Caldwell: sources, style, performance, historiography*, ed. Emma Hornby and David Maw (Woodbridge: The Boydell Press): 259–69

Kathleen Rose PALTI 2008, '"Synge we now alle and sum": three fifteenth-century collections of communal song: a study of British Library, Sloane MS 2593; Bodleian Library, MS Eng. poet. e.1; and St John's College, Cambridge, MS S.54' (PhD dissertation, University College London)

Kathleen PALTI 2008a, 'An unpublished fifteenth-century carol collection: Oxford, Lincoln College MS Lat. 141', *Medium ævum* 77: 260–78

Kathleen PALTI 2011, 'Representations of voices in Middle English lyrics', in *Citation, intertextuality and memory in the middle ages and renaissance*, ed. Yolanda Plumley, Giuliano Di Bacco and Stefano Jossa (Exeter: University of Exeter Press): 141–58

Kathleen PALTI 2011a, 'Singing women: lullabies and carols in medieval England', *The journal of English and Germanic philology* 110: 359–82

William J. PHILLIPS 1921, *Carols: their origin, music, and connection with mystery-plays* (London: G. Routledge & Sons)

Edward Bliss REED 1932, *Christmas carols printed in the sixteenth century including Kele's Christmas carolles newely inprynted reproduced in facsimile from the copy in the Huntington Library* (Cambridge, MA: Harvard University Press)

Karl REICHL 2003, 'James Ryman's lyrics and the Ryman manuscript: a reappraisal', in *Bookmarks from the past: studies in early English language and literature in honour of Helmut Gneuss*, ed. Lucia Kornel and Ursula Lenker (Frankfurt am Main: Peter Lang): 195–227

Karl REICHL 2005, 'The Middle English carol' in *A companion to the Middle English lyric*, ed. Thomas G. Duncan (Cambridge: D. S. Brewer): 150–70

Karl REICHL 2012, *Medieval oral literature* (Berlin: De Gruyter)

Edith RICKERT 1910, *Ancient English Christmas carols MCCCC to MDCC* (London: The New Medieval Library; 2nd edition, London: Chatto and Windus, 1914)

Joseph RITSON 1790, *Ancient songs from the time of King Henry the Third to the Revolution* (London: J. Johnson)

Rossell Hope ROBBINS 1938, 'The earliest carols and the Franciscans', *Modern language notes* 53: 239–45

Rossell Hope ROBBINS 1942, 'The burden in carols', *Modern language notes* 57: 16–22

Rossell Hope ROBBINS 1943, 'Two new carols (Hunterian MS. 83)', *Modern language notes* 58: 39–42

Rossell Hope ROBBINS 1952, *Secular lyrics of the XIVth and XVth centuries* (Oxford: At the Clarendon Press)

Rossell Hope ROBBINS 1957, 'Friar Herebert and the carol', *Anglia* 75: 194–8

Rossell Hope ROBBINS 1959, 'An early rudimentary carol', *Modern language review* 54: 221–2

Rossell Hope ROBBINS 1959a, 'The Middle English carol corpus: some additions', *Modern language notes* 74: 198–208

Rossell Hope ROBBINS 1959b, 'Middle English carols as processional hymns', *Studies in philology* 56: 559–82

Rossell Hope ROBBINS 1959c, *Historical poems of the XIV and XV centuries* (New York: Columbia University Press)

Rossell Hope ROBBINS 1960, 'The early English carols', *The choir* 51: 126–8

Rossell Hope ROBBINS 1961, *Early English Christmas carols* (New York and London: Columbia University Press)

Rossell Hope ROBBINS 1963, review of Greene 1962 in *Speculum* 38: 484–7

Rossell Hope ROBBINS 1966, 'The Bradshaw carols', *PMLA* 81: 308–10

Rossell Hope ROBBINS 1980, 'The Middle English court love lyric', *The interpretation of medieval lyric poetry*, ed. W. T. H. Jackson (New York and London: Columbia University Press): 205–32

192 Bibliography

Erik ROUTLEY 1959, *The English carol* (London: Oxford University Press)

Margit SAHLIN 1940, *Étude sur la carole médievale: l'origine du mot et ses rapports avec l'église* (Uppsala: [no named publisher], 1940)

Rebekka SANDMEIER 2012, *Geistliche Vokalpolyphonie und Frühhumanismus in England: Kulturtransfer im 15. Jahrhundert am Beispiel des Komponisten John Dunstaple* = Abhandlungen zur Musikgeschichte 25 (Göttingen: V & R unipress)

Bertram SCHOFIELD 1946, 'A newly discovered 15th-century manuscript of the English Chapel Royal – part I', *The musical quarterly* 32: 509–36

Manfred SCHÖPF 1969, 'Zur Strophenform einiger Carols', *Anglia* 87: 394–7

Manfred SCHULER 1966, 'Die Musik in Konstanz während des Konzils 1414–1418', *Acta musicologica* 38: 150–68

Ann-Marie SEAMAN and Richard Rastall 1977, 'The music of Oxford, Bodleian Library, MS Lincoln College Latin 89', *Research chronicle of the Royal Musical Association* 13: 95–101

Adele Margaret SMAILL 2003, 'Medieval carols: origins, forms, and performance contexts' (PhD dissertation, University of Michigan)

J. F. R. STAINER and C. Stainer 1898, *Dufay and his contemporaries: 50 compositions . . . with an introduction by E. W. B. Nicholson . . . and a critical analysis of the music by Sir John Stainer* = Early Bodleian Music 1 (London: Novello, 1898)

Sir John STAINER, with J. F. R. Stainer and C. Stainer 1901, *Sacred & secular songs, together with other ms. compositions in the Bodleian Library, Oxford, ranging from about A.D. 1185 to about A.D. 1505, with an introduction by E. W. B. Nicholson, M.A., Bodley's Librarian and transcriptions into modern notation* = Early Bodleian Music 2: 2 vols. (London: Novello, 1901)

Eric G. STANLEY 1997, 'The verse forms of Jon the Blynde Awdelay' in *The long fifteenth century: essays for Douglas Gray*, ed. Helen Cooper and Sally Mapstone (Oxford: At the Clarendon Press): 99–121

Judith STELL and Andrew Wathey 1981, 'New light on the biography of John Dunstable?', *Music and letters* 62: 60–63

John STEVENS 1950–51, 'Carols and court songs of the early Tudor period', *Proceedings of the Royal Musical Association* 77: 51–62

John E. STEVENS 1951, 'Rounds and canons from an early Tudor songbook', *Music and letters* 32: 29–37

John STEVENS 1952, *Mediæval carols* = Musica Britannica 4 (London: Stainer & Bell for the Royal Musical Association; revised edition 1958; reprinted 1970, 1976; further revision, prepared by David Fallows, 2018) [Reviews in Bukofzer 1954, Dart 1953, Gombosi 1953, Greene 1954a, Harman 1953, Jacquot 1953, Miller 1953, Miller 1953a]

J. E. STEVENS 1952a, 'Carol', in *Die Musik in Geschichte und Gegenwart*, ed. Friedrich Blume (Kassel: Bärenreiter), ii: cols. 856–9, lightly updated as C. Paulette CATHERWOOD, 'Carol: I: Vom Mittelalter bis zum 17. Jahrhundert', in *Die Musik in Geschichte und Gegenwart . . . Zweite, neubearbeitete Ausgabe*, ed. Ludwig Finscher, *Sachteil* 2 (Kassel, etc.: Bärenreiter and Stuttgart, etc.: J. B. Metzler, 1995): cols. 460–62

John STEVENS 1953, *Mediæval carols . . . selected from the collection of 135 Carols published as Volume IV of Musica Britannica*: eleven leaflets with photographic reprints from Stevens 1952 (London: Stainer & Bell); reprinted with new outside pages in about 1958, still retaining the 1952 music but with an inaccurate copyright statement 'Revised Edition © Copyright 1958'. The series comprises: set 1: *MC* 2–5 (from pp. 2–3); set 2: *MC* 8, 114 (from pp. 6 and 104); set 3: *MC* 9, 105 (from pp. 7 and 94); set 4: *MC* 17–19 (pp. 12–13); set 5: *MC* 25–26 (pp. 18–19); set 6: *MC* 37, 55 (pp. 26, 44); set 7: *MC* 27, 16, 5^A (from pp. 20, 11, 111); set 8: *MC* 59, 4^A (from pp. 48–9, 110); set 9: *MC* 79–80 (pp. 66–7); set 10: *MC* 1, 107 (pp. 1, 96); set 11: *MC* 28, 95 (pp. 21, 83).

John Stevens 1954, 'Carol', in *Grove's dictionary of music and musicians*, 5th edition, ed. Eric Blom, 9 vols. (London: Macmillan): ii.78–88 [his most extensive and wide-ranging statement about the early carols]

John STEVENS 1958, *Mediæval carols: second, revised edition* = Musica Britannica 4 (London: Stainer & Bell for the Royal Musical Association; with unaltered reprints 1970, 1976)

John STEVENS 1961, *Music and poetry in the early Tudor court* (London: Methuen)

John STEVENS 1963, *There is no rose of such virtue: medieval carol* (London: Stainer & Bell)

John E. STEVENS 1967, with Margaret Bent, Howard M. Brown, Richard L. Greene, Frank Ll. Harrison, Rossell Hope Robbins and Brian Trowell, 'The English carol', in *Report of the tenth congress [of the International Musicological Society]: Ljubljana 1967*, ed. Dragotin Cvetko (Kassel: Bärenreiter): 284–309

John STEVENS [1974], *Tidings true: medieval carols selected from volume 4 of Musica Britannica* (London: Stainer & Bell) [all newly reset]; reprinted 1987 as Invitation to Medieval Music 6

John STEVENS 1975, *Early Tudor songs and carols* = Musica Britannica 36 (London: Stainer & Bell for the Royal Musical Association) [Reviews in Charles 1976, Fallows 1976]

John STEVENS and Dennis Libby 1980, 'Carol', *The new Grove dictionary of music and musicians*, ed. Stanley Sadie, 20 vols. (London: Macmillan): v.162–73

Reinhard STROHM 1993, *The rise of European music, 1380–1500* (Cambridge: Cambridge University Press)

Reinhard STROHM 2001, 'Music, humanism, and the idea of a "rebirth" of the arts', in *Music and concept and practice in the late middle ages*, ed. Reinhard Strohm and Bonnie J. Blackburn (Oxford: Oxford University Press): 346–405

Andrew TAYLOR 1991, 'The myth of the minstrel manuscript', *Speculum* 66: 43–73

Sir R. R. TERRY [1932], *A medieval carol book, the melodies chiefly from mss. in the Bodleian Library, Oxford, and in the Library of Trinity College, Cambridge* (London: Burns Oates & Washbourne)

Brian TROWELL 1959, 'Faburden and fauxbourdon', *Musica disciplina* 13: 43–78

Brian TROWELL 1960, 'Music under the later Plantagenets' (PhD dissertation, University of Cambridge)

Brian TROWELL 1980, 'Faburden – new sources, new evidence: a preliminary survey', in *Modern musical scholarship*, ed. Edward Olleson (Oxford: Oriel Press): 28–78

Brian TROWELL 1980a, 'Fauxbourdon', in *The new Grove dictionary of music and musicians*, ed. Stanley Sadie (London: Macmillan, 1980): vi.433–8

Ernest TRUMBLE 1959, *Fauxbourdon, an historical survey: volume I* = Wissenschaftliche Abhandlungen/ Musicological studies 3 (Brooklyn: Institute of Mediaeval Music)

Ernest TRUMBLE 1960, 'Authentic and spurious fauxbourdon', *Revue belge de musicologie* 14 (1960): 2–28

Ernest TRUMBLE 1990, 'Dissonance treatment in early fauxbourdon', in *Beyond the moon: Festschrift Luther Dittmer*, ed. Bryan Gillingham and Paul Merkley = Wissenschaftliche Abhandlungen/ Musicological studies 53 (Ottawa: Institute of Mediaeval Music): 243–72

Daniel WAKELIN 2001, 'Lightning at Lynn, 1363: the origins of a lyric in Sloane 2593', *Notes and queries* n.s. 48: 382–5

Daniel WAKELIN 2006, 'The carol in writing: three anthologies from fifteenth-century Norfolk', *Journal of the Early Book Society* 9: 25–49

Daniel WAKELIN 2010, 'Instructing readers in fifteenth-century poetic manuscripts', *The Huntington Library quarterly* 73: 433–52

Andrew WATHEY 1986, 'Dunstable in France', *Music and letters* 67: 1–36

Andrew WATHEY 1989, 'The production of books of liturgical polyphony, in *Book production and publishing in Britain 1375–1475*', ed. Jeremy Griffiths and Derek Pearsall (Cambridge: Cambridge University Press): 143–61

Rob C. WEGMAN 2003, 'New music for a world grown old: Martin Le Franc and the "contenance angloise"', *Acta musicologica* 75: 201–41

Rob C. WEGMAN 2010, 'The state of the art', in *Renaissance? Perceptions of continuity and discontinuity in Europe, c.1300–c.1550*, ed. Alexander Lee, Pit Péporté and Harry Schnitker (Leiden: E. J. Brill): 129–60

Siegfried WENZEL 1979, review of Greene 1977 in *Speculum* 54: 140–42

Siegfried WENZEL 1986, *Preachers, poets, and the early English lyric* (Princeton: Princeton University Press)

Jessie L. WESTON 1911, *Old English carols from the Hill MS* (London: David Nutt)

J. A. WESTRUP 1932, 'Song' in H. E. Wooldridge, *The polyphonic period, part II: Method of musical art 1400–c. 1600* = The Oxford history of music 2: 2nd edition, revised by Percy C. Buck (London: Oxford University Press): 256–375

Ella Keats WHITING 1931, *The poems of John Audelay* = Early English Text Society, Original series 184 (Oxford: Oxford University Press)

Edward WILSON 1973, *A descriptive index of the English lyrics in John of Grimestone's preaching book* = Medium Ævum Monographs, New series 2 (Oxford: Basil Blackwell)

Edward WILSON 1980, 'Two unpublished fifteenth-century poems from Lincoln College, Oxford, MS. Lat. 141' in *Notes and queries* n.s. 27: 20–26

H. E. WOOLDRIDGE 1905, *The polyphonic period, part II: Method of musical art, 1300–1600* = The Oxford history of music 2 (Oxford: At the Clarendon Press)

Peter WRIGHT 2000, 'Binchois and England: some questions of style, influence and attributions in his sacred works', in *Binchois studies*, ed. Andrew Kirkman and Dennis Slavin (Oxford: Oxford University Press): 87–118

[Thomas WRIGHT] 1836, *Songs and carols printed from a manuscript in the Sloane collection in the British Museum* (London: William Pickering)

Thomas WRIGHT 1841, *Specimens of old Christmas carols, selected from manuscripts and printed books* (London: The Percy Society)

Thomas WRIGHT 1847, *Songs and carols now first printed from a manuscript of the fifteenth century* (London: The Percy Society)

Thomas WRIGHT 1855, *Songs and carols from a manuscript in the British Museum of the fifteenth century* (London: The Warton Club)

J. Ernst WÜLFING 1896, 'Der Dichter John Audelay und sein Werk', *Anglia* 18: 175–217

David WULSTAN 1968, *An anthology of carols* (London: J. & W. Chester)

David WULSTAN 1985, *Tudor music* (London: J. M. Dent)

David WULSTAN 2012, review of Mullally 2011 in *Plainsong and medieval music* 21: 212–13

J. H. WYLIE, completed by W. T. Waugh 1914–29, *The reign of Henry V*, 3 vols. (Cambridge: Cambridge University Press)

Beth Ann ZAMZOW 2000, 'The influence of the liturgy on the fifteenth-century English carols' (PhD dissertation, University of Iowa)

John J. ZEC 1997, 'The relationship of the carol, the processional, and the rhymed office of the nativity cycle as influenced by the mendicant orders in the late middle ages in England' (PhD dissertation, The Catholic University of America)

Julius ZUPITZA 1892, 'Die Gedichte des Franziskaners Jakob Ryman', *Archiv für das Studium der neueren Sprachen und Litteraturen* 89: 167–338

Julius ZUPITZA 1894–7, 'Anmerkungen zu Jakob Rymans Gedichten', *Archiv für das Studium der neueren Sprachen und Litteraturen* 93 (1894): 281–338 and 369–98; 94 (1895): 161–206 and 389–420; 95 (1896): 259–90; 96 (1896): 157–78, 311–30; 97 (1897): 129–53

General index

Adam of Usk: 183n2
Adam von Fulda: 50
adaptation of earlier poems to become carols: 27, 28–9, 31–2
Agincourt, Battle of (1415): 96n9, 100–1, 132, 139–41, 161–2, 180, 184
Ailly, Pierre d': 173
Alcock, John: 156–7
Alfonso the Wise, King of Castile: 21
anonymity: 88, 178
Apel, Willi: 21n7
Arras, Peace of (1435): 171
Arthur, Prince of Wales: 167n1
Atlas, Allan W.: 182
Audelay, John: xi, 12–13, 57–8, 67, 84, 152

Bacon, Francis: 15n13
ballade: 21
ballata: 21–3, 26, 62, 66
Barbieri, Francisco Asenjo: 114n1
Bardel (Bardwell), Johannes: 56
Basel, Council of (1431–49): 124
Becket, St Thomas: 130n19, 138n9, 143–4, 172–3
Bedyngham, John: 121, 170
Benskin, Michael: 137
Bent, Margaret: 9n10, 49n10, 53n2, 148n25–6, 163n8, 164n10, 170n5, 174n17, 178n22
Bernard, Edward: 81
Bernard of Clairvaux: 138
Besseler, Heinrich: 45–6, 48–50 (Ex. 6.3a), 171–2
Beverley: 57
Binchois, Gilles de Bins dit: 50n15, 124–9, 131–2, 169–72, 174–8
Boffey, Julia: 3n8
Boklund-Lagopoulou, Karin: 57n3, 58n12
Book of XX songes (1530): 168

Bourges: 95
Bowers, Roger: 93, 134, 138, 145, 149, 163, 167
Brackley, John: 78
Bramley, Henry Ramsden: 87
Briçeño, Luis de: 83
Bridge, Sir Frederick: 180
Brook, G. L.: 60
Brown, Carleton: 3, 28n21, 64n9–10, 95n8
Buckle, Alexandra: 163n8
Bukofzer, Manfred F.: achievements: 3, 36, 45–6, 181; agreements with: 18, 54n3; disagreements with: 26, 33, 34n2, 36–7, 56n1, 134–5, 149, 159n17, 171
burden: definition: 14–17; and double burden: 33–42, 159
Burney, Charles: 80, 82–3
Burrell, John: 163
Byrd, William: 168
Byttering: 163n7

Caldwell, John: 89n2, 92, 182
Camargo, Martin: 1n4
cantiga: 21–4
Cantigas de Santa Maria: 21–2, 34
Capgrave, John: 183
Carmen, Johannes: 170–1
carol: definition: 5, 12–14; with music for burden only: 69–70, 168; suggested impact: 169–78
Catherine de Valois, Queen of England: 94–5, 165n16
Catherwood, Paulette: 1n5, 8n7, 60n1, 93n4, 149, 154n2
Cattin, Giulio: 174n18, 175n20
Cesaris, Johannes: 170–1
Chaganti, Seeta: 14n10
Chambers, Sir Edmund: 12n2, 14, 15n13, 58n11, 149n1, 180–1

Chapel Royal: 95, 97–8, 134–5, 155, 163–4, 174
Charles VI, King of France: 94–5
Charles VII, King of France: 94–5
Charles d'Orléans: 22n10
Chaucer, Geoffrey: 162
'Childe': 89
Childe, Iohannes: 89
Childe, William, 'clericus': 89
Childe, William, of Eton College: 89
chorus: 17–18, 22, 33, 34, 45, 184
Christine de Pizan: 22n10, 175
Ciconia, Johannes: 47n9
Clark, Sir Kenneth: 134n1
Clercx, Suzanne: 47n9
Collier, Heather: 1n5, 58n12
Cologne: 172
Colton, Lisa: 170n5
Constance, Council of (1414–18): 124, 144, 162, 169–74
contenance angloise: 169–78
Cooke, John: 140n13, 163–4
Cooney, Helen: 182
couplet: 22
Curry, Anne: 96n9, 101, 142n14, 144n15
Cutler, John L.: 3n8

Damett, Thomas: 140n13, 163–4
Dart, Thurston: 2
Davey, Henry: 95n6, 179
Day, Timothy: 181n2
Decembrio, Pier Candido: 100n15
decorative initials: 121, 154
Deeming, Helen: 100n15, 149,
Deschamps, Eustache: 26
Dibble, Jeremy: 117
Diederichs, Elisabeth: 175n19–20
Dufay, Guillaume: 46, 48–50 (Ex. 6), 50n16, 169–78, 184
Duffy, Eamon: 113n3
Dunstable, John: 89–90, 131, 132, 145, 163–5, 169–72, 175–9 (Ex. 24.2), 184
Duncan, Edmondstoune: 179–80
Dunstan, St: 66
Dürrer, Martin: 25n18
Dyboski, Roman: xi, 13, 59, 180

Early Bodleian Music: 115–18
Edward III, King of England: 142n14
Edward IV, King of England: 66
Edwards, A. S. G.: 1n4, 3n8, 18n17
Elmham, Thomas: 101n16, 139n11, 164

English language: 161–3
'English nation': 162
Exeter Cathedral: 10, 89, 132–3

Fallows, David: 5, 10n15, 123, 163n8, 169–70
Faulkes, Anthony: 1n4
fauxbourdon: 31–2, 43–51, Fig. 4, 151, 153, 166, 179, 182, 184
Fehr, Bernhard: 119
Fein, Susanna: xi, 58n8
Feragut, Beltrame: 49
Ferreira, Manuel Pedro: 24n14
Fétis, François-Joseph: 170n5
Finscher, Ludwig: 182
Flasdieck, Hermann: 50
Fletcher, Alan: 62n3
Flood, W. H. Grattan: 95n6
Flügel, Ewald: 58n12, 119, 180
foot/fote: 16–17
Ford, Boris: 182
formes fixes: 21–3
Fortunatus, Venantius: 19
Franciscans: 25–6
French spoken in England: 6, 161n3
Froissart, Jean: 22n10

Gafori, Franchino: 50
Gennrich, Friedrich: 21n7
George, St: 101–2, 113
Georgiades, Thrasybulos: 45
Gerber, Rudolf: 50
Gesta Henrici Quinti: 101n18, 164, 183n2
Gombosi, Otto: 54
Gower, John: 56
Greene, Richard Leighton: achievements: x, 2–3, 5, 122–3; agreements with: 8n8, 10n15, 12–18, 78, 132n22; disagreements with: 56, 58n9, 58n11, 60–7, 89n4, 92–3, 96n10, 104–5, 120, 134–47, 156–7
Greer, David: 89n2
Griffiths, Jeremy: 1n4
Grimestone, John of: 28, 62–4
Gros, William le, Earl of Albemarle: 136
Grossin, Etienne: 46, 49
Guilelmus Monachus: 49n10, 50

Hadow, Sir Henry: 180
Halliwell, J. O.: 57n8
Hamm, Charles: 5, 171–2
Harding, Stephen: 138
Hardman, Phillipa: 102n19

General index

Harrison, Frank Ll.: achievements: 54, 171; agreements with: 134, 136, 138, 155–6; disagreements with: 23n12, 89n2, 89n4, 90, 96n10, 165n16
Haughmond Abbey: 57
Hawkins, Sir John: 45n2
Hearne, Thomas: 100n16
Helms, Dietrich: 122n9
Henry V, King of England: 94–103, 113, 132–3, 147, 153, 156, 161–6, 171, 174, 178, 183–4
Henry VI, King of England: 95, 96n10, 99, 163–4
Henry VIII, King of England: 120
Herebert, William: 64
Hill, Richard: xi, 12–14, 16–17, 58–9, 104–6
Hirsh, John C.: 58n11
Hoffmann-Axthelm, Dagmar: 45n2
Hortschansky, Klaus: 164n9
Hughes, Andrew: x, 9, 155–6
Hughes, Dom Anselm: 29n22
Huloet, Richard: 17n15
Humfrey, Duke of Gloucester: 96n10, 165
Hythe: 134, 137–8

Isaac, Henricus: 55

Jacob, E. F.: 113
Jacquot, Jean: 14n11
Jeffrey, David L.: 26n19
Joan, Queen of England, mother of Henry V: 165
John, Duke of Bedford: 164–5
John of Gaunt: 156n11
Johnson, Robert: 168
John the Fearless, Duke of Burgundy: 94
Josquin Desprez: 55

Kanazawa, Masakata: 49n10
Kaye, Philip: 124
Kele, Richard: 14
Kenney, Sylvia: 120n2, 145, 171
Kerby-Fulton, Kathryn: 182
King, Jonathan: 1n5, 8n8, 9, 149–50
King's Lynn: 65
Kirkman, Andrew: 124, 128

Lacy, Bishop Edmund: 89–90, 132–3, 163
Laird, Paul R.: 122n9
Landini, Francesco: 48n9, 52
Lane, Eleanor: x, 120n2, 121n4, 123, 131–2

Lang, Paul Henry: 171
Langland, William: 162
lauda spirituale: 21, 25–7
Ledrede, Richard: 14
Le Franc, Martin: 169–72, 178
Le Gentil, Pierre: 24n14
Lens, Jean de: 174
Lewis, Sir Anthony: 2
Liebert (Libert), Reginaldus: 46, 49
Liuzzi, Fernando: 25n16
London, Wymondus: 70
Luisi, Francesco: 31
Lydgate, John: 56, 96n8

Machaut, Guillaume de: 22–3 (Ex. 4.2), 26, 109, 170
McInnes, Louise: 2n5, 36n3, 62n3, 68n1, 70n9, 71n11, 76n2, 134, 138, 145n24
McPeek, Gwynn S.: x, 8n8, 95, 134, 136n6, 145, 148
Maitland, J. A. Fuller: x, 114–15, 180n1
major prolation: 8, 33, 53, 96, 147–8, 159, 171, 174
Marguerite d'Anjou, Queen of England: 95
Marix, Jeanne: 124n13, 171
Mary Newarke College, Leicester: 155–6
Massé, H. J. L.: 180n2
Matteo da Perugia: 22n10
Mauser, Siegfried: 182
Meaux Abbey: 9, 134–9
Mersenne, Marin: 83
metrical irregularity: 54–5
metrical regularity: 6, 15–16, 31–2, 52–4
Mettingham College: 149
Miller, Catherine Keyes: 120n2
Milsom, John: 168
Mitchell, Robert: 124
Mooney, Linne R.: 3n8
Morelli, Cesare: 83
Mullally, Robert: 12n1, 14
muwashshah: 24

Nelson, Alan H.: 113n3
Nicholson, E. W. B.: 115–18, 154
Nicolas, Nicholas Harris: 81n5
Noble, Jeremy: 165n16
Nosow, Robert: 164n10

Obrecht, Jacob: 55
Ockeghem, Johannes: 55
Olivier, Laurence: 100n15
oral transmission: 45, 104–10
Orme, Nicholas: 90–1, 132

General index

Packe, Thomas: 123
Padelford, Frederick Morgan: 154
Page, Christopher: 66, 83n9, 155n7
Palti, Kathleen: xi, 2n5, 13, 56–7, 68, 111
parchment quality: 138n8, 148, 155
Paris: 95, 97
Parker, John: 87n12
Pepys, Samuel: 80–85
Percy, Bishop Henry: 80–1, 83–4
perfect time: 9, 33, 53, 72, 99, 101, 147, 150, 159, 175
Petri, Theodoricus: 27–31
Petrucci, Ottaviano: 82
Phillips, William J.: 180
Piæ cantiones (1582): 27–31
Piccard, Gerhard: 131
Pirro, André: 171
Pirrotta, Nino: 171
Planchart, Alejandro Enrique: 173–4
Plummer, John: 157–8
Plymtree: 90
Polton, Thomas: 162
'popular by destination': 92–3, 99, 111
Power, Leonel: 131, 163, 165, 179
Probus: 90
pseudo-score: 9, 11, 154
Pyamour, John: 157
Pyggott, Richard: 168

Raby, F. J. E.: 69, 96n10
Radomski, Mikołaj: 46, 49
Rastall, Richard: 1n4, 71n10
Reese, Gustave: 182
refrain: 15–17
refrain: 22
Regis, Johannes: 55
Reichl, Karl: 24n15, 58n11, 70, 134
Richenthal, Ulrich von: 172–3
Riemann, Hugo: 45n2–3, 48n9, 114n1
Ritson, Joseph: x, 57n3, 76n2, 77–8, 84
Robbins, Rossell Hope: 3, 14n10, 19n2, 26, 36n4, 56, 62n4, 64, 121, 155n6
Rockstro, W. S.: 115
rondeau: 21
Rouen: 95–8
Ryman, James: xi, 58, 69–70, 110n3, 119

Sahlin, Margit: 12n1, 62n4
Saltwood Castle: 134, 138n8
Sandmeier, Rebekka: 170n5
Sandon, Nicholas: x, 120n2, 121n4, 123, 131–2
Saunders, Suparmi: 128

Schofield, Bertram: 3, 8n8, 134–5, 155, 181
Schöpf, Manfred: 62n5
Schuler, Manfred: 172n10
Scott, Kathleen L.: 145n20
Scrope, Archbishop Richard le: 65–6
Seaman, Anne-Marie: 1n4, 71n10
Sedulius: 65
Seine, Battle of the (1416): 164
Selden, John: 80–1
Sheppard, John: 168n4
Sigismund, King of the Romans (from 1433 Holy Roman Emperor): 183
similis ante similem: 53, 106
Slavin, Dennis: 178n21
Smaill, Adele: 1n5, 14n10, 58n9
Smert, Richard: 89–90, 129, 132
Smith, John Stafford: 80, 82–4
Solage: 22n10
Squire, William Barclay: 179n1
Stainer, Cecie (Elizabeth Cecil): 116–18
Stainer, Charles Lewis: 116
Stainer, John Frederick Randall: 116–18
Stainer, Sir John: x, 80, 87, 115–18
Stanford, Charles Villiers: 115
Stanley, Eric G.: 58n9
stanza: 18, 19
stave-ruling: 8, 9, 77, 123, 128n18, 155
Stevens, John: achievements: x, 2–6, 69, 121–2, 130, 137, 181; agreements with: xii, 28, 33–4, 43–6, 54, 76–7, 96n10; disagreements with: 9, 26, 36, 39, 89, 120, 137
Strecche, John: 183n2
Strohm, Reinhard: 157, 165n16, 170n5, 171–2
Sturgeon, Nicholas: 132, 163–4
Sumption, Jonathan: 95n7
Sutkowski, Adam: 49n12
Syon Abbey: 134, 136

Takamiya, Toshi: 1n4, 18
Talbot, James: 83
Tapissier, Johannes: 170–1
Taruskin, Richard: 182
Taylor, Andrew: 56n2
Terry, Sir Richard Runciman: 181
Thomas, Duke of Clarence: 148, 163
Thomas, Earl of Lancaster: 155–6
Thomas Becket, St: 130n19, 138n9, 143–4, 172–3
tierce: 22
Tinctoris, Johannes: 50, 169

Tours, Treaty of (1444): 95n8
Toward, Richard: 83
Trouluffe, John: 89–90, 129, 132
Trowell, Brian: 43n1, 45–6, 50–1, 70, 165n16
Troyes, Treaty of (1420): 94–6, 165n16
Trumble, Ernest: 45–6, 49n10
Turbet, Richard: 181n2

Vale, Malcolm: 161n2, 162n5
Van den Borren, Charles: 171
verse: 18
villancico: 21
virelai: 21–3, 26, 34n2; English style: 76n1
Vita et gesta Henrici Quinti: 100
vuelta (*volta*): 22, 26

Wakelin, Daniel: 56, 57n5, 65n11, 111
Walker, Ernest: 179
Walsingham, Thomas: 183n2
Wanley, Humfrey: 81
watermarks: 131
Wathey, Andrew: 8n9, 157, 165n13–14
Wegman, Rob C.: 170n5
Wenzel, Siegfried: 62n3, 62n6, 63n7

Weston, Jessie L.: 180
Westrup, Sir Jack: 4, 77
White, John: 77
Whiting, Ella Keats: xi, 58n8
Wilson, Blake: 25n16
Wilson, Edward: 1n4, 62n6
Windsor, Chapel of St George: 9, 134–5, 139–44
Wolf, Johannes: 118
Wooldridge, H. E.: 45n3, 179
Worcester: 156–7
Wright, Craig: 165n16
Wright, Peter: 53n2, 124–8
Wright, Thomas: xi, 57n1, 57n5, 87
Wülfing, J. Ernst: 57n8
Wulstan, David: 14n11, 24n14
Wylde, John: 43n1
Wylie, J. H.: 94–5, 97–8, 100n14–15, 144n15, 162n4
Wynkyn de Worde: 14

zajal: 24
Zamzow, Beth Ann: 1n5, 134
Zek, John: 1n5, 25n17, 134
Zupitza, Julius: xi, 58n11, 110n3, 119

Index of carols

Abide, I hope it be the best (*MC* 10/42): 8, 33, 39, 72–5 (Ex. 10.2), 150, 152, 159–60
Agincourt carol: see *Deo gracias, Anglia*
Ah, man, assay (*MC* 17): 17, 69
Alleluia, Pro virgine Maria (*MC* 28/69): 15–17 (Ex. 3.1), 52, 148
Alleluia: A newë work (*MC* 30): 17, 39, 72, 155n7, 159
Alleluia: Now well may we mirthës make (*MC* 20): 17, 34, 163
Alleluia: Now may we mirthës make (*MC* 105): 38
Alma Redemptoris mater (*MC* 4): 53, 152, 162
Alma Redemptoris mater (*MC* 23): 72, 159, 163
Anglia, tibi turbidas (*MC* 56): 38, 146–7
As I lay upon a night (*MC* 11[A]): 28–9 (Ex. 4.5), 52, 64
As I lay upon a night (*EEC* 149): 63–4
Ave, plena gracia (*MC* 66): 147
Ave domina (*MC* 24): 53
Ave Maria: Hail, blessëd flower (*MC* 36): 17, 37, 72, 159–60

Be merry, be merry (*MC* 6): 111, 152
Benedicite Deo Domino (*MC* 57): 93–6, 145, 147

Comedentes convenite (*MC* 71): 136n6, 138–9

David ex progenie (*MC* 34/46): 37, 39, 159–60, 163
Deo gracias, Anglia (*MC* 8/29): 8, 17, 33, 39–41 (Ex. 5.2), 52–3, 72, Fig. 3, 100–2, 150, 152–3, 159, 162, 179

Deo gracias, Persolvamus alacriter (*MC* 22): 112
Do well and dread no man (*MC* 104): 38

Ecce, quod Natura (*MC* 37): 10, 26–8 (Ex. 4.3), 45, 52, 147, 163, 179
Enforce we us with all our might (*MC* 60): 101, 112, 139–42 (Ex. 19.1), 147
Enixa est puerpera (*EEC* 191): 62, 66
Exultavit cor in Domino (*MC* 61): 101, 139, 142–3, 147
Eya, martyr Stephane (*MC* 12): 52, 152, 162

Farewell lo (*MC* 20[A]): 17, Fig. 5
For all Christen soulës (*MC* 118): 18, 34
From stormy wyndis and grevous wethir (Turges): 167n1

Gaudeamus pariter (*MC* 72): 112
Goday, my lord (*MC* 18): 17

Hail Mary, full of grace (*MC* 2/31): 6–7 (Ex. 2.1), 43, 45, 52–4, 152, 156
Have mercy of me (*MC* 88): 38
Hay, hay, hay, hay,/ Think on Whitsun Monday (*EEC* 425): 65–6

I have loved so many a day (*MC* 3[A]): 71, 78
In every state, in every degree (*MC* 85): 38
I pray you all with one thought (*MC* 15/65): Fig. 7, 109–10 (Ex. 15.2), 89, 137, 147, 176
I pray you all with one thought (*MC* 100): 38
Ivy is good (*MC* 55): 37, 53, 135, 137–8

Jesu, fili virginis (*MC* 111): 38, 113
Jesu, for thy mercy (*MC* 112): 38

202 Index of carols

Jesus autem hodie (*MC* 108): 38
Johannes assecretis (*MC* 77): 17

Laus honor virtus gloria (*MC* 39): 39, 159–60, 163
Letare, Cantuaria (*MC* 96): 38
Lovely tear of lovely eye (*EEC* 271): 63, 66
Lullay, lullay: As I lay (*MC* 1^A): 71, 79
Lullay, lullay, la lullay (*EEC* 149): 64, 67
Lullay, lullay, little child, (*EEC* 155): 63, 67
Lullay, lullow: I saw a sweet (*MC* 1): 72, 76, 78, 84, 160
Lullay, my child and wepe no more (*MC* 2^A): 71, 77

Make us merry this New Year (*MC* 83): 113
Make we joy now in this fest (*MC* 26/97): 112
Man assay, assay, assay, And ask mercy while thow may (*MC* 17, 110, 17^A): 69, 71
Man, be joyful (*MC* 82): 121n6
Man, be wise, and arise (*EEC* 357): 65–6
Marvel not, Joseph (*MC* 81): 34, 87, 123, 128–9 (Ex. 18.3)

Nova nova: ave fit ex Eva (*MC* 5^A): 70, 71
Novo profusi gaudio (*MC* 47): 112
Novus sol de virgine (*MC* 48): 137
Nowell, nowell: In Bethlem (*MC* 3/38): 34, 52, 152, 159
Nowell, nowell: Out of your sleep (*MC* 25): 34, 76, 159–60
Nowell, nowell: Out of your sleep (*MC* 14^A): 11, Fig. 2
Nowell, nowell to us is born (*MC* 38): 39
Nowell, nowell: The boarës head (*MC* 79): 18, 84, 87
Nowell, nowell: this is the salutation of th' angel Gabriel (*MC* 4^A): 26n17, 70–1
Nowell, nowell. Who is there (*MC* 80): 34, 84, 87
Nowell sing we both all and some (*MC* 7/16): 52, 111, 150–1 (Ex. 20.1), 152, 162–3
Now make we mirthë (*MC* 9): 112, 152
Now may we singen (*MC* 5): 52, 111, 152

O blessed Lord (*MC* 116): 38, 123, 129–30 (Ex. 18.4)
O clavis David (*MC* 91): 18, 33n1, 34, 38
Of all the enemies (*MC* 10^A): 70

Of a rose sing we (*MC* 19): 112, 160, 163
Of thy mercy (*MC* 8^A): 69
Omnis caterva fidelium (*MC* 70): 38

Parit virgo filium (*MC* 73): 38, 71, 78
Pray for us (*MC* 13/106/115): xii, 38, 104–6, 112, 124–8 (Exx. 18.1 and 18.2), 152, 162
Princeps pacis (*MC* 45): 98–101, 145, 147
Princeps serenissime (*MC* 62): 96–8 (Ex. 14.1), 112, 135, 139, 145, 147
Proface, welcome (*MC* 107): 34, 121n6
Psallite gaudentes (*MC* 93): 38, 113

Qui natus est de virgine (*MC* 51): 17, 37

Regi canamus glorie (*MC* 89): 38, 113

Saint Thomas honour we (*MC* 59): 38, 112, 137, 139, 143–4
Salve sancta parens (*MC* 6^A): 70
Sing we now (*MC* 7^A): 69
Sing we to this merry company (*MC* 21): 112
Sing we to this merry company (*MC* 76): 87, 112, 163
Soli Deo sit laudum gloria (*MC* 87): Fig. 8
Sol occasum nesciens (*MC* 49): 37
Sonet laus (*MC* 78): 17
Spes mea in Deo est (*MC* 99): 38

Te Deum (*MC* 95): 33n1, 43, 46–7 (Ex. 6.2)
That holy [Martyr Steven] (*MC* 22^A): 17
The best rede (*MC* 117): 39
The boar's head in hand bear I (*EEC* 132): 84
The holy martyr Stephen (*MC* 50): 112, 137, 147
There is no rose of such virtue (*MC* 14): 44 (Ex. 6.1), 52, 54, 152
The rose is the fairest flower of all (*EEC* 427): 102–3
Think, man, of mine harde stundes: 65–6
Think we on our ending (*MC* 18^A): 71
Though I sing and mirthës make (*MC* 9^A): 70
Tibi laus, tibi gloria (*MC* 44): Fig. 1, 147
Tidings true (*MC* 102): 38
To many a well (*MC* 114): 38

Veni, Redemptor gencium (*MC* 41): 39, 72, 159–60
Verbum Patris hodie (*MC* 67): 17, 39

Welcome yule: Welcome be thou, Heaven king (*EEC* 7): 84
What tidings bringest thou? (*MC* 11/27): 17, 34–5 (Ex. 5.1), 54, 150, 152

Worship we this holy day (*MC* 94): 54–5 (Ex. 7.1), 113

Y-blessed be that Lord (*MC* 40): 89, 160, 163

Index of other songs and poems

Adieu ces bons vins de Lannoys (Dufay): 178n21
Adieu ma doulce (Binchois): 176n21
Adieu m'amour et ma maistresse (Binchois): 176n21
Adieu ma tres belle maistresse (perhaps Binchois): 178n21
Alma proles (Cooke): 140n13, 164
Amours, merchi (Binchois): 176n21
Ave regina celorum (I) (Dufay): 175–6 (Ex. 24.2)

Beata viscera: 52
Benedicta es celorum regina (de Anglia): 174n17
Bien puist (Binchois): 176n21
Blow northern wind (EEC 440): 60–1, 66

Cantemus socie Domino (Sedulius): 66, 136n6, 145n19
Cras amet qui nunquam amavit: 19
Cluchi cách, gaine cách: 24–5

Da gaudiorum premia (Dunstable): 165n16
De plus en plus (Binchois): 176n21
Douce dame jolie (Machaut): 22–3 (Ex. 4.2), 52, 54

Ecce, novum gaudium: 27–8 (Ex. 4.4)
Ecco la primavera (Landini): 52
En Katerine solennia (Byttering): 163n7

Fair and discreet (Ritson): 122n8

Gaude terra tenebrosa: 9, 159
Gentil madonna (Bedyngham): 122n8
Glad and blyth mote ye be (Selden): 9
Gloria, laus et honor: 20–1

Hand by hand we shall us take (EEC 12): 61–2, 66

I heard a maiden wepe for herë sonnÿs passion: 70
Io zemo (Galfridus de Anglia): 122n8

J'ay mis mon cuer et ma pensee (Dufay): 178n21

Ma belle dame, je vous pri (Dufay): 178n21
Man of might, that all had i-dight (EEC 424.1): 62n5
Marguerite, fleur de valeur (Binchois): 176n21
Mary, mother, come and see (EEC 157): 63, 66
Miles Christi gloriose: 155–6
Miserere mihi Domine: 70
Mon seul voloir/ Certes m'amour (Cesaris): 70n4
My folk what have I do thee (William Herebert): 64n9
Myn hertis lust (Bedyngham): 122n8
My woeful heart (Ritson): 122n8

Nesciens mater: 90, 121, 132
Now has Mary born a flour: 77 (Ex. 11.1)
Now springs the spray (EEC 450): 62, 66

O aquila magna (Venice): 175n20
O blessed Lord (Ritson): 39, 121n7, 122n8
Of one that is so fair and bright (EEC 191): 62
[O] lux beata trinitas: 121, 123
Omnes una gaudeamus (MC 15[A]): 8, 106–9 (Ex. 15.1)

O potores exquisiti (Egerton): 136, 139, 144–5
O Redemptor, sume carmen: 20n4
O Rosa bella (Bedyngham): 90n6

Padre del cielo (Venice): 175
Pastime with good company (Henry VIII): 120, 130–1
Pervigilium veneris: 19
Pour ce que veoir ne je puis (Dufay): 178n21
Preco preheminencie (Dunstable): 145, 164–5
Psallimus cantantes: 70
Puer natus in Betlehem: 78

Quant je suis mis au retour (Machaut): 109
Qui nos fecit ex nihilo (Venice): 174–5 (Ex. 24.1)

Salvatoris mater pia (Damett): 140n13, 164
Salvator mundi Domine: 70

Salve, festa dies: 19–20 (Ex. 4.1), 134, 139, 147
Salve mater Domini (Sturgeon): 164
Salve regina (Dunstable or Power): 131
Sancta Maria virgo intercede: 174n17
So ys emprentid (Bedyngham): 122n8
Sub Arturo plebs (Alanus): 174n17

Táin Bó Cúalnge: 24–5
Tappster, dryngker (Selden): 157n15
This enders night (*EEC* 150): 62n5
Tota pulchra es (Plummer): 157–8 (Ex. 20.1)
Toutes mes joyes (Binchois): 176n21
Triste plaisir (Binchois): 175–7 (Ex. 24.3)

Veni sancte Spiritus/ Veni creator (Dunstable): 145, 163–5
Verbum caro factum est: 29–32 (Ex. 4.6, Ex. 4.7), 176n20
Vostre tresdouce regard (Binchois): 131

Welcome be ye when ye goo (Selden): 157n15

Index of manuscripts

Aosta, Biblioteca del Seminario Maggiore, cod. 11: 23n12
Aosta, Biblioteca del Seminario Maggiore, cod. 15: 49n11, 170, 174n17

Bologna, Museo Internazionale e Biblioteca della Musica, MS Q15: 46, 48, 49n14

Cambridge, Corpus Christi College, MS 167 (Capgrave): 183n1
Cambridge, Gonville and Caius College, MS 383/603: 70
Cambridge, Magdalene College, Pepys Library, MS 1236: 82
Cambridge, Magdalene College, Pepys Library, PL Ballads 1: 80, 85–6 (Ex. 12.1), Fig. 5, Fig. 6
Cambridge, St John's College, MS F. 25: 165
Cambridge, St John's College, MS S. 54: 57, 64
Cambridge, Trinity College, MS B. 14. 39: 62
Cambridge, Trinity College, MS O. 3. 58 (Trinity carol roll): contents: x, 6–13, 33–4, 39–41, 104–6, 114–15, 162, 179–80; date: 149, 153; geographical origin: 149; music: 43, 67, 72, 74, 90n6; notation: 149–50; structure: 6–7
Cambridge, Trinity College, MS O. 9. 38 (Glastonbury miscellany): 78
Cambridge, Trinity College, MS R. 14. 26: 71n11
Cambridge, University Library, MS Add. 2764(1): 10, 17, 43, Fig. 5
Cambridge, University Library, MS Add. 5943: 64, 77, 79
Cambridge, University Library, MS Add. 9414: 71 (Ex. 10.1)
Cambridge, University Library, MS Ee. 1. 12 (Ryman): xi, 58, 69–70, 110n3, 119
Cambridge, University Library, MS Gg. 4. 12 (Capgrave): 183n1
Cambridge, University Library, MS Ll. 1. 11: 11, Fig. 2
Cortona, Biblioteca Comunale, MS 91: 25

Edinburgh, National Library of Scotland, MS Advocates 18.7.21 (John of Grimestone): 28, 62–7

Florence, Biblioteca Nazionale Centrale, Banco Rari 18: 25

Glasgow, University of Glasgow, MS Hunter 83: 70

London, British Library, Add. MS 5465 (Fayrfax book): 119, 167–8
London, British Library, Add. MS 5665 (Ritson): contents: x, 9–10, 12, 18, 34, 38–9, 84, 90–1, Fig. 8, 104–6, 119, 163, 167; date: 3n8, 120–33; geographical origin: 10, 132–3; music: 54–5, 124–30; notation: 43, 46–7; structure: 121–3
London, British Library, Add. MS 5666: 71, 76–9, 84, 160
London, British Library, Add. MS 31042: 102
London, British Library, Add. MS 31922 (Henry VIII book): 120, 168
London, British Library, Add. MS 34888: 78
London, British Library, Add. MS 43736: 117
London, British Library, Add. MS 46919: 64n9

Index of manuscripts

London, British Library, Add. MS 47214: 65n11
London, British Library, Add. MS 57950 (Old Hall): 47n9, 87n12, 148, 163–5
London, British Library, Egerton MS 613: 62
London, British Library, Egerton MS 3307 (Egerton): contents: x, 2n6, 3, 17, 20, 34, 163; date: 95–101, 134–48; geographical origin: 134–48; music: 37–8, Fig. 1, 106–10; notation: 26; structure: 8–9
London, British Library, Harley MS 978: 82
London, British Library, Harley MS 2253 (Harley lyrics): 60
London, British Library, Harley MS 2330: 64
London, British Library, Harley MS 4294: 104–6
London, British Library, Lansdowne MS 763: 43n1
London, British Library, Royal MS 12 C 12: 155n7
London, British Library, Royal MS 12 E 1: 64–5
London, British Library, Sloane MS 2593 (Sloane): xi, 56–7, 65, 68–9, 79, 87, 104
London, Lambeth Palace Library, MS 84: 139n11
London, Lincoln's Inn, MS Hale 135: 62
London, University Library, MS 657: 61

Modena, Biblioteca Estense Universitaria, alfa X. 1. 11 (ModB): 157–8, 170
Munich, Bayerische Staatsbibliothek, clm 14274 (St Emmeram): 49n13, 50n15, 53n2

Oxford, Balliol College, MS 354 (Hill): xi, 12–14, 58–9, 104–5, 119
Oxford, Bodleian Library, MS Arch. Selden B. 26 (Selden): contents: x, 9, 17, 37, 64, 80–1, Fig. 3, Fig. 7, 117–18, 150–53; date: 154–60; geographical origin: 154–60; music: 26–7, 28–9, 34, 45, 72–6, 89–90, 106–10; notation: 39–42, 53; structure: 9
Oxford, Bodleian Library, MS Ashmole 1393: 10, 26, 62
Oxford, Bodleian Library, MS Bodley 26: 61
Oxford, Bodleian Library, MS Bodley 88*: 10, 17, 39, 42
Oxford, Bodleian Library, MS Canonici misc. 213: 116–18
Oxford, Bodleian Library, MS Douce 302 (Audelay): xi, 12–13, 57–8, 67
Oxford, Bodleian Library, MS Eng. poet. e. 1 (OxEng): xi, 57, 70, 77, 87
Oxford, Bodleian Library, MS Lat. liturg. e. 7: 135n3
Oxford, Lincoln College, MS Lat. 89: 71

Paris, Bibliothèque nationale de France, f. lat. 1139: 31
Paris, Bibliothèque nationale de France, f. lat. 1343: 31
Paris, Bibliothèque nationale de France, Rés. Vm^8. u. 1: 83n7

Trento, Castello del Buonconsiglio, MS 90 (1377): 122n8, 157
Trento, Castello del Buonconsiglio, MS 92 (1379): 31–2 (Ex. 4.7), 49n13, 122n8, 124–8, 164, 178n21

Venice, Biblioteca Nazionale Marciana, MS. Ital. Cl. IX. 145: 50n15, 174–5 (Ex. 24.1)

Warsaw, Biblioteka Naradowa, MS III.8054 (Krasinski): 49n11, 49n12
Windsor, Eton College Library, MS 178 (Eton choirbook): 54–5, 167–8